Too many schools think that SEL ___ once-a-week activities for 30 minutes. In this incredibly impactful book, the authors show us - through concrete, specific examples - how deeper, more authentic inquiry- and problem-based learning experiences are the true path to achieving those SEL competencies that we know our children need. The pulse metaphor of this book is a perfect fit and the learning stories contained within resonate powerfully. I can't recommend this book highly enough for any educator who believes in whole child education, student agency and voice, and deeper, more meaningful learning.

Scott McLeod, J.D., Ph.D
Professor of Educational Leadership and founding director, CASTLE

Pulse of PBL might be the best Project Based Learning book I've ever seen. And it's not just because it's full of concrete, usable practices for educators rather than just theories and ideas, but because it successfully shows how to plan learning experiences that connect content with the heart. Mike and Matinga teach us how to tie SEL into authentic PBL projects. Using the power of authenticity that comes from PBL, while considering the diverse backgrounds, needs, and passions of students, we can create deep and meaningful learning. This book is full of stories, research, and practices that can absolutely transform the way you teach, and more importantly, it can transform the way you see your students. When this happens, the potential for their success in and out of your classroom is limitless.

Trevor Muir
Teacher, speaker, and author

In *The Pulse of PBL*, authors Kaechele and Ragatz avoid buzzwords and quick fixes as they make a convincing case for integrating Social and Emotional Learning and Project Based Learning. Instead, they guide readers to understanding with compelling examples, practical strategies, and their own deep commitment to providing students with the education they deserve. This is a resource that teachers will return to again and again as they put these concepts into action with their own students.

Suzie Boss,
PBL advocate and author

If you are a practitioner of PBL and SEL, this book must be part of your knowledge library! This is one of the more comprehensive guides that not only walks you through step-by-step about the implementation of inter-linked PBL and SEL practices but explains "why" it works. As the original co-founder and designer of one country's first all project-based learning schools, the Napa New Technology High School and co-founder of the organization that has evolved to become the New Tech Network, this book resonates. For me, PBL and SEL are inseparable–and when they are connected, the magic switch turns on and students' engagement, happiness and learning capacity "light up."

Ted Fujimoto
Co-founder of New Tech Network

I'm excited for educators to digest "Pulse of PBL", an important and vital examination of what makes for great Project Based Learning. Integrating SEL and Equity into PBL design aligns beautifully with the evidence-based benefits of learning through inquiry, which sits at the heart of PBL.

Lydia Dobyns,
President & CEO of New Tech Network

Add this to your PBL bookshelf! We've been hearing for some time why PBL and SEL are compatible -- now Matinga and Mike have provided the blue-print for making it happen. They're clearly expert, caring teachers, and draw from their own experience and others like them to give practical guidance and plenty of examples of teaching tools and classroom-tested strategies, with engaging and detailed stories of a variety of PBL projects. This book will help PBL teachers deepen their practice by supporting the social and emotional needs of students, which is so essential for the success of a project. And it will help SEL advocates recognize that rather than teaching SEL competencies in isolation, they need to be interwoven with the kind of powerful, in-depth, authentic learning experiences the authors describe.

John Larmer,
Former editor in chief, PBLWorks

Matinga and Mike offer a fresh and thoughtful look at two high profile concepts in education. With humility and practicality, they address some of the misconceptions and challenges that face educators when implementing these concepts. They also provide high quality protocols and learning activities that can be used in any learning environment. This is a book that you'll reference often and wear out your highlighter.

Dean Shareski,
Author, speaker, consultant at Advanced Learning Partnerships

Pulse of PBL, by Mike Kaechele and Dr. Matinga Ragatz, has successfully "married" a great instructional practice (Project Based Learning) with a critical support that our students need now - more than ever - (Social Emotional Learning). It provides an important guide for any teacher who wants to intellectually challenge their students and help them develop resilience.

Larry Ferlazzo
High school teacher, author, and Education Week advice columnist.

Pulse of PBL

**Cultivating Equity Through
Social Emotional Learning**

**Mike Kaechele
Matinga Ragatz, Ph.D**

BLEND

Blend Education

PO Box 5953

Salem, OR 97304

blendeducationpublishing.com

Pulse of PBL: Cultivating Equity Through Social Emotional Learning / Mike Kaechele and Matinga Ragatz. -- 1st ed.

ISBN: 978-1-7341726-1-4 (Blend Education)

Table of Contents

Index of Graphics

Chapter 1

Introduction

SEL should be at the heart of every project because SEL is the *Pulse of PBL*.

- Profile of a Graduate
- SEL & PBL
- What Makes a Weak Pulse?
- ILevas: Remedies for a Transformational Classroom

"Jambo," greeted Matinga, smiling.

"Jambo," shouted back the fifth grade students.

The students at the central Michigan suburban middle school loved learning that in Swahili, *simba* means *lion*, *rafiki* means *friend*, *safari* means *journey* or *travel*, and that *hakuna matata* is not just a Disney cartoon song but a common phrase that Tanzanians use to encourage calm in the face of adversity: "Don't trouble yourself."

Vickie Weiss's students sat mesmerized as their guest speaker, Matinga, introduced them to the culture and customs of the Maasai, a seminomadic people with a traditional lifestyle in Tanzania and Kenya. Matinga told Weiss's students about the Kilimanjaro International Airport (KIA) Learning House, a Project Based Learning (PBL) school she founded in 2017. The school was designed to meet the needs of Maasai children, who as young as six or seven years old spend much of the day far from home, taking their cattle from field to field to forage for grass. Traditional schools do not accommodate the daily schedules of the cattle drive, so Maasai children do not usually attend school. At the KIA Learning House, the children's daily schedule and chores are different. Through PBL, they learn to grow and preserve food to feed their families alongside important academic skills. The students speak Maa as their first language, Swahili as their second, and learn English at KIA Learning House as their third language.

KIA Learning House had a problem: their students had no books due to the high cost of shipping to Tanzania and the difficulty finding preschool books for Maasai children that highlight the beauty of their cultural values and traditions instead of solely showcasing western lifestyles and story lines. When the fifth graders heard about this predicament, they immediately suggested authoring books for the KIA students. Weiss collaborated with Matinga and the KIA Learning House teachers to design a PBL experience fulfilling the students' request. Weiss, who had been teaching PBL for fifty-two years (yes, fifty-two years—that is not a typo!), disclosed the Driving Question: "How can we, as authors, write and illustrate English Pre-K books for KIA Learning House students that are culturally appropriate?" Each student team created an illustrated, preschool level book that was culturally responsive. Then they recorded themselves reading their books in English.

To learn about the Maasai people, students embarked in a historical and cultural study of what they ate, where and how they lived, and what a day in the life of a Maasai child was like. The fifth graders needed to include concepts familiar to three to six-year-old Maasai children in their books. For example, one group of students wanted to create an alphabet coloring book but couldn't simply use the familiar "A is for Apple" because the Maasai children do not have easy access to fruits grown in temperate regions of the world. The students dug deeper in research to learn more about the Maasai diet and values to ensure that each letter of the alphabet represented recognizable ideas to the KIA Learning House students and their families.

Brief Historical Background

The Maasai practice a seminomadic herder lifestyle that extends back centuries. During the colonial era, they lost much of their sovereignty and autonomy when Europeans drew the borders of Kenya and Tanzania. However, as fierce warriors and hunters, they were able to fend off British slavery and human trafficking. Due to unfair treaties and sociopolitical maneuverings, the Maasai people gradually lost sovereignty of their extensive land and today are under constant government pressure to abandon their traditional culture. Their land attracts political and economic interest from outside entities desiring to profit by expanding national parks for safari tours, mining for precious stones, and extending large commercial farming operations. As a result of these land problems, the Maasai today face a drastic increase in poverty and a series of social ailments that beset disenfranchised communities, such as ignorance of indigenous rights, degradation of their traditional culture and language, alcoholism, and vulnerability to abuse and discrimination by outsiders.

The fifth grade students in Michigan discovered another example of cultural differences between themselves and Maasai children when they opted to tell original stories about cattle, which are the prominent economic status of the Maasai. But soon, the fifth graders in Weiss's class realized that the clipart of black-and-white Holstein cows, so recognizable in the United States, were unfamiliar to Maasai children. The Maasai people raise zebu, a large, humped-back breed of cattle. The fifth graders edited their books to include zebu instead of

Holsteins. Then each book was written in English and translated into Swahili with the help of Google Translate and Teacher Jacky, the Head Teacher at KIA Learning House.

Upon completion of the project, Weiss emailed the book files to Teacher Jacky who printed, bound, and presented the stories to her students. Teacher Jacky sent back pictures and videos of the KIA Learning House students holding the books that the fifth graders had written. These were their first take-home books! Weiss revealed the pictures and videos to her students at a parent showcase night. It was a moving moment to watch Weiss's class see their work in the hands of children a world away. Both the parents and the students cheered in amazement.

The throughline of the project was the Social and Emotional competency of Social Awareness. Weiss's students learned the importance of cultural influences and the benefits of respecting indigenous social norms. The project encouraged them to delve into the history and current ramifications of British colonization on Maasai lands and culture. Students considered other children's perspectives and understood the privilege of being a student in a well-appointed school in the United States.

In Weiss's PBL class, students expanded their viewpoint to a more global perspective. Through the PBL process, they acquired a set of skills beyond the academic content: confident and compassionate problem-solving, intentional collaboration, and advocation for others. These skills were not adopted magically by the students but were intentionally taught in the Project Based Learning design. Traditional lessons often focus on empathy for the plight of others in a detached way without necessarily creating opportunities for students to act upon the human conditions of others. In contrast, Weiss's students practiced empathy with a far-reaching impact by learning about the Maasai children in Tanzania for the purpose of creating stories that would connect with the Maasai readers.

Like Weiss's fifth graders, all students deserve an education focused on boosting their academical, social, and emotional strengths through authentic PBL. No matter how much pressure from politicians to mandate standardized curriculum, and no matter how much the evaluation of schools and teachers depends on raising test scores, educators still recognize that they have a responsibility to teach children by developing every student's intellectual, emotional, and social potential. No one becomes a teacher just to teach content from a textbook. People become educators to teach real, breathing children to help them develop into productive adults.

Profile of a Graduate

What outcomes does one expect when they teach a child? When leading PBL workshops, Mike and Matinga often open with a protocol to figuratively paint the profile of a graduate for that particular school, taking its location, cultural context, and grade levels into consideration. As a group, educators are asked to brainstorm qualities and characteristics they would like to see in their students upon completion of their classes. After facilitating this exercise with thousands of educators, they have rarely seen teachers include a list of academic content skills. Instead, educators list descriptors such as collaborative, strong communicator, kind, critical thinker, empathetic, and perse-vering. Sometimes there are no content- related qualities at all, and Matinga and Mike jokingly remind participants that we want to teach content standards too! It is not that teachers don't believe content is important, but when thinking about their students, teachers realize the responsibility of teaching important life skills that may not explicitly appear in the academic content.

The set of skills listed in the profile of a graduate activity has been labeled many things. Traditionally the business world has referred to them as "soft skills," implying that they are weak or less necessary. However, recently there has been a shift in the way people view soft skills because they are in high demand in the workplace. In 2019, qualifiers like creativity, persuasion, collaboration, adaptability, and time management ranked among the top five soft skills that employers are seeking.[1] Calling them "soft" doesn't do justice to how essential these skills are!

Recently it has been popular among educators to call them 21st Century Skills. This is misleading because these skills are not new. Early humans practiced these skills! They survived through collaboration in hunting together. They demonstrated problem-solving by discovering how to start fires for warmth and cooking. Although this set of skills was not recently invented, they have become more crucial than ever. Others use the term "college and career readiness," and while this applies to many of them, these skills are about more than advancing to higher education and better jobs. The skills encompass becoming a productive human in your family and society beyond the world of academia and work.

More recently the profile of a graduate characteristics have been grouped as part of a learning process known as Social and Emotional Learning (SEL) competencies. This term has become a recognized standard. It doesn't tie the skills specifically to preparing for college or work but is broader. The Collaborative for Academic, Social, and Emotional Learning (CASEL) has identified the five broad categories of Self-Awareness, Self-Management, Social Awareness, Relationship Skills, and Responsible Decision-Making.[2] In the following chapter, we will dive deeper into defining these ideas.

SEL & PBL

Project Based Learning and *Social and Emotional Learning* have become buzzwords in the United States and around the world. Their popularity stems from the pendulum swinging back from the extreme obsession of standardized testing and curriculum in the early 2000s. Guess what—national initiatives to standardize curriculum such as the Common Core didn't work![3] There are still millions of children who are "below grade level," whatever that means. It turns out that we cannot mandate and legislate children's academic success. Therefore, more and more school systems are shifting to a learner-centered environment.

The problem with many traditional learning experiences is that they are teacher dominated. The main design centers around the teacher's lecture while students take notes of information that will be regurgitated on a test later (and then promptly forgotten). This type of classroom values compliance, obedience, and passivity. Student autonomy and divergent thinking can be seen as threats or distractions. In some school districts, adherence to pacing guides require teachers to be at the exact same place as their colleague across the hall, leaving little room for students to practice Self-Management or Responsible Decision Making because all meaningful decisions have been made by the teachers or curriculum directors. Students speaking to each other or collaborating mid-lesson can be seen as committing off-task behavior rather than being part of the learning process.

Teachers may find this assessment to be outdated or harsh, but a 2019 Gallup survey reveals that even though teachers believe that school is relevant, the students disagree. Fifty-two percent of teachers believe that "students work on projects or assignments that can be used in the real world," but only twenty-six percent of students do.[4] Students believe that they do not get to choose relevant topics or do authentic projects in school. This dichotomy underlines that the problem isn't students' lack of motivation, but rather the learning approach is seen as irrelevant and outdated by the target audience. The content and standards-driven classroom structure leaves little room to learn about SEL competencies, let alone practice and assess them.

The SEL competencies that students develop are the "final product" of Project Based Learning as they transform students into the profile of a graduate.

But there is a better way—enter Project Based Learning. PBL is a student-centered framework where children work individually or in groups to attack authentic problems and generate solutions. It is an interactive structure giving ample opportunity to teach, practice, and assess any of the SEL competencies. PBL is a natural fit with SEL, like a hand in a glove. The development of Social and Emotional Learning skills is not only an essential partner to PBL but the end goal. It is the throughline of this pedagogical approach. Without SEL, PBL becomes a string of artificial activities without any deep mean-ing or lasting essential skills. Project Based Learning is the perfect framework to seamlessly integrate SEL into any class-room.

What Makes a Weak Pulse?

Students gathered around the items in the center of the room: a pineapple, a toy speedboat, a black-and-white picture of Marilyn Monroe, a sugar packet, a bag of chips, a tabloid pa-per, and a teddy bear, all sitting on top of a landscaping paver. The song "Panama" by Van Halen blasted from the classroom speakers. Mike told students that each item was a symbol for something in their next project and challenged them to make connections. (Author's note: all projects attributed to Mike in this book were codeveloped and cotaught with his in-credible partner, Andrew Holly. For the sake of brevity, only Mike is mentioned throughout.) Students quickly associated the pineapple with Hawaii and the teddy bear with Theodore Roosevelt. Next, he shared a slide deck of images from primary sources, such as a newspaper photo of the sinking of the *RMS Lusitania*. By the end of the hour, students had collectively made enough connections to guess that the project covered the Spanish-American War time period. However, they were stumped by how the paver related to the topic.

The following day students eagerly arrived in Mike's classroom, confident that they knew what the paver represented. "I have been thinking about this all night and I know it. The paver represents the 'foundation' of America."

"Sorry, that's incorrect," replied Mike as he secretly beamed at the thought of students thinking about his class outside of school.

After two days of research, the students concluded that the paver represented the Philippines, the "stepping-stone" to China. Mike realized that the topic of the Spanish-American War was not particularly interesting to students, so he thought that a fun final product would gloss over this blunder. Students created "Common Craft" style videos with cutout drawings to tell the story of one of the countries from this time period.

The excitement of the mystery items wore off as students researched to write their video scripts. Mike did not intentionally teach any skills beyond the content, and there was no intended audience for the student videos outside of the classroom. As they watched the final products together as a class, Mike thought that the Pineapple Project went fairly well.

The following day students reflected on the project in a Google Form and in a class Talking Circle. Mike was surprised by what he heard:

"I hated this project. It was so boring."

"If we are going to learn like this, I might as well return to my traditional school."

"Why did we learn this? I have no idea."

After licking his wounds, Mike realized that the Unfortunate Pineapple Project had no emotional connection to the students. In fact, the students had absolutely no interest in the historical links between the Philippines, pineapples, and the paver. He tried to disguise a traditional history lesson as a PBL experience, and it blew up in his face. As a new PBL teacher, Mike was missing the infusion of SEL competencies.

The project did not include Social Awareness lessons to help students empathize with the colonized people of Cuba, the Philippines, and Hawaii, who first suffered under the oppression of the Spanish and then saw no improvements with the new American regime. The project neglected Responsible-Decision Making components by not applying the historical content to current events. Students did not have opportunities to evaluate the long-term consequences of the colonizers' socio-economic and cultural impact on the original inhabitants. Since the project lacked a real purpose as well as an authentic audience for the final product, students lacked motivation to develop effective communication skills when creating their videos. It was a project, but not Project Based Learning.

Have you designed and implemented a project experience in your classroom that fell flat? Do any of the following symptoms describe your efforts?

- The kids started off excited but slowly lost enthusiasm, and the project fizzled out.
- Students had fun with a project but didn't actually learn anything.
- Your students never bought in at all, and it felt like you were dragging them, kicking and screaming through the whole process.
- A few students did decent work, but the majority contributed minimal effort, resulting in shabby products.
- Your students wasted weeks of class time and then threw something together the night before it was due.

You might have felt embarrassed, thinking, "I am never trying PBL again!"

On the other hand, maybe you have implemented Social and Emotional Learning into your practice. You set aside time each day to practice mindfulness or use a character-building curriculum. Do the results below sound familiar?

- At the elementary level, SEL did not seem to impact your students beyond the one-off time slotted for it.
- At the secondary level, some students didn't take SEL seriously and treated it as time to goof off.
- Your experience with PBL or SEL had been mostly positive, but you see other teachers taking it to a higher level and wonder how to get your students there.

Chances are your project has a weak pulse. When your pulse is weak, your heart does not provide enough oxygen to your limbs. You may become disoriented and confused. In a worst-case scenario, you could die of a heart attack. A project with a weak pulse has no oxygen to ignite students' motivation and personal development. A project with a weak pulse causes students to become confused and lose interest. In a worst-case scenario, your project is DOA, dead on arrival, just like Mike's Pineapple Project.

PBL without SEL is listless and rudderless because the projects do not connect emotionally with the students. SEL without PBL can be shallow and feel like a detached set of exercises. Teaching SEL skills within a project creates a bridge between the core content and each individual child. Students master the SEL competencies in purposeful and authentic ways. The antidote leading to successful PBL lies in the intentional introduction of Social and Emotional Learning Skills as a foundational element. We are convinced that the PBL framework is the ideal structure to cultivate SEL competencies.

SEL should be at the heart of every project because SEL is the *Pulse of PBL*.

ILevas: Remedies for a Transformational Classroom

This book will not focus on the plethora of research arguing the need for SEL or PBL in schools. There is plenty of literature available that addresses the validity and effectiveness of Social and Emotional Learning[5] and Project Based Learning.[6] This book is not a step-by-step guide for implementing Project Based Learning in your classroom. There are plenty of other books out there that explain the PBL process. Our assumption is that readers have pondered the research and are ready to implement both practices. Our goal is to give you practical examples and resources to infuse SEL and PBL in any classroom setting.

Given the fast-paced nature of teaching, it is hard to keep up on the latest, constantly shifting research. Teachers are busy planning lessons, grading, and meeting the needs of the children in front of them. The number of daily decisions and responsibilities feels overwhelming, even before COVID-19 made teaching even more challenging. The expertise of classroom teachers needs to be honored more as they are professionals in the field. Matinga and Mike are both experienced classroom teachers who have worked with teachers around the country to hone their PBL and SEL proficiencies. This book shares practical wisdom based on their experiential lens as teachers and practitioners.

One important tool in this book is *ILevas* (ee-LAY-vahs), practical methods for teachers (student versions available online) to implement the concepts contained in the chapter. Matinga is from an ethnic group called the Kombe (also known as *Ndowe* or "beach people") in the tiny country of Equatorial Guinea on the coast of West Africa. In traditional Ndowe culture, when one is going through mental or physical pain, it is common to seek the wisdom of an auntie, an elder, or a healer. These elders often impart helpful advice known as ILevas in the

Ndowe language of the Kombe people. Most recommendations tend to encourage decelerating the rhythm of life to make room for self-reflection, the practice of moderation, and the development of an intrinsic change in mindset.

Historically, people around the world have looked to the wisdom of healers in their community to restore harmony between the body, mind, and community. For example, headaches are a common symptom of today's fast-paced world. People normally treat a headache as a nuisance, take some oral pain relief, and then jump back into the rat race. From a more traditional perspective, an elder, recognizing the symptoms, would invite you to sit for a chat and drink sweet country tea (West-African citronella or lemongrass leaves). However, the invitation is actually to practice what Matinga calls *sotto voce*, "tea yoga."

Though the tea leaves and ingredients may vary from place to place, tea yoga is practiced all over the world. Consider the detailed process of drinking a cup of tea. First one is forced to put the kettle on, wait for the water to boil, wait longer for the tea to steep, then pause for the tea to cool a bit while intimately blowing on the hot surface and enjoying the stimulating aroma. Next one must approach the lip of the mug shyly and carefully so as not to get burned. As with yoga, this changes the breath and uses it more purposefully. One cannot drink hot tea while hectically running around but instead must snuggle up to a steaming mug in the cold winter or stimulate sweat glands to cool the body in hot weather. Healers recognize that a headache is a cry from your body to slow down, moderate and stretch your thinking, and approach life's issues in a deliberate way.

Just like traditional ILevas, our ILevas in this book are meant to work like tea yoga and are integrative approaches based on years of practice in the classroom. We will demonstrate how to cultivate Social and Emotional competencies within your academic practice. The ILevas in this book are not based on trends or abstract ideas but tried-and-true practices that have proven results in Matinga and Mike's classrooms through decades of experience. When the pulse of your classroom is weak, use our ILevas to analyze and bring harmony and healing to your teaching practices.

Just like wellness, many of our ILevas should be preemptive strategies. Your doctor doesn't want you to wait until after a heart attack to start an exercise plan and a healthy diet. Practicing meditation to alleviate stress is important before a traumatic encounter. Our ILevas are best introduced at the beginning of school and implemented throughout the year, creating a sustainable culture of wellness.

Our ILevas are designed to teach SEL coping skills to encourage productive behaviors and decision-making in students. Instead of lamenting or grumbling about certain dispositions in your students, you should aim to restore or "heal" unproductive attitudes. In our journey as teachers, we have learned that one cannot simply assume that students know and understand their role in productive thinking. We have lectured, nagged, threatened, punished, and even bribed our students to encourage them to think the way we expect them to think. But it doesn't work! Our students engage in constructive PBL work because we have taught them the role they are expected to play. We have seen "difficult" students become more engrossed in their learning when they recognize the usefulness of better coping skills.

Ignoring the cultivation of Social and Emotional Learning competencies in children to focus solely on the transfer of academic content should be considered malpractice.

ILevas must be personalized with intention. Before a healer applies treatment, they ask you about your personal and family medical history, including any allergies, drugs prescribed, and risk factors such as high blood pressure, asthma, or diabetes. Next the healer discusses your symptoms and performs a thorough examination. Finally, they offer healing practices tailored to you based on your age, weight, medical history, and specific health issues. ILevas should be fully customized—the exact inverse of standardization. Our ILevas should be personalized for your students in your setting.

This book includes many stories that we have collected from elementary and secondary classrooms across the country. They represent the gamut of schools, from rural to urban and early elementary to high school. SEL is the pulse of learning for all students, not a subset of children perceived as either gifted and talented at one end of the spectrum or remedial at the other end.

This book takes the following path: Before considering how to integrate SEL into PBL, one needs a clear understanding of what each is in its own right. Chapter 2 will give an overview of CASEL's five competencies, define the three levels of SEL, and address some misconceptions about SEL. In Chapter 3 we define PBL by giving an overview of what it looks like in an elementary and secondary class through two concrete project examples, tracing them from start to finish. It might be helpful—but not mandatory—to already be familiar with the PBL pedagogical framework. You may have already attempted some projects and struggled or were not satisfied with the outcomes. Chances are, SEL was the missing pulse needed to modify your PBL project into something highly impactful for your students.

Chapters 4 through 8 are the heart of this book. Each one highlights one SEL competency and how it fits into the PBL framework. The bullets at the beginning of these chapters are specific aspects of the PBL process where that particular SEL skill is addressed. Since, in practice, SEL and PBL are intricately woven together, many of the PBL elements cross into multiple chapters addressing several SEL competencies simultaneously. Chapter 9 dives into how to assess SEL in PBL, and Chapter 10 tells the story of an exemplar integration of SEL and PBL from the perspective of a student, parent, teacher, principal, and community partner.

Reflection Questions

- What skills beyond content are most important for you to teach your students?
- How would you define SEL and PBL?
- What aspects of SEL and PBL have you tried in your classroom?

PULSE OF PBL

Chapter 2

Transformative Social and Emotional Learning

Character, confidence, and self-esteem are best developed by students engaging in authentic, meaningful work, rather than an artificial, canned program of character building.

- Three Levels of SEL
- The Five CASEL Competencies
- Six Misconceptions of SEL
- Teacher SEL Self-Work

Three Levels of SEL

The term *emotional intelligence* (EI) gained popularity from Daniel Goleman's 1995 book of the same name. He originally defined EI by five components: self-awareness, self-regulation, internal motivation, empathy, and social skills.[7] The previous year, he had cofounded CASEL, and the term *social and emotional learning* was coined.[8] The CASEL framework has shifted slightly over the years as it has grown in popularity and as a result of extensive research on learning and how the brain functions.

In this book, it is not our intention to reinvent a new model of SEL (or PBL for that matter). Rather the goal is to demonstrate for the reader how SEL competencies can be taught, practiced, and assessed to transform any PBL classroom. Therefore, we have chosen the CASEL framework because of its long-standing recognition in the field of education as the basis of our explanation.

More important than the choice of a specific framework is the form of its implementation in the classroom. We divide SEL into three levels:

- Level I: Individual SEL
- Level II: Collaborative SEL
- Level III: Transformative SEL

FORMS OF SOCIAL & EMOTIONAL LEARNING

LEVEL I INDIVIDUAL	LEVEL II COLLABORATIVE	LEVEL III TRANSFORMATIVE
WORK ON SELF	**WORK WITH OTHERS**	**CHANGE YOUR WORLD**
Focused on self-awareness, self-control, and coping skills to understand one's identity for personal well-being.	Balance of individual and collaborative skills to learn how coping skills and strengths affect others.	Centered on critical self-analysis, collaborative problem-solving, and leadership for social justice.

Pulse of PBL

Individual SEL is commonly found in the character-building aspect of many SEL programs available for purchase. In these programs, students are taught how to identify and articulate their emotions, placing significant focus on adherence to school rules and displaying appropriate classroom behavior. Students learn self-control to mitigate disruptive be-haviors, and normative values are usually in isolation from the rest of the curriculum. Individual SEL helps students improve their understanding of themselves for their personal wellness.

Collaborative SEL focuses on teaching students the CASEL competencies through a lens of how their emotions and coping skills affect others. This second level of SEL expands upon In-dividual SEL emphasizing team building, collective problem-solving, and clear communication skills. At this level, students learn the synergy of a productive group that respects one another and forges together individual's strengths.

There can be situations when Individual and Collaborative levels of SEL are misused. For example, most Western tradi-tional learning focuses on preserving the rugged individualism narrative (the myth of the American cowboy). Assessment is competitive (standardized testing to rank children), and every-one must stand on their own (collaboration is seen as cheating).

When detached from the academic context, SEL can be-come weaponized. Dena Simmons describes Weaponized SEL as "white supremacy with a hug" when white children are taught SEL competencies to prepare them for college and career readiness, but Black and Brown children are taught SEL as a behavioral management strategy.[9] Weaponized SEL fosters all of the competencies in the sense of a motivational poster or pithy social media post: "Teamwork: let's all work together." Students learn the social skills that can lead to successful mid-dle-class jobs and harmonious relationships within the Western normative culture, void of current and historic issues of social injustice.

The subtext of Weaponized SEL is an avoidance of conflict, which hinders authentic relationships and the Social and Emo-tional learning process. It is full of messages like "I don't want to talk about the implications of racism, immigration, gun laws, capitalism, American imperialism, or politics in general be-cause they are too contentious. Parents in the community might get upset." This avoidance sterilizes academic content so that it is absent of relevance and context to students' life expe-riences. It especially diminishes the reality of our socially and historically marginalized students. Weaponized SEL neglects systemic injustices and forces all students to assimilate to the normative culture, ignoring their unique personal journey.

Transformative SEL, on the other hand, is centered on equity and social justice.

CASEL researchers Jagers, Rivas-Drake, and Williams have coined the third level "Transformative SEL," which scrutinizes structures and systems for democratic solutions with social justice for all students, especially disenfranchised groups. It builds on the coping skills of Individual SEL and the rest of the CASEL competencies of Collaborative SEL, tasking students to apply them to the tangible injustices of power, privilege, discrimination, social justice, empowerment, and self-determination. Transformative SEL acknowledges inequity and challenges students to find solutions to the root causes of injustice.[10] Transformative SEL is, by definition, culturally responsive and equitable. Thus, all students' socio-cultural backgrounds are seen as a source of identity and strength.

The three levels of SEL are not linear steps for how to teach SEL in sequence to students. In other words, teachers should not start at Individual SEL and work their way up to Transformative. Students at any age and maturity level can develop Transformative SEL skills from the beginning. Since Collaborative and Transformative levels include Individual SEL skills, students should be engaging in aspects of all three levels at once. Some of the lowest-skilled SEL students get stuck in Level I Individual SEL with the focus on self-control and behavior management. Teachers can become frustrated at their low engagement and developmental progress. If students are challenged with authentic purpose in Transformative SEL, the "why" behind the SEL practices, their motivation and growth in SEL competencies will greatly increase. The three categories are tools for teachers to analyze and reflect on their SEL strategies to ensure they include all levels.

The Five CASEL Competencies

According to CASEL, Social and Emotional Learning (SEL) is defined as "the process through which people acquire and effectively apply the knowledge, attitudes, and skills necessary to understand and manage emotions, set and achieve positive goals, feel and show empathy for others, establish and maintain positive relationships, and make responsible decisions."[11]

There are five CASEL core competencies, and each one is comprised of sub-competencies for further clarity. In the CASEL framework, the five SEL competencies are encircled by four circles representing the scope of practice. The two inner rings represent the classroom and school where educators have the most influence, whereas the outer rings represent families and communities where students spend most of their time. A common weakness of many SEL instructional approaches is the primary focus on the academic settings (classroom and school) while ignoring the transfer of SEL skills to the larger family and community settings. Through authentic partnerships in the community, Project Based Learning is the ideal approach to support the integration of SEL into all four of the environments encircled in the CASEL framework at once.

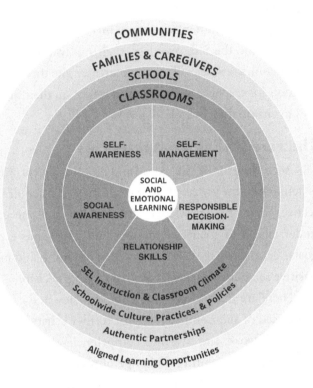

Source: ©2020 CASEL. All Rights Reserved. [https://casel.org/sel-frame-work/].

Let's consider what the three levels of SEL look like for each of the five CASEL competencies:

Self-Awareness[12]
<ul><li>Integrating personal and social identities</li><li>Identifying personal, cultural, and linguistic assets</li><li>Identifying one's emotions</li><li>Demonstrating honesty and integrity</li><li>Linking feelings, values, and thoughts</li><li>Examining prejudices and biases</li><li>Experiencing self-efficacy</li><li>Having a growth mindset</li><li>Developing interests and a sense of purpose</li></ul>

Self-Awareness is the art of understanding one's true self in terms of character, emotions, strengths, and shortcomings. Most SEL programs begin with an Individual focus on Self-Awareness by teaching young learners to notice and name their feelings beore moving on to the rest of the SEL competencies. They emphasize character-building and a growth mindset. Students focus on discovering who they are as an individual and what social or cultural factors have influenced their identity.

At the Collaborative level, students see their identities as part of the community that surrounds them. They become aware of how their cultural and developmental assets align with and affect others. Students comprehend that their individual integrity and personal choices have consequences for others. Their knowledge of Individual SEL skills is applied to the collective as opportunities to reflect and demonstrate these competencies in their social demeanor and academic development.

Due to persistence of historic inequities, Transformative Self-Awareness is a critical skill for both teacher and students to aid in identifying and processing complex emotions around events that are uncertain or socially turbulent. Biases should be checked and unique cultural aspects viewed as assets, not deficits or threats to the norm. Discovering the relevance and significance of their cultural and social identities encourages students to feel empowered, builds self-confidence, and improves self-efficacy. In addition, through Transformative Self-Awareness, students recognize how their identities color their personal worldviews.

Self-Management[13]
• Managing one's emotions
• Identifying and using stress management strategies
• Exhibiting self-discipline and self-motivation
• Setting personal and collective goals
• Using planning and organizational skills
• Showing the courage to take initiative
• Demonstrating personal and collective agency

Self-Management is the art of regulating one's actions and taking responsibility for one's wellbeing. Traditional teacher-controlled instruction leaves few opportunities for students to manage their learning and development autonomously. Therefore Individual SEL instruction often focuses on students regulating their feelings and behavior, addressing mainly the first bullet point on the list above. Students are taught to control their impulses and process their emotions of anger, stress, or sadness. Students craft personal goals, usually addressing individual classroom behavior.

Collaborative Self-Management, on the other hand, requires students to work together to manage their time, tasks, and teams. Goals are set as a group as members plan and organize their projects. In addition to regulating their behavior, students roleplay the essential social skills of listening, advocacy, speaking, teamwork, and relationship-building.

When students use productive individual skills to summon the collective agency of the group and work to organize for changes in their community, their Self-Management effort is Transformative. Students use their skills not just to empower the group but to tackle difficult challenges beyond their immediate team. Like Marvel's *Avengers©*, students assemble their collective Self-Management skills to engage in tasks bigger than themselves. They create plans to dismantle systemic injustices, providing equity of opportunity for others.

Social Awareness[14]
• Taking others' perspectives
• Recognizing strengths in others
• Demonstrating empathy and compassion
• Showing concern for the feelings of others
• Understanding and expressing gratitude
• Identifying diverse social norms, including unjust ones
• Recognizing situational demands and opportunities
• Understanding the influences of organizations and systems on behavior

Social Awareness is the art of experiencing empathy with people from all backgrounds. It is the ability to hold multiple perspectives at the same time. Individual Social Awareness focuses on tolerance by getting along with others. Often, the goal in teaching Social Awareness is to maintain a peaceful and harmonious classroom environment, rather than to truly make students aware of the complexity of diverse people of the world.

Collaborative Social Awareness moves beyond tolerance of others into the realm of actively appreciating them for their unique perspective. In this context, diversity is celebrated for the strengths of multiple viewpoints. Collaborative Social Awareness highlights the practice of empathy for outside groups, but without necessarily addressing social systems or beliefs that keep groups on the outside in the first place.

Transformative Social Awareness deeply empathizes with the perspective and circumstances of others of different backgrounds and cultures. In a project that encourages Transformative Social Awareness, students might investigate cultural and socio-economic norms to understand conditions that lead to inequality with the intent of aligning them with their circle of influence. Transformative Social Awareness has a bias toward action, with students actively seeking to use their skills and apply their research to dismantle unequal systems in their communities.

Relationship Skills[15]
• Communicating effectively
• Developing positive relationships
• Demonstrating cultural competency

- Practicing teamwork and collaborative problem-solving
- Resolving conflicts constructively
- Resisting negative social pressure
- Showing leadership in groups
- Seeking or offering support and help when needed
- Standing up for the rights of others

Having great Relationship Skills includes the art of negotiation, listening, and cooperative abilities to manage social pressure and conflicts productively. The teaching of Individual Relationship Skills focuses on building effective personal relationships. In order to create a harmonious classroom environment, lessons in taking turns and talking kindly to others are standard.

Collaborative Relationship Skills emphasize students' abilities to work well with their team. They learn to contribute to their groups, negotiate conflicts, and collectively solve problems. In PBL, students collaborate with multi-generational community members outside of school, spanning culture and other demographic differences. The goal is for students to realize their capabilities as productive members of the community.

When students passionately advocate for a cause, it is Transformative. Students combine their joined voices to eloquently defend principles of truth, justice, and unity with historically marginalized people. They discover the power of organization to stand up against systemic oppression and unfair social structures. Transformative Relationship Skills create leaders who look to the future with solutions that benefit all.

Responsible Decision Making[16]

- Demonstrating curiosity and open-mindedness
- Learning how to make a reasoned judgment after analyzing information, data, and facts
- Identifying solutions for personal and social problems
- Anticipating and evaluating the consequences of one's actions
- Recognizing how critical thinking skills are useful both inside and outside of school
- Reflecting on one's role to promote personal, family, and community well-being
- Evaluating personal, interpersonal, community, and institutional impacts

Responsible Decision Making is the art of weighing decisions about personal behavior and social interactions in a manner that is considerate of social norms and ethical standards. Individual Responsible Decision-Making concentrates on students inwardly thinking about their personal behavior decisions and how it affects the wellbeing of others: "Is it a good choice to hit another student?" or "What happens to other children when you blurt out in class?" In the classroom, emphasis is placed on providing time to reflect through the probable impacts of actions ahead of time to make choices that will not distract or harm others.

Collaborative Responsible Decision-Making moves students beyond personal choices to solving problems plaguing the community. Students may use a design thinking process to observe, analyze, brainstorm, critique, test, and propose solutions based on reliable sources and thoughtful consideration of diverse viewpoints. Responsible Thinking Skills lead to robust, peer-reviewed solutions to real life dilemmas.

Transformative Responsible Decision-Making happens when student address the complex issues in society with a lens of equity. For example, a team of students might explore and design a plan for their community to support one of the United Nations' Sustainable Development Goals.[17] Students work on global issues by making Responsible Decisions at the local level to bring about lasting changes.

Now that we have explored the five CASEL competencies and how they intersect the three levels of SEL integration, let's further define Transformative SEL by debunking some fallacies that many educators believe about Social and Emotional Learning.

Misconception 1: SEL is equivalent to mindfulness, yoga, breathing, and meditation.

Many educators mistakenly equate SEL with mindfulness, meditation, yoga, breathing, and other calming techniques. Keep in mind that those types of activities are tools to develop SEL competencies, but they are not the actual SEL skills themselves. The SEL competencies are the habits and characteristics that result from these and many other practices, not the specific techniques themselves. When educators incorrectly correspond specific activities with the SEL competencies, they may be missing the "why" behind the practices.

Students learn routines such as mindfulness, yoga, and calming techniques to control their emotions. We are not opposed to practicing these approaches, but we will focus on the aspects of SEL that are naturally embedded in the PBL framework. Those other coping techniques can always be used too, but they are not explicitly in the PBL framework. Think of PBL as the big-picture pedagogy toolbox—and mindfulness, yoga, and calming techniques as tools that fit inside of it.

We are not arguing that tools and techniques such as mindfulness, meditation, and yoga have no place in schools. They have helped many students and adults develop some of the SEL competencies. Regulating oneself is an important piece of SEL, but what is missing is the communal side of SEL competencies. Yoga and breathing don't address communication, collaboration, and problem-solving. Mindfulness does not teach students how to set goals, organize themselves and their teammates, and achieve their objectives. Meditation may help students self-regulate in emotionally charged situations but does not build empathy toward social injustices. These are all helpful tools, but they miss the holistic picture of teaching students the entire collection of SEL competencies.

We distinguish mindfulness, yoga, breathing exercises, and meditation as tools to teach centering skills and not the SEL competencies themselves.

Several dangers can result from focusing only on specific techniques such as the popular mindfulness exercises. First of all, there is concern that SEL becomes an add-on approach, relegated to a few minutes during morning meetings or part of a separate advisory class. Skillful teachers will integrate mindfulness throughout the day as students deal with content and relational challenges. But for many teachers, SEL can become an extra activity—the equivalent of kids leaving class for an elective class such as music, art, or PE—valuable experiences, but segregated from the core instruction of the day. Worse yet, it may be seen as the latest mandated program from administration, leading to the mindfulness activities not being implemented with fidelity and care.

A second danger is that teaching mindfulness and similar activities in isolation means that students will remain at Level I Individual SEL and will not intentionally reach the Collaborative and Transformative Levels. These activities are all about the student identifying their feelings and monitoring their behavior choices. Early childhood PBL experts Lev, Clark, and Starkey divide SEL skills into two broad categories: those that promote independent learning and those that build collaboration. They categorize independence skills as self-regulation, self-efficacy, perseverance, and self-management.

Collaboration consists of "sharing, turn-taking, empathy, communication, and developing and sustaining relationships."[18] Mindfulness and similar approaches focus primarily on the independent learning skills, neglecting the more communal, collaboration categories.

Furthermore, we advocate for an additional set of tools centered on teaching oracy (Chapter 6) to reach the higher levels of Collaborative and Transformative SEL. In this book, we will present Project Based Learning as a framework that includes many tools that develop all the SEL competencies infused into every classroom moment, not limited to the internal focused ones of Individual SEL.

Misconception 2: SEL is a waste of academic time.

Closely related to the last misconception is that SEL is all extracurricular fluff. Some teachers, especially at the secondary level, view mindfulness and similar practices as nonacademic exercises that divert precious class time from teaching content. They have a million standards to cover and don't have time for "touchy-feely" moments. Instead of SEL being infused throughout the day, the isolated mindfulness practices become an additional activity with little apparent relevance to the class and content discipline. Therefore, they wholesale reject teaching SEL because they misunderstand its broader purpose and goals.

Social and Emotional Learning is not all Kumbaya around the campfire at summer camp. Research demonstrates that developing SEL competencies improves academic outcomes.[19] Our personal experiences in the classroom and in working with thousands of teachers from around the world validates the research that SEL improves academic outcomes. Once we understand and can successfully put into practice a more complete definition of what Transformative SEL is, we can begin to see its value in improving our students.

Perseverance and growth mindset in Self-Awareness teach students to work through academic difficulties. The organizational skills of Self-Management lead to quality work completed on time. Social Awareness helps students analyze situations from multiple perspectives. Communication and collaboration of Relationship Skills enables students to exchange complex ideas in written and verbal forms. The problem solving of Responsible Decision-Making leads to deep understanding of academic content and application to real-world problems. SEL competencies are intricately intertwined with academic skills and are at the heart of deeper learning. Throughout this book, we will examine how a shift to a PBL framework infuses the development of SEL as central to the cultural fabric of class and not as an addition to overcrowded lesson plans.

Misconception 3: SEL is about building relationships and checking on our students' emotional states.

With the COVID-19 quarantine and the Black Lives Matter protests in 2020, students (and teachers too) were all experiencing mental stress or trauma to some degree. The shifts in the national social consciousness and the personal upheaval in many families, as well as the global school shifts to virtual, hybrid, or socially distant in-person learning, meant everyone had to adapt their teaching and learning patterns. The majority of teachers launched the year with a focus on SEL, by which they meant building relationships and checking in on their students' personal health and wellbeing. Educators were wise to concentrate on students as human beings first—listening, caring, and establishing personal connections with them. We needed, and continue to need, to check in on students' mental wellness.

The rallying cry of teachers everywhere was "We need to Maslow before we can Bloom."[20] Educators were calling for establishing a climate of safety and belonging per Maslow's hierarchy of needs before engaging students with academic content on Bloom's taxonomy of cognitive objectives. While connecting with students and building classroom culture is crucial work, it again is only a fraction of SEL, not the entire package. It is trauma-informed education, a necessity for students, especially dealing with a cross-section of a highly contagious virus, racial inequity, isolation, grief, and poverty. But trauma-informed education, or the implicit understanding of how trauma affects student behavior and ability to learn, needs to be distinguished from SEL as a separate practice. During emergency COVID-19 instruction, teachers monitored students' social and emotional states of being, which is a critical first step of SEL but doesn't address most of the competencies. Just like mindfulness, trauma-informed instruction is a piece of the Individual SEL puzzle but inadequate by itself. Checking in on students doesn't foster SEL growth in children.

Transformative SEL instruction goes beyond trauma-informed education, building the entire set of SEL competencies in ALL of our students.

A danger is that trauma-informed instruction can all too easily become a "start of the year" initiative but tail off as the year progresses. A teacher might start off strong with community-building activities but revert to more traditional practices as they face the pressures of standardized testing and curriculum demands. Developing SEL skills in our students is not something that can be relegated to the first week and then checked off as completed. It must be prioritized for the entire school year. If one only does meaningful activities to build relationships the first week and then in the second week shifts to teacher-dominated lessons focused entirely on content for the rest of the year, then that first week seems disingenuous.

- If you only work on building relationships in week one and shift to an emphasis on content, then how will students develop Self-Awareness?
- If students are consistently passive listeners and never discuss your content in meaningful ways with each other or community members, then how will they forge Relationships Skills with each other?
- If students only passively listen to lectures, fill out worksheets, and take traditional tests, then how will students apply what they learn to their world to sharpen their Social Awareness?
- If students are not offered multiple options to show how and what they are learning, then how will they build Self-Management by completing a project?
- If students only read the chapter and take notes, then how will they exercise Responsible Decision Making without opportunities to question your course content?

Relationships and community-building take time. They can't be "accomplished" the first week and then set aside. The beginning of the academic year should set the tone for what your learning environment will be like for the rest of the year, not some kind of one-off fun time before "real" learning begins.

Misconception 4: SEL will fix my classroom management issues.

Educators should not envision SEL curriculum as a behavior-management strategy to make their classroom run more smoothly.[21] Research has shown teaching integrated SEL competencies improves student behavior, leading to higher achievement in both classroom grades and standardized tests.[22] Hence SEL education does improve how students act, but controlling students' behavior should never be the rationale for implementing SEL.

The purpose of SEL instruction is for personal student growth and improving important life skills, not to help with classroom management for the teacher. Do not use SEL competencies to manipulate children into compliance with adult needs. The focus should always be on developing individual students for their own sake, not to make instruction easier for the adults in the room. As mentioned, compliance and control have a long history in the culture of education institutions worldwide. The traditional teacher played the role of the unquestioned authority figure, and in their traditional classroom students needed to do as they were told or suffer the consequences. This rigid approach left little space for students to practice and cultivate SEL skills. Today we know better!

In her formative years, Matinga attended Catholic boarding school in Spain with strict nuns who watched her every move. When she went through her teacher education program, she was advised to be an exacting teacher and rule with a firm hand. Hence, she started her career in much the same way as the nuns in her school, a strict teacher with tons of classroom rules. But she soon found that the more rules she created, the more opportunities students had to break her rules.

In class, Matinga loved to share stories about her world travels with her students to inspire them to dream big and achieve their goals. One day a student queried, "You always tell us that we can do these amazing things, then why are you just a teacher?" Matinga drove home in tears. The student was right. After a painful self-inventory, she realized that her identity as a teacher was an enforcer of rules rather than someone who inspired a love for life-long learning and personal development. Matinga and her colleagues were the first close relationships many of her students had with college-educated professionals. Yet what Matinga's students saw was an overworked, uninspired, and uninspiring example of a college graduate. She projected all her stress toward the students. Matinga embarked on a self-development journey to become a role model students would find inspiring. On her quest for a new mindset, she began experimenting with integrating technology and PBL in her classroom. The freedom to learn pioneered new ways of instruction, which in turn invigorated her to learn more and widen her network as she confidently embraced emerging pedagogies. Life-long learning became a pastime. Then it hit her like a ton of bricks! Just as she was motivated by the autonomy of becoming a high-performing educator, her students could be sparked by some sense of freedom and wonder in her class. Most adults learn through self-directed learning experiences, but students are rarely given this opportunity in schools.

Her draconian rules began melting away until eventually she was left with only one: "If you make it my problem, I will have to do something about it!" Incredibly the less rules she had, the more her students rose to each challenge. Instead of being so punitive, Matinga began explicitly teaching targeted coping skills to help students manage themselves. As a result, they intrinsically developed productive behaviors and often fashioned their own strategies to manage their projects. Her classroom became a hub of self-directed and constructive learning.

Students deserve freedom to develop SEL skills to become independent, self-sufficient learners.

When teachers focus on controlling behavior, they are implementing the worst form of Individual SEL. They are teaching the aspects of self-control but neglecting broader collaborative skills necessary for society. The danger of this misconception is that teachers misuse coping skills as tools for compliance and ignore Collaborative SEL skills that prosper the entire child.

Misconception 5: SEL will "save" students of color.

The previous misconception of SEL as a classroom management remedy is particularly problematic when it is imposed on students of color. A common approach, especially among schools with a majority of Black, Indigenous, People of Color (BIPOC)[23] students, is to use Self-Management lessons to focus on teaching students to assimilate to normative behavior at school,[24] mostly for the benefit of teachers. While it is true that Self-Management skills are an indicator of success in school, there is a danger in focusing on those skills above all else. This deficit thinking perpetuates a narrative for BIPOC children that says that fitting into the dominant white norms is more important than honoring students' unique cultural values and gifts.[25]

Social and Emotional Learning should not be used to impose white, middle-class values on Black and Brown students. However, done improperly, SEL programs can be veiled racism, assimilating students of color to white, middle-class values. "Weaponized" SEL blames the victim in a form of behaviorism, ignoring questionable systemic practices that amplify unproductive behaviors. It's like someone brutally kicking you in the knee, but then telling you how to manage the pain on their terms, without considering the origin and effects of the pain. Rather than stop kicking you, your assailant minimizes the effects of their aggression by revising the history of assaults, reverses the roles of victim and aggressor, and blames you for your constant complaints, creating a system to teach you to accept the kicking as normal behavior. Transformative SEL is not about choosing one cultural set of values over another but creating the conditions in which students' beliefs do not become obstacles to their learning. In explicit SEL lessons, students become self-experts, using their own cultural values as constructive perspectives to help them flourish.

When we require BIPOC students to tone down their cultural affectations to match the norm, we are guilty of an unintended yet dehumanizing microaggression: "Leave your spices at the door; we only use salt and pepper here." For example, "use your inside voice" is a common class-management practice that can turn into an inadvertent microaggression. Students, especially in elementary school, are reminded to use their inside or quiet voice to minimize disruptions. The belief is that kids learn best in a quiet environment, so there is a general expectation that children ought to maintain a library-like atmosphere in the classroom. Notably we tend to fixate on BIPOC voices and expression as noise pollution rather than to focus on listening to the words they are actually saying. African-American and Latino communities, places of worship, and households are often a vibrant bouquet of verbal, physical, and emotional expressions. Whether inside or outside, boisterous greetings, laughter, and even loud, casual conversation is not a sign of disrespect or anger. Young brown and black students who are less fluid in code-switching (see page 175) carry their own cultural expressions into school and may particularly be subject to unjust reprimands and punishments that leave them feeling confused and picked-on:

Teacher: *Jameson, keep your voice down? If I have to remind you again to use your inside voice, you are going to have to work alone in the office.*

Jameson: *What? I'm just working with Juan and Tyrone on our project.*

Teacher: *I know, but I can hear you clearly from over here. Please tone it down!*

In this short exchange, who is disrupting the learning process? The teacher can clearly hear that Jameson, Juan, and Tyrone are hard at work, yet the notion of the "inside voice" seems more important than the learning effort. We have experiential confirmation that people have meaningful conversations and work productively in noisy environments such as social gatherings, a large city, or a sidewalk cafe on the corner of a busy street. Kids are able to concentrate and work collaboratively in a playground full of their screaming peers.

Notably there are BIPOC cultural affectations that value quiet and contemplative spaces where everyone is encouraged to slow down to listen, provide wait time for others to process, and to build consensus quietly. The PBL classroom may be dynamic and lively, especially during student work time, but additionally educators should flex to create space for cultural perspectives that default to a quieter zone. Teaching students these simple personal and cultural differences and then norming their learning environment around student-made principles allows them to self-manage rather than feel blamed for something they do not understand:

Aiyana: *Hey, Jameson, our group is trying to read some articles we found.*

Jameson: (lowering his voice) *Oh, are we being too loud?*

Aiyana: (smiling) *Just a little. You guys don't mind dialing it down a bit?*

Jameson: *Not at all. It's my bad, I get loud when I am trying to make a point! Sorry about that.*

Aiyana: *Don't apologize. We are good, right?*

Jameson: *We always good.*

This short student exchange might seem laughable, but it is plausible in a space where multiple perspectives are valued, and students have been taught how to make the learning space work for others. Transformative SEL requires teachers to be sensitive to the cultural norms that their students bring into the classroom.

When flexing to be more inclusive, do we prioritize teachers' levels of comfort or students' cultural ways of interacting?

Weaponized SEL asks BIPOC students and students furthest from opportunity to understand and navigate systemic issues by themselves. As part of our efforts to develop productive young adults, we need to level up to Transformative SEL where young people are raised to identify structural biases and develop the skills to mitigate them. Transformative SEL has equity baked in. Equity is not and should not be an independent practice, divorced from high-quality pedagogy. The idea of separate equity strategies for a specific subset of students indicates that the norm is not for everyone.

Consider the simple act of buying shampoo. When Matinga buys products for her amazing hair, she must find the ethnic beauty product aisle. Many stores still keep ethnic beauty products in locked glass cases located in a section of the store that is monitored by video or near the pharmacy.[26] Her shampoo and hair styling products are not located in the "normal" beauty aisles. The implication is that shampoo for Black hair is not shampoo but a different kind of product that doesn't belong in the beauty aisle. There is shampoo for "normal" (aka white) people, and then there is the ethnic aisle for other people. Similarly, when educators implement disconnected equity policies rather than weaving inclusivity into everyday school culture, they are guilty of *othering* students by putting conversations about injustice and bias in the "ethnic aisle." The focus should not be about a reactive practice but about a reflective practice.

Equity should be the main dish, not just an optional ingredient.

We talk about equity in coded language when referring to BIPOC students. Try taking the word *equity* and substituting it with "Black people." How does it sound to say "Black-people-based practices" instead of "equity-based practices"? Or here are some "strategies for Black kids" instead of "strategies for equity." When we separate students of color under the guise of equity, we are guilty of othering. We refer to this as Equity with a capital "E."

Practicing Equity with a capital "E" implies including *other* resources. For example, when we bring in a book by a Black author about Black struggles during the month of February but ignore BIPOC contributions throughout the year. Educators need to interrogate the ways they deliver the curriculum and why they are holding on to a traditional system that pushes out so many students.

Equity is not a separate branch in the teaching tree.

It is the vital root.

In this book, the SEL practices and the strategies have equity baked in. Equity is the very fiber of Transformative Social and Emotional Learning. The most effective strategies for teaching Black and Brown students are not some special ways to teach them because of their skin color. Transformative SEL and PBL are, quite simply, excellent strategies to teach ALL children. Don't put Black and Brown students in the "ethnic aisle" of your lesson plans. Teach all kids in constructivist, humanistic ways; honor their unique culture and gifts; build on their strengths in authentic tasks seated in their community.

SEL must be culturally responsive. If it is not culturally responsive, is it really SEL? Kids will not develop self-awareness if we deny their core identities. Author Dr. Ibram Kendi describes his school experience: "I hated what they called civilization, represented most immediately by school. I loved what they considered dysfunctional—African American culture, which defined my life outside school."[27] Every culture has its unique strengths that should be honored and amplified in the classroom.

Teachers can prioritize systemic injustice as the focus of student projects and SEL skill development. Dena Simmons, founder of LiberatED, an organization focused on intersectionality, asks, "Why teach Relationship Skills if the lessons do not reflect on the interpersonal conflicts that result from racism? Why discuss Self- and Social Awareness without considering the imbalance of power and privilege, even if that means examining controversial topics like white supremacy?"[28]

Do not reserve topics of race, privilege, and power for "diverse" students. White students, especially, need to explore these topics if we expect to challenge existing structural inequities.

Low teacher expectations of students are harmful. Dr. Bettina Love, an award-winning author and cofounder of the

Abolitionist Teaching Network (ATN), talks about children of color being "spirit murdered" when schools have such low expectations of them that they never offer them any opportunities to show what they can do.[29] Black and Brown students deserve the opportunities afforded by authentic PBL to cultivate SEL competencies in culturally responsive ways. "Research suggests that it is precisely these students [disadvantaged and BIPOC] who would benefit most from an approach that integrates mastery, identity, and creativity."[30] SEL cannot be viewed as a behavior-management system for students of color! All students need to grow in Transformative SEL competencies to positively impact society. Smoother behavior in the classroom may sometimes be a bonus effect, but it is not the end goal of Transformative SEL.

Teacher SEL Self Work

Educators should examine their SEL skills first, before they lead students in Transformative SEL. In the classic book, *Teaching as a Subversive Activity*, Postman and Weingarter explain, "There can be no significant innovation in education that does not have at its center the attitudes of teachers, and it is an illusion to think otherwise. The beliefs, feelings, and assumptions of teachers are the air of a learning environment; they determine the quality of life within it."[31] Educators who have not reflected on their own SEL strengths, weaknesses, and biases will be ill-equipped to cultivate Transformative SEL in students.

It is particularly important for teachers to reflect on their beliefs about BIPOC children, realizing that they may have implicit bias that they are unaware of. Teachers often have less constructive relationships with BIPOC and lower-income students than with higher income white students.[32] The Education Trust study, *Social, Emotional, and Academic Development from an Equity Lens*, recommends changing adult beliefs from

- "deficit to strength-based mindset,
- one-size-fits all to recognizing cultural and contextual influences,
- allowing bias to impact students to targeted and continuous efforts to reduce bias." [33]

When educators focus only on scaffolds and supports for deficiencies, it sends a hidden message that adults have low expectations for that student. (See Chapter 5 Self-Assessment for more details on scaffolding learning in PBL.) When our curriculum only highlights the dominant white, middle-class culture and values, it "others" those students who don't match the norm. When teachers don't recognize their own implicit bias as a result of growing up in a culture with structural racism, they fail to notice when their students are victims of bias from other children, the school system, or even from the teacher themselves. Instead, teachers should discover and build upon the many assets that diverse students bring to the classroom, paying particular attention to cultural strengths such as family and community cohesiveness, multilingual aptitude, and cultural heritage. Educators should practice Self-Awareness by making a habit of learning about their students' cultural perspectives and reflecting on their own implicit beliefs, recognizing that actions speak louder than words. In Chapter 4, we include an

Identity Inventory exercise to help students build strong Self-Awareness skills through implicit self-assessment. These are strategies that we also have used in our teacher professional de-velopment workshops to encourage profound self-reflections about implicit bias. Consider these ten implicit bias reflection questions:

10 Implicit Bias Reflection Questions

1. What current issues do I care about?
2. What socio-economic, religious, physical, or racial advantages do I have?
3. What lived experiences helped form my implicit biases?
4. Do I actively interact with people that have different life experiences?
5. How well do I understand intersectionality (or how social groupings like race, class, gender, sexuality, age, etc. affect people's lived experiences)?
6. Am I comfortable participating in difficult conversations about social issues?
7. Do I listen or judge during conversations about controversial social issues?
8. How are my biases reflected in the way I teach or relate to my students?
9. What steps do I take to learn more and increase my implicit bias awareness?
10. What steps do I take to dismantle implicit institutional biases when they are identified?

School administrators should provide time and space for teachers to reflect and define the SEL competencies in their context. Educators should explicitly interrogate their own SEL strengths and weaknesses, workshopping how to effectively integrate the instruction of SEL into the school day in culturally appropriate ways.[34] Personal interrogation must go beyond listening to an inspirational keynote or a one-off professional development day. There must be a long-term commitment by the district to replace the ubiquitous mounds of paperwork, the pointless teacher meetings, and fruitless alignment sessions with ongoing support that is differentiated and personalized for specific teacher needs in their school context.

Misconception 6: Schools can just purchase a canned, add-on SEL program.

In 2020, when the COVID-19 pandemic raged throughout the world, the majority of schools shifted to virtual or hybrid learning. With the stress of the pandemic lockdown, the protest against police brutality, and the lack of consistent contact with many children, educators were rightly concerned about their students' wellbeing. Districts scrambled to purchase one of the numerous add-on or stand-alone SEL curriculums that are readily available. While well intentioned, buying SEL curricula is misguided because it is based on the flawed assumption that SEL is another subject area. SEL should not be separated, taking up valuable class time, but integrated throughout the entire day. Stand-alone SEL curriculum is an example of schools compartmentalizing learning. Schools already have false divisions of subject matter between math, English, science, and social studies that reinforce the idea that school is separate from the real world. Stand-alone SEL curriculum relegates it to becoming just another disconnected "subject" that is learned in the abstract, rather than personally applied to life. Not to mention that the one-size-fits-all nature of these out-of-the-box SEL curricula, by definition, cannot also be culturally responsive to the plethora of cultural and social-economic demographics any one school may find in their student body.

The add-on approach to SEL is not recommended. Frey, Fisher, and Smith argue that SEL should be the "fabric" of school. It should be modeled by adults and integrated into the daily classroom routines. SEL is best taught through practicing the competencies in authentic learning experiences.[35]

SEL should be the heart and soul of everything that happens in the classroom all day, every day.

Social and Emotional learning should not feel like the latest fad program added onto teachers' already overwhelming list of mandates. Yet SEL is vital to students' academic and social success. Therefore, what is the best way for teachers, who are already paralyzed by too many demands, to find time for it? Project Based Learning is the perfect framework to seamlessly integrate SEL into any classroom. In PBL, students are practicing (a) Responsible Decision-Making as they address real-world problems, (b) Relationship Skills as they communicate in their groups, and (c) Social Awareness, as they collaborate with the community.

A further weakness of many SEL programs is a focus on the individual aspects of Self Awareness and Self-Management. It is a common practice to introduce SEL competencies sequentially. The result is that Social Awareness, Responsible Decision Making, and Relationship Skills are left until later in the school year, or in worst case scenarios never taught at all. We disagree with the need to teach SEL competencies in sequence. SEL should not be seen as a hierarchy. PBL starts with an authentic problem for student groups to research that emphasizes Responsible Decision-Making and Relationship Skills first. As a result of success at the end of a project, students become more Self-Aware of their abilities and their Self-Management limitations. These limitations can be improved throughout the school year with additional opportunities to make meaningful decisions and build larger networks. Zaretta Hammond tells us that "competence precedes confidence."[36] PBL creates an environment where students can foster all of the SEL competencies simultaneously.

Character, confidence, and self-esteem are better developed by students engaging in authentic, meaningful work, rather than an artificial, canned program of character-building.

The best approach is to directly teach SEL skills to all students infused into daily classroom routines. Start by assessing students for strengths to build on and gaps to improve. Just as when introducing content, tailor the instruction of SEL skills to data gathered from formative assessments of each child. If one truly believes that SEL competencies matter, they need to plan their implementation, teach, practice, and assess them in every student. The best framework to integrate SEL into daily classroom routines is Project Based Learning. It is the ideal structure to make practicing SEL skills an integrated part of your class. In the next chapter, we will look at an overview of the key components of PBL.

Reflection Questions

- Which of the SEL competencies have you already used in your practice?
- Which of the SEL competencies are new or unclear to you and require further investigation?
- Have the examples of SEL that you have observed been Individual, Collaborative, or Transformative?
- Which of the SEL competencies seem most important to teach your students?
- In what contexts have you heard misconceptions about SEL?
- How can you be certain that your SEL is Transformative for all your students?
- What self-work do you need to do before teaching?

PULSE OF PBL

Chapter 3

Components of
Project Based Learning

PBL is the ideal framework to structure the instruction, practice, and assessment of SEL Competencies.

- Entry Event
- Driving Question
- Need to Knows
- Structured Inquiry
- Benchmarks and Formative Assessment
- Community Partners
- Voice and Choice
- Reflection
- Feedback and Refinement
- Final Product Presentation

Having defined the three levels of Social and Emotional Learning in each of the five CASEL competencies, let's examine the components of Project Based Learning. Keep in mind that PBL is an interwoven process, not a strict sequence of steps like a recipe. While a few aspects are linear—particularly in the way projects launch and end—most of these things are happening simultaneously throughout the project cycle. In this chapter, we describe two PBL examples, one elementary and one secondary, observing the PBL journey from start to finish and noting the SEL competencies occurring during each step.

Entry Event

Most students do not come to class in love with our course content. Therefore, teachers need to generate some excitement by launching projects with a compelling entry event. It is helpful to remember famed TV scientist Bill Nye's rule for kids: ABC—Action Before Content.[37] The purpose of the entry event is to generate a buzz around the targeted topic, build curiosity, and give students some initial background and experiential knowledge. An effective entry event naturally leads to student questions about the project. An entry event could be as simple as a short video or as complex as a multiple-day simulation. Guest speakers, field trips, and fieldwork are other popular types of entry events. Excellent entry events often have an element of mystery or surprise to them. The best entry events have both a cognitive and an empathetic hook. We want to capture students' hearts and minds. Remember that young people do not have the life experience that we have had, and it is not enough to ask them to imagine things or introduce a topic that bears no relevance to them.

Before students' minds go deep, their bodies must actively engage with content.

The Trickster Tales Project was a third-grade project launched at Leonardo da Vinci Health Sciences Charter, a diverse urban school in San Diego, California. Children studied folk tales in a project that integrated literature, writing, art, science, math, and social studies.[38] Teacher Erin Gannon based the project on a cross section of folktales from around the world that involved a trickster character who overcomes a weakness in a cunning or funny way. This project had an extended entry event that spanned over a few weeks. Since the school had limited resources, the project began when students launched a Donors Choose campaign to raise money to purchase "trickster tales" books. Students employed math as they practiced graphing and addition skills when charting the funds donated toward their goal.

Once the money was raised and books were purchased, the main entry event commenced. Gannon had an "unboxing" of the delivered packages. Students opened the boxes and were given time to explore the trickster tales. They placed a sticky note on their top book choice, claiming it to read later. Gannon read some of the books out loud to the class, and they created a wall chart of common elements between the stories. Students started asking questions and making connections between the stories. They knew that all of the books were about trickster tales, but Gannon had not explained what that term meant. Students discovered the meaning of the term through a whole class conversation about the themes of the stories.

A few days later, students began a series of inquiry lessons on light and shadows in science. Gannon introduced shadow and light kits from a local science center. Students performed multiple experiments to observe how different sizes and colors of bulbs affected the pattern of the shadows. At the time, they were unaware that the science content would ultimately be a part of their Trickster Tales Project. Students were intrigued and came to class wanting to know more.

Similarly, Mike's Civil Rights Project integrated American History and English Language Arts (ELA) for his high school sophomores at Kent Innovation High, a comprehensive Project Based Learning school. Located in Grand Rapids, Michigan, the school serviced diverse students from rural, urban, and suburban districts across the county. Like the Trickster Tales, this project started with a multiple-step entry event as well. In step one, students watched a 2012 episode of the hidden camera TV show *What Would You Do?* that staged groups of Black and white teenage actors vandalizing a car in a city park to see how passersby would react.[39] The Black kids were confronted by many people and numerous calls were made to the police. The white kids were not confronted by anyone, and the only call made to the police was to report that there were Black kids (family members of the Black actors) sleeping in a different car in the parking lot. This first step illustrated implicit biases of the people that passed by. (Note: this project was first implemented in 2015, five years before the Black Lives Matter movement led world-wide protests of the graphic murder of George Floyd).

For the second step of the entry event, students took the online implicit bias test from Harvard University[40] to start a conversation on whether they may have some implicit preferences toward white or Black people that they were unaware of. For the final step, students were shown historical slides of a Ku Klux Klan (KKK) rally on July 4, 1925. The KKK are an American white supremacist hate group who historically have terrorized Catholics, Jews, non-whites, leftists, and immi-grants. Mike blotted out the location of the rally, and students researched only to discover that the event took place in their city, Grand Rapids. Now students had the background knowledge to capture their attention about the history and per-sistence of racism, their personal subconscious biases, and the sobering proximity of horrific racist events.

Entry events address several of the SEL competencies. First of all, students practice intense observation, demonstrating cu-riosity and open-mindedness of Responsible Decision-Making. The students' role in entry events is not to sit back and be entertained, but to actively take note of what they are experiencing with the mindset of a crime scene detective. The elementary students in Gannon's classroom were investigating and making conjectures from the start about the relationships between light, objects, and shadows. Transformative entry events, such as the Civil Rights Podcast example, place students in other's perspectives, building Social Awareness skills of compassion and empathy.

Driving Question

In PBL, the Driving Question (DQ) helps frame the project for both students and the teacher. It gives a purpose and focus both to the teacher's planning and to student inquiry. The most important aspect of a good DQ is that it is engaging. It should be a question that students want to answer. DQs should not be "schooly" like a state standard but should be written using language that connects with the students. Mike often uses trending slang or popular song lyrics. To create her DQs, Matinga aligns the lesson content with current issues relevant to students' daily lives. Great DQs should work like internet clickbait and entice student interest.

The Driving Question is different from the traditional "hook" teachers use at the beginning of a lesson to grab students' attention. The traditional "hook" is used to prepare students for the upcoming teacher-led lesson. Though it might serve as a reference later in the learning, it does not drive the lesson or the learning. Hooks do not compel the student to scrutinize the topic nor mobilize actions. The Driving Question, on the other hand, is used not only to create a buzz but to sustain interest throughout the project. More importantly, DQs oblige students to react, research, and execute a plan to answer them.

In addition to a Driving Question, students are given a Framing Question. Framing Questions specify student roles, final products, audience, and purpose. They are more structured than DQs, usually using the following format:

How can we, as _____ (role) . . .
Do _____ (task) . . .
So that _____ (audience and/or purpose)?

Framing Questions make clear to students what they will be doing in the project and for what purpose. Note that the role is sometimes omitted for secondary students as it is often implied.

> The Driving Question for the Trickster Tales Project was as follows:
> *"How do trickster tales teach cultural values?"*

The goal of this project was for students to experience the power of stories to teach cultural values—primarily to children, but also to adults. Gannon's students came from diverse backgrounds, and she wanted them to explore how different cultures and households teach norms through the differences and similarities of their stories. She used the ancient tradition of storytelling to develop an inclusive culture in her classroom.

> The Framing Question for the Trickster Tales Project was as follows:
> *"How can we, as storytellers, use art and science to share trickster tales in a puppet show for our parents?"*

Another purpose of Gannon's project was to integrate art and science into the students' storytelling skills. Artistic shadow puppets were created to perform the stories. They studied the science of how light and shadows worked so that they could move the puppets closer and farther from the light source for dramatic effects in their performance.

> The Driving Question for the Civil Rights Podcasts Project was as follows:
> *"How can a social movement effectively cause change?"*

One of the goals of the Civil Rights Podcast project was for students to learn about the historical discrimination against African Americans from post-Civil War to present and how protest and resistance shifted legal and tangible changes in American society. Students had to determine which resistance methods were most effective with the implied purpose of supporting the continued struggle for equity today.

> The Framing Question for the Civil Rights Podcasts Project was as follows:
> *"How can we create a podcast walking tour documenting Grand Rapids civil rights events to tell the story of how our city worked toward equity?"*

Another goal of this project was for students to realize that the Civil Rights Movement did not just happen in Alabama, Mississippi, and the deep South but in the North too, including their hometown. Additionally, Mike wanted students to go beyond the famous heroes of the Civil Rights Movement and appreciate the thousands of lesser-known people who fought for equal rights for African Americans. The framing question revealed to students that they would be creating podcasts to share their town's stories.

The Trickster Tale Driving Question cultivated Social Awareness by asking students to understand beliefs and values from various cultures around the world and the impact of their traditional stories in building their personal identities. Its Framing Question presented a scientific challenge: the use of light and shadows in storytelling. This scientific challenge re-quired Responsible Decision-Making skills to solve it. Students practiced open-mindedness, analyzed information, and identi-fied possible solutions to answer the DQ and the Framing Question. This challenge encouraged students to reflect on the origin stories of their community or family beliefs and social norms—an exercise that in turn created a healthier and more inclusive learning environment.

The Civil Rights Driving Question developed the Social Awareness competencies of examining prejudices and biases while giving a sense of purpose to the project. Its Framing Question identified the social problem that students would in-vestigate, employing Responsible Decision-Making to propose ways to apply historic resistance actions and methods to cur-rent injustices to promote the well-being of BIPOC communities. The analysis of the students' research challenged their perspectives and encouraged them to identify unjust so-cial norms and use their voices to express empathy, compassion, and change.

Need to Knows

Immediately after the entry event and the revealing of the DQ and Framing Question, students start the Need to Know (N2K) process. This is a version of the well-known KWL protocol:

1. What do you **Know** about . . . ?
2. What do you **Want** to know about . . . ?
3. What have you **Learned** about . . . ?

In PBL, the first two questions are emphasized when a project is launched. What do you **know**, or what background knowledge do you have about the topic? Then what do you **Need to Know** in order to answer the DQ and complete the task in the Framing Question? Teachers use a wide variety of processes to gather these questions. Student questions range from content knowledge to skills required to complete the final product. The result is a list of key N2Ks that drive inquiry through the rest of the project.

Don't Get in Your Own Way:

To promote structured inquiry and interest throughout the project, refrain from answering students' questions as you collect N2Ks. If you treat the N2K exercise as a Q&A, students will continue to defer to you and will not be encouraged to answer the questions through their research and collaborative work. Instead answer student questions with questions that prompt inquiry. "I wonder, what is a good source to find that infor-mation?" Or encourage them to add questions to

---

be considered later. "That is a great question, please add it to our N2K list." Use students' N2K list to guide what information or breadcrumbs you need to include in the coming days to ensure students "find" information themselves.

Gannon used an organic process of gathering N2Ks throughout the Trickster Tales Project. Rather than reveal the entire project on the first day, she let the students drive the project through activities that built up to the final product. She started a list of N2K questions during the whole class discussion after the "unboxing" of the trickster tales. After playing with the light and shadow kits, students added more science questions to the class N2Ks.

Not all kids have easy access to background knowledge, so Gannon had students write down the questions in a note catcher inside of their science notebooks. They wrote daily entries, adding observations, questions, and solutions. Then she created a "Notice and Wonderings" anchor chart from listening to students during project exploration time.

The gathering of the N2Ks in Mike's Civil Rights Podcast Project started in a Google Doc that listed the DQ, Framing Question, state social studies standards, and Common Core ELA standards. Below this information, each student wrote their first name on a line and list their N2Ks after it.

Many of their questions focused on the KKK as students were curious about this organization from the photo gallery that they had seen in the entry event. Other questions originated from the state standards. At the beginning of the year, Mike taught students how to break down the state social studies standards to help them focus their research. The Civil Rights Podcast Project was implemented toward the end of the school year, so students asked questions about the components of the state standards that were either unfamiliar to them or piqued their interest. Other students asked general questions that they had about the Civil Rights Movement and the history of racism.

Student-Generated N2Ks in Mike's Civil Rights Movement Project

Entry Event Questions	<ul><li>Were there specific events that brought about the (KKK) march on July 4, 1925?</li><li>Why didn't people stand up for other people's rights?</li><li>Why was there so much hate back then, even though it wasn't all that long ago?</li><li>How did the KKK convince so many people to join them? Why did their methods of convincing people work?</li><li>Why is the KKK still allowed to be around today and is not classified as a terrorist organization?</li></ul>
Standards-Based Questions	<ul><li>How have certain court cases impacted the movement?</li><li>How was gender integration a part of the Civil Rights Movement?</li><li>Why is *Plessy v. Ferguson* important?</li><li>What is the Harlem Renaissance, and how did it affect the movement?</li></ul>

	• What are Jim Crow laws?
General Topic Questions	• Why do people feel the need to degrade other people based on their skin pigmentation? • How does our generation behave toward a different race compared to the previous generation? • Are we just focusing on the time frame of 50s–60s? And are we just focusing on civil rights that have to do with race or civil rights for gender or LGBTQ?? • Why did it take so long for people to realize that what was happening is wrong? • How can we stop racism completely if it is passed on from generation to generation? • How do you get rid of a problem that has become rooted in our society as instinct rather than choice? • Can we please talk about systematic racism, pleaseeeeeee????

After generating all these questions in the Google Doc, students worked in groups to choose their top three questions. These questions were then shared out to the whole class, and a student wrote them on butcher paper that was then posted on the wall for reference during the remainder of the project.

The purpose of the N2K process is to teach students to ask better questions to create a platform to practice Responsible Decision-Making. It is a structure for student initiative to access their personal agency and to organize themselves under Self-Management. Student questions guide the project process as they set their goals motivated by their interests in the subject matter.

Structured Inquiry

Now that students are excited about the project and the class N2Ks are posted on the wall, they dive into a cycle of inquiry that extends throughout the project. Inquiry in PBL is the art of investigating intriguing questions embedded across all subject areas. During the inquiry phase of a project, student teams plan out their "next steps" to answer the N2K questions through a combination of research, interviews, experiments, surveys, observations, discussions, and teacher instruction. Inquiry is the meat of the PBL project and extends until the final showcase. Through the lens of SEL, structured inquiry focuses not only on academic content, but also on the essential investigation skills needed to produce a successful final product.

In the Trickster Tales Project, the inquiry phase started during the entry event and continued throughout. Students determined the theme of each tale and how the themes related to one another. This led to the use of a wall chart documenting trickster character traits in each story and how that character interacted with others.

Story (Include country/ culture)	Who is the **trick-ster**? (List character traits)	Who gets **tricked**?	Why? What does the trickster **want**?	Is the trickster a **teacher** or a **fool**?	What do **we learn**?

Wall chart documenting descriptors and interactions of the trickster

At the same time, in science, students began experimenting with shadows and lights. They used transparent objects and toys to investigate which kind of objects light gets "stuck on." Students played with different types of bulbs and wattages, and they moved objects closer and further away from the light, noting the effects.

As students began creating their own folk tale, a master storyteller visited their classroom and shared how to block their story into chunks to present a more natural narrative to their audience, instead of memorizing it word for word. An artist came and demonstrated Indonesian shadow puppets. She brought several different kinds of puppets and introduced the idea of colored shadows. Students immediately wanted to make their own shadow puppets to share their folk tales. Structured inquiry continued as the children soon realized that manipulating puppets and making lighting adjustments simultaneously throughout their performance made it difficult to focus on telling the story. They solved this issue by deciding to prerecord the narration of their stories and play the audio files while they manipulated the puppets during their presentation.

Likewise, in the Civil Rights Podcast Project, the inquiry phase began as students researched key vocabulary and historical events listed in the state standards from post–Civil War through the Civil Rights Movement. Students participated in literature circles on the books *Beloved* by Tony Morrison, *The Autobiography of Malcolm X* by Alex Haley and Malcolm X, *I Know Why the Caged Bird Sings* by Maya Angelou, and *Native Son* by Richard Wright. They analyzed primary source writings and watched videos alongside contemporary writings on civil rights.

Inquiry continued with a trip to the city archives at the local public library. Students delved into old books and newspaper clippings of local civil rights leaders and events. They even went old-school and scrolled through microfiche records. Next students interviewed their own family and community members to gather their perspectives on Civil Rights Movement events in Grand Rapids. Students lacked podcasting experience, so they listened and critiqued existing podcasts, noting their structure and elements. Allowing students to choose their podcast style based on product analysis is the type of learning scaffolding that empowers the students because it gives them the opportunity to analyze various types of podcasts options rather than merely receiving direct instruction about what a quality podcasts sounds like. Additionally, students attended workshops on storyboarding and scriptwriting to prepare them for the final product.

Inquiry encompassed the student-centered design thinking process that is at the core of Responsible Decision-Making. Students were researching, experimenting, testing ideas, reflecting, discovering solutions, and considering their impact on the community every step of the way. Similarly, the Trickster Tales Project centered on perseverance. Using Responsible Decision-Making strategies, students problem-solved hurdles that arose as they blocked out their stories and created puppets. Students rec-orded audio versions of their stories to address the difficulty of telling their story and working the puppets simultaneously. They persisted through all of these challenges. Students showed perseverance by using Self-Management skills as they made agreements for partner work, structured goal setting for each day, established clear deadlines with the class timeline, and held themselves responsible to take their work seriously, especially during audio recording and puppet performance.

Relationship Skills was the SEL focus of the Civil Rights Project. Students used team contracts and scrum boards (see Chapter 5) to communicate effectively about their project progress. Students reflected on their learning by completing a weekly exit ticket on one of the capacities of Relationship Skills in the CASEL framework. Students led a Talking Circle (page 181) to discuss issues of group cohesion throughout the project.

Benchmarks and Formative Assessments

Benchmark assessments are major checkpoints throughout the project cycle to check students' understanding of content standards and expected progress on the project. Examples might include outlines, rough drafts, prototypes, written scripts, or storyboards. Formative assessments are daily check-ins for understanding and misconceptions. They can take almost any form, from written exit tickets to teacher observations

(See "Protocols" in Chapter 9 for more examples). By the end of the project, group project outcomes should not be a surprise to the teacher because these daily check-ins allow a window into each step of the groups' progress.

Assessment is not limited to the teacher; frequent peer and self-assessment are part of the culture of the PBL classroom. Additionally, community experts can provide feedback on student work. Every activity in the classroom can be a potential formative assessment from daily protocols to conversations and observations. The PBL teacher is constantly checking their students, evaluating what knowledge or skills are lacking, and adjusting by providing small group workshops or scaffolding as needed for student success.

The Trickster Tales Project was primarily an English Language Arts project but included multiple content areas with specific benchmarks for each one. In ELA, students had to recount fables and folktales to determine the central message, lesson, or moral of each story. A second literacy standard required them to "tell a story with appropriate facts and relevant, descriptive details, speaking clearly at an understandable pace."[41] Speaking and listening standards required students to fluidly tell an engaging story on an audio recording. Additionally, the project met social studies standards about folklore traditions around the world through the variety of books read.

Gannon used observations and conversations with students as formative assessments, and she documented details on a clipboard chart. Each student had to analyze the trickster in their chosen story and record in their notebook a chart similar to the class wall chart as part of their summative assessment.

The students wrote the moral of their story in their notebooks before participating in the whole class debrief sessions as formative checks of understanding. The audio recordings were used as summative assessment for the speaking and listening standards. For social studies, students demonstrated mapping skills documenting the places around the world where their stories originated.

For science, students investigated standards about the effects of placing objects made of different materials in a beam of light. In math, they charted the funds they raised prior to starting the project, and they practiced measurement while investigating the effect on shadows when moving objects different distances from the light source.

Students drew diagrams in their science notebooks to demonstrate what they learned about the effects on shadows of different kinds of objects located at various distances from the light source. They defined the concept of shadow and explained how they are made. Students applied their learning in another context by going outside and drawing diagrams of shadows of objects in the sun. For math, students measured the distances between light sources and objects, then labeled them in their shadow diagrams. During the fundraiser, they divided the fundraising goal by the number of students in their class to learn how much each family would need to raise in donations.

In the Trickster Tales Project students learned and practiced Self-Awareness skills as they analyzed their chosen stories. For example, they learned that in some of the stories, the trickster is typically a smaller, weaker animal that uses its wit to outsmart the bigger, stronger animals. The class discussed which characters in their stories reflected their own personal strengths and how to use them to their advantage while at the same time being humble and modest. Gannon assessed perseverance by walking around with a checklist, documenting behavior as she observed evidence of this important skill. She led whole group discussions about perseverance and had students write reflections about their stamina and "stick-to-it-ness" in their notebooks.

The Civil Rights Podcast Project contained two social studies benchmarks and two ELA ones. The first social studies benchmark required students to draw sketches detailing Jim Crow–era events and policies. For the second benchmark, students created a timeline of their top ten events of the Civil Rights Movement. Both assignments required students to verbally explain the history and rationale of their choices.

The social studies content was formatively assessed primarily through conversations and observations. Primary and secondary sources were the basis of whole class and small groups discussions. Mike used exit tickets to check for gaps in understanding and daily check-ins of their sketches and timelines to ensure that students were staying on pace.

For the first ELA benchmark, students scrutinized the theme of their Civil Rights novel in a literary analysis. They explained how their novel reflected the African American experience of the time period it was written in. The second benchmark was the podcast script. Each script was written collaboratively, with individual group members typing in a different font color to show their contributions.

The ELA content was formatively assessed by teacher observations and peer feedback in literature circles. Students were prompted through their exit tickets to reflect on the theme and character development in their story. The podcast scripts cycled through several peer feedback protocols and checkpoints to ensure accuracy and improve the quality of writing.

Student's Social Awareness skills increased as they empathized with the historical injustices that African Americans struggled against in the United States. They understood how social norms and systems reinforced the unjust idea that BI-POC were less valued than white people. Students used effective communication skills as an integral part of their Civil Rights podcasts. They demonstrated heightened Relationship Skills through their collaborative scriptwriting, recording audio in an informative, engaging manner, and sharing their newfound in-sights with the community.

Community Partners

The next two components of PBL are the secret sauces that take a project from bland to spicy. Community partnerships give an authentic purpose to the projects. Instead of creating an assignment that only the teacher sees, students work with area experts to polish their skills and publish their work. Sharing their work publicly adds healthy stress, encouraging students to produce quality work because they know it has a purpose beyond the bottom of the recycling bin. PBL not only prepares students for the future, but it also affords them the opportunity to make a difference doing meaningful work right now!

The Trickster Tales Project was codesigned with a retired teacher and master storyteller, who suggested to Gannon the idea of using trickster tales as a focus for the project. The retired teacher recommended stories to read and, as a guest storyteller, was instrumental in demonstrating performing techniques to her students. Finally, when students decided that they needed to record their stories, he returned, set up a recording studio in the classroom, and helped students choose effective intro and ending music. Through his outside expertise, students created professional-level recordings that they were proud of.

A second community partner was the local puppeteer, who shared her knowledge of Indonesian shadow puppets through a short puppet show. She talked with students about her art and how shadow puppets used the science concepts that they had been studying. They learned that traditional performances are based on literature and often involve thought-provoking story-lines while engaging audiences with humor and drama. The puppeteer taught the students how to make the hinged puppets that they used in their final show. Both the master storyteller and the puppeteer made authentic connections between the content and the real world.

The Civil Rights Podcast Project had important connections to the community as well. During the research phase, Mike worked with the library archivist to find civil rights stories in the community. He brought in guest speakers from the local chapter of the National Association for the Advancement of Colored People (NAACP) and activists who challenged segregated busing by riding interstate buses in the Freedom Rides of 1961. Students interviewed family and community members about their memories of the Civil Rights era and events in their city, such as the integration of a local high school, which led to protests from white citizens. Through social media, some students even connected with eyewitnesses who no longer lived in the Grand Rapids area.

The students' completed podcasts were shared with the community by ExperienceGR.com, a website that is the primary tourism advertiser for local attractions, businesses, and hotels in the city of Grand Rapids, Michigan. The students were thrilled that the creators of such a public website valued and agreed to share their work. Students were proud that their stories would be heard by a larger audience beyond their school peers.

In both projects, community partners modeled for students specific SEL skills. The storyteller and puppeteer taught the third graders the Relationship Skill of effective communication. The archivist taught the high school students Responsible Decision-Making skills of how to make reasoned judgment after analyzing information, data, and facts. In general, community partners can model any of the competencies, but are especially impactful when they bring Social Awareness of a different cultural or social perspective.

Voice and Choice

The second secret sauce of PBL is student voice and choice. The traditional classroom is teacher-centered and often offers a one-size-fits-all learning experience that falls short of reaching all students. In PBL, students have choices in areas such as content, style of learning, how they demonstrate their learning, group roles, and who they learn with. These choices give students buy-in to the content and motivate them to deeper learning. Many PBL teachers allow the students to choose their final products or even dig deep into a particular passion related to the project focus.

Student choice does NOT mean that PBL is a free-for-all.

Choices are balanced by the need for deep exploration of academic content to meet the expectations for the class. The amount of choice should match the PBL experience level of the teacher as well as students and be age appropriate, although younger students can handle much more choice than they are often given credit for. If students are new to PBL, then choices should be gradually granted for the sanity of the teacher so that students aren't overwhelmed by a less structured learning environment.

Don't forget about voice! PBL is about more than giving students a choice board. PBL is transformative when students share their ideas and passionate viewpoints on important issues in the world and in their community. They don't need to wait until they are adults to be active citizens. Some of the world's most powerful role models are young activists such as Malala Yousafzai, Autumn Peltier, and Greta Thunberg, who are speaking out on issues that adults are neglecting. Like these dynamic influencers, our students should be empowered to seek out their strong interests and act upon them to make a positive difference right now!

Students had significant choices throughout the Trickster Tales Project. They picked a partner, their folk tale, and wrote their own stories. They flexed their creativity in designing and building custom puppets. When students struggled with the puppet hinges, they were given the choice of whether to use them. During the podcast recording session, they chose the music. Student voice happened with Gannon's guidance throughout the PBL process. She never told them that they were performing a trickster tale shadow puppet show. Instead, she introduced guests and concepts along the way, creating "breadcrumbs" that led students to suggest shadow puppets as the final product.

In this project, choice and voice decisions were limited in some areas. For example, everyone had to tell a tale using shadow puppets, and everyone had to record and perform to the audio. For younger students, it often makes sense to limit choices in some areas while allowing it in others. Too many choices can be paralyzing for young learners. Consistency in final products makes managing the process easier for the teacher.

In the Civil Rights Podcast Project, students had many choices. As in every project, they determined the N2K questions that drove their research. Students chose a partner to work with, and the teachers matched the pairs to form groups of four to create the podcasts. For the benchmark assessments, students showed creativity in their drawings of the Jim Crow era and chose which events to include on their Civil Rights Movement timelines. Each group researched and selected their podcast topic including who to interview. The groups chose their scriptwriting style, their podcast narrator, and artistic aspects such as open-source music and sound effects.

Similarly to the Trickster Tales Project, Mike's students did not have a choice in the final product. Everyone had to create and record a podcast episode. The idea was driven by their community partner who was interested in creating a walking tour of Grand Rapids Civil Rights events and experiences. In this case, it would not have made sense to let students have other choices as a final product on this project.

The students curated a lasting source of local Civil Rights legacy knowledge for any resident or visitor to the Grand Rapids website. Students' voice will live on powerfully through this final product. Just as importantly, students learned to talk from informed positions and defend civil rights with a new depth of knowledge. The podcast project sparked lifelong skills that students will wield in future civic participation fostering a more just society.

Their voices did not end with these podcasts but were just getting warmed up!

Student voice and choice in PBL leads to a greater sense of self-efficacy. Students develop agency as they are motivated to make plans for success. Students learn to advocate for themselves and, in the case of the Civil Rights Podcasts, for those who were historically oppressed. Students practiced Transformative SEL, becoming aware of systemic racism and understanding the power needed to implement equitable changes.

Reflection

In recent years, educators have reemphasized the importance of metacognition or the act of thinking about one's own thinking. Of course, the concept is not new as over one hundred years ago, John Dewey emphasized reflection in hands-on learning. The anonymous quote "We don't learn from experience but from reflecting on experience" is based on his writings. Reflection is "remembering with analysis."[42]

We define reflection as a learning tool that helps ground students' focus in the learning process rather than fixating on the final product. Taking time to think about both content and processes is an integral part of PBL that cements deeper learning. It is important that students reflect on their learning at regular intervals, not just at the conclusion of the project.

The Trickster Tales Project reflection experiences took place in two ways. First, during frequent whole class discussions, students reflected on the progress of the project. They then wrote their reflections in their notebooks along with key takeaways from the day. At the end of the project and before the project showcase, the class created a project wall timeline to summarize the story of their work. They displayed their project progress, related their perseverance through obstacles, and showed off the content knowledge that they had learned. This reflection experience was a visible reminder of their cognitive and emotional growth throughout the project.

Reflection began in the Civil Rights Project with the questions generated in the N2K process. It continued throughout the project in the form of daily exit tickets and think-pair-share conversations. Some days reflection questions measured the group's content knowledge and other times they ranked their team's Relationship Skills. Students considered which N2Ks were answered and added new questions to the list. At the conclusion of the project, there was a final reflection in a Google Form about the project itself, their personal collaboration, and enduring takeaways.

Reflection is a key component in all levels and aspects of SEL. It is how students learn and practice the skills along the way. When students reflect on how to improve society to make it more equitable, the project practices Level III Transformative SEL.

Feedback and Refinement

No one achieves their best work on their first try. PBL skills are developed through practice and over time. During a project, students revise their work constantly based on feedback from peers, the teacher, and community partners. The consistent use of procedures and protocols instructs students on how to both give and accept appropriate feedback, leading to personal growth and high-caliber final products.

Feedback for the Trickster Tales Project, for example, came from the master storyteller. He coached students on how to tell the story in chunks instead of memorizing their whole script. When the children struggled to tell the story and manipulate their puppets at the same time, he helped them manifest their idea of prerecording the audio by teaching audio-recording techniques so they could focus on manipulating the puppets. Students immediately listened to their stories and re-recorded if necessary. Many students who had been nervous and fearful of presenting in front of others felt more successful after listening to their recorded stories. Once students finished their Trickster Tales audio recordings and practiced their puppet shows, they performed for their kindergarten reading buddies. As one group performed, their classmates paid attention to the reactions of their young audience and offered suggestions for improvement the following day.

One of Mike and Matinga's favorite feedback protocols is the Tuning Protocol[43], in which students take turns providing focused feedback to help each other fine-tune their final products before presentation day (see Chapter 8). In the Civil Rights Project, Mike divided the class in half for a smaller number of groups. The students took turns reading their podcast scripts out loud to each other. The rest of the class used a rubric to give specific feedback on their content and the engagement level of their writing.

In addition, students peer reviewed their scriptwriting. Each team had two other teams review their writing for style, spelling, and grammar. Mike's ELA coteacher suggested final refinements of the scripts. It was important that all revisions were completed before the recording phase started. Students practiced reading their podcast scripts out loud multiple times before they were given a microphone to record.

Feedback and refinement are a combination of Responsible Decision-Making and Relationship Skills. Students carefully analyze each other's work and respond with feedback that is specific and thoughtful. Receiving feedback and acting on that feedback is an SEL skill that demonstrates maturity and a growth mindset.

Final Product Presentation

The culmination of any project is sharing it publicly with an audience. This can happen in a variety of ways. For example, a school open house day for parents and the community is a common choice for a learning showcase. Another option is posting student work online for the general public. Sometimes it is more powerful to bring in a few experts from the field related to the project to evaluate student work. The purpose of public presentations is for students to show off their work to the community and to bring a more authentic audience to view their work. An authentic audience outside of their peers and teacher is highly motivating to students.

When students work for you, it is acceptable. When they work for a public audience, it is exceptional.

After weeks of hard work, Gannon's third grade students performed their shadow puppet shows as part of a schoolwide education expo. After the performances, guests toured the project wall, the timeline of the entire process with anchor charts, content vocabulary, and photos from throughout the project. In addition, students showed off their reflection notebooks, explaining how they persevered through the successes and challenges during the project. Science experiment materials were displayed on tables for students to demonstrate to guests what they had learned. Gannon's students felt immense pride telling their stories and explaining how light and shadows work.

The final destination for the student podcasts project was a host page on Soundcloud.com with a Google Maps walking tour that connected each podcast to a specific location in the city of Grand Rapids. The students shared the page with ExperienceGR, the local advertising organization for the tourism and hotel industry, who posted a permanent blog post about the Civil Rights Walking Tour and podcasts on their website, which in turn sent many visitors to the Soundcloud site.[44] In addition, ExperienceGR mentioned the students' work on their Facebook feed and received over six hundred Facebook likes and over one hundred shares. Students were thrilled to see the positive community reaction to their project.

The culmination of a project demonstrates all of the SEL competencies. Students use Relationship Skills to communicate the solutions of their Responsible Decision-Making. They demonstrate empathy and justice while standing up for others. Reflections on the project process, not just the final product reveal the Self-Management used to complete the task. Finally, students develop confidence of Self-Awareness as they share their high-quality work.

PBL is about more than delivering content knowledge. Instead, it takes a holistic view of student learning. PBL explicitly develops SEL skills concurrent with content acquisition. As mentioned in Chapter 1, most school's profile of a graduate characteristics are equivalent to the SEL competencies. Educators recognize that these skills are critical in today's workplace and in meaningful relationships. The remainder of this book will focus on how to teach these Transformative SEL competencies in a project framework because they are the Pulse of PBL.

Reflection Questions

- What aspects of PBL have you already tried in your practice?
- What aspects of PBL are new or unclear to you and require further investigation?
- What aspects of PBL could you use in your classroom all the time, even if you are not "doing a project"?
- How might you add the "secret sauces" of community partners and student voice and choice to your projects?
- Can you start to predict some ways that SEL works inside of the PBL framework?

Chapter 4

Developing Self-Awareness

Develop students who advocate for themselves when they
need help, and then give them the tools to be independent.

- Classroom Culture
- Group Roles
- Student Identity
- Voice and Choice
- Reflection
- Public Presentations
- Self-Directed Learning

Cami was a freshman in the original class at Kent Innovation High (KIH), Mike's high school, where the Civil Rights Podcast Project took place. KIH was a PBL lab school, busing in students from twenty districts across the county. There was nervous energy as students met each other and made new friends during the first week. Cami was excited about this new opportunity but had a secret that had caused her pain at her home district and ostracized her at church. She was timid, suffered social anxiety, and refused to use the microphone to speak in front of the class.

Back at her local school, Cami had been pulled out of the classroom due to a reading disability. At KIH, Cami was a special education student who thrived in the mainstream PBL classroom. Mike remembers an art piece that she was proud of, made with the symbolism of the Holocaust. In a PBL classroom, Cami gained confidence through authentic work. With time she was no longer afraid to speak out, and she started confidently giving guest tours of the school.

During a Civil Rights project in Cami's sophomore year, students volunteered stories of personal discrimination that they had experienced. She stood up in front of the class and told **his** struggles as a transgender male in a rural community. He had experienced discrimination from his church and at his home school but felt safe and respected enough to share his story in Mike's class. It was a powerful moment as Cami had found his voice. During his junior year, Cami changed his name to Chris. Upon graduating, Chris shared with Mike that he didn't know who he was when he showed up at KIH and never would have made it through high school if it wasn't for finding himself in the PBL environment. Chris taught Mike that labeling students can be harmful and can lead to low expectations of students. Instead, students should be accepted and supported for who they are, wherever they are in their life's journey.

> "I mean I hope you and everyone at Kent Innovation High knows that what that school did for me was amazing. I had social anxiety and didn't know who or what I was, did not read in my age range, and COULD NOT do public speaking. And you and Mr. Holly's class was my favorite and I just felt so comfortable and free. I'll never forget that you made me speak through that mic for the first two weeks till I wasn't nervous anymore." –'Chris'[45]

Self-Awareness focuses on accurately perceiving who you are as a person and developing confidence based on your individual strengths. Many students like Chris are made to doubt themselves, their value, and their abilities because non-academic skills like his are deemed unimportant in the traditional classroom. However, Project Based Learning gives all students the opportunity to gain confidence through opportunities to create meaningful work that bridges academic and nonacademic abilities. Stories like Chris's are echoed in many schools, making it essential to consider one's classroom culture.

Classroom Culture

Meeting students at the door to welcome them to class is a common teacher practice. An exit ticket or even a high five on the way out of the door is another familiar routine. You have probably seen viral videos of teachers who have elaborate, personalized handshakes for each one of their students. You may not take it to that level, but daily check-ins and check-outs are an important part of getting to know students and building a culture of acceptance in your classroom. In order for students to develop Self-Awareness, they must feel safe to be their whole selves in your room even if they are still developing the person they want to be.

One of the first steps in teaching Self-Awareness is to encourage students to accurately depict their identity and develop an understanding on how to cope with their evolving emotions. For an SEL spin on the check-in ritual, use our version of the Mood Meter. The image features a four-colored spinner that students use to identify how they feel each day based on their energy level and disposition. Display the Mood Meter in a visible location near the doorway and ask students what color they are feeling as they enter the classroom. This quick visual formative assessment informs the teacher how ready students are to learn. Based on the mood of the group, the teacher may need to adjust the lesson before class begins. If an individual student is "blue" or "red," the teacher can have a conversation, de-escalating or offering support before the student is triggered into unproductive behavior.

GREEN

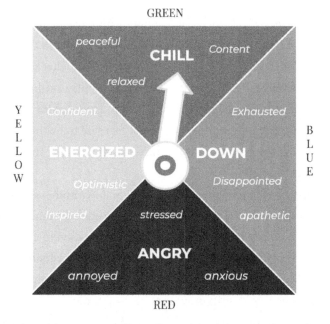

RED

Adapted from *Emotionally Intelligent Schools LLC Mood Meter*[46]

Second grade teacher, Wendy Turner uses mood bracelets as a way for students to communicate their disposition. Near the door of her classroom, she keeps a pail of red, blue, yellow, and green rubber bracelets with a simple sign asking, "How are you feeling today?" As students enter the room, they choose the color to wear based on how they are feeling. Mood bracelets give nonverbal messages to everyone about how each student is feeling. Throughout the day, students can go back to the pail and exchange the bracelet for a different color as their mood changes. When students choose a red bracelet, Turner checks in with them to see if they want to share their feelings. This is always a request, not a demand for the student to talk. Not only has she taught her students that it is normal to communicate their feelings in productive ways, but she has seen them grow in empathy as they support one another.[47]

After naming basic emotions, students need to learn skills to handle difficult emotions such as visible anger or sadness in healthy and productive ways. One simple but often overlooked aspect of the PBL classroom is that the teacher is not always locked in front of the room delivering whole class direct instruction. More often than not, PBL teachers are coaching and facilitating small groups of students. They have time to check in with students during this daily work time. While students are self-managing effectively during group work, the teacher can easily pull aside a student that needs emotional support or coaching. Since conferencing with students is a common PBL practice, quiet conversations can take place right in the room, and the other students will not be distracted from their projects.

Teachers need to establish classroom culture at the beginning of the year. Instead of simply handing out the course syllabus and focusing on the typical dos and don'ts on the first days of school, Matinga devised a student orientation process to onboard her students into her learning environment. Her first weeks of school were modeled after the practices of the typical new employee orientation. When starting a job, there is an expectation that new hires will be trained in each aspect of it.

They might be qualified to do the job, but they must be made familiar with the nuances of the role. Employee orientation is an everyday, real-world concept. After this training, there is an expectation that the new hire will do the job properly without constant oversight. Teaching SEL skills at the front end of the school year and every time there is a major change in processes and roles should be framed in similar terms. During the student orientation period, Matinga did not simply tell students what behavior was expected in her class. Rather she explicitly trained them to use Social and Emotional Learning skills that would keep them in an iterative path of self-reflection, self-direction, and Self-Management.

Explicitly training students to cope in a variety of circumstances mitigates problematic assumptions about "age appropriate" or culturally expected behaviors. By taking the time to lay down definitive lessons you help students become more *self-aware*. Then train them to use a set of universal scaffolds to analyze situations, putting everyone on the same page. Ultimately specifically training students to cope makes their role in their academic journey make more sense. Take, for example, Matinga's "Actionable vs. Circumstantial" T-chart scaffold:

ACTIONABLE	CIRCUMSTANTIAL
Stuff I can control	Stuff I cannot control

Many of the unproductive thinking and behaviors that students might understandably display in school are often prompted by how little control they feel over their lives as minors. As they become young adults, students gain more control of their world but need a clear understanding that life does not simply hand one a Harry Potter wand at age eighteen. The Actionable vs. Circumstantial lesson begins by creating a shared definition of the word *control*. Students are urged to collect and display definitions of the word *control* as a noun and as a verb (there are surprisingly many definitions). Then in small groups, they are asked to narrow their definitions of the word as it applies to people. Using a Talking Circle (see Chapter 6), the students create a shared definition of both the noun and verb forms.

The next step is to examine how the word *control* applies to their young lives by using the Actionable vs. Circumstantial T-chart. For this activity, the word *actionable* is simply defined as "stuff that you can control or act upon," and the word *circumstantial* is defined as "stuff you cannot control or that depends on circumstances outside of your control". Using an In2Out Protocol[48], students first audit their own beliefs by listing actionable and circumstantial aspects in their own lives (In). They then share their lists with one partner ("2"), finding commonalities to add to their list. Finally, they share in a whole class Talking Circle (Out). Matinga wrote question prompts and scenarios on small pieces of paper, folded them, and placed them inside of a basket. She fished the papers out one at a time and read them to prompt the discussion. The Talking Circle might include prompts such as these:

- How do you usually feel when faced with circumstances that are out of your control?
- Share an event or something that has happened that was out of your control. What was your reaction? What might you have done differently?

What students discover through this activity is that, even though they cannot rule the world, there is a great deal they can currently control. Help your students focus on the T-chart column that they can control, encouraging them to discuss the merits and personal benefits of adopting productive reactions to events and issues that they cannot control. Rather than teaching students to follow a list of dos and don'ts in a docile way, provide space for self-reflection to arrive at constructive behaviors on their own. Better yet, through this process they identify unproductive behavior in others. In the event that a student opts to be disruptive, everyone in the room is aware that the meltdown is not a personality issue but a selfish choice.

During project work time, if one of their peers is in the weeds or anxious about possible obstacles, students can reach for the Actionable vs. Circumstantial T-chart scaffold to narrow their options and guide their thinking. If the issue is circumstantial and there is no way to get over it, under it, or around it, then they need to walk away. If it is actionable, then they can use the KARE Gap ILeva (see Chapter 5) to diagnose the problem and choose a strategy to help them bridge the gap, resolving the issue.

Demand quality work with high expectations of each student because you have taken the time to train them how to cope before they face demanding work.

Address students' concerns with simple questions: "Is this actionable or is it circumstantial? If it is circumstantial, why are we still talking about it? If it is actionable, what strategies can you use to resolve or overcome this issue?" When the student shares a set of possible strategies, then you can workshop their chosen strategies to find feasible solutions together (some students just need to process aloud). Soon they will stop expecting you to solve their problems but instead see you as a mentor or facilitator.

The rest of Matinga's orientation is customized for her students. She lists the coping skills her students commonly seem to lack and creates interactive lessons, scaffolds, and activities to explain the purpose of each needed skill. She designs the stu-dent orientation using games, role-plays, movie clips, discussion sessions, or special speakers. Before starting any academic content, Matinga uses the student orientation process to put in place relevant classroom culture and high-performance expectations.

Group Roles

Another aspect of the student orientation process is defining how students will work in groups and what roles they will take on. Matinga and Mike's students begin the year by filling out an inventory that identifies their passions and skills. Every time they launch a new project, students take on different roles in their groups based on the information in the inventory. Students exercise personal agency when they select and manage their roles. Matinga and Mike recommend starting students off in roles that maximize their strongest skill set so they know their value to the group, then shift them to progressively challenging roles throughout the year to stretch their abilities.

Many students have never considered what makes them unique or that everyone else does not think and function exactly the same way as they do. The Myers-Briggs personality test is an easy way to have students reflect on their personal traits and possible tendencies.[49] Matinga uses the Personality Diagnostic ILeva to instruct students on how to first understand themselves and then create a plan to work with others.

She does not use this controversial test to determine students' personalities but to open conversations with young people about what might be their stress triggers that lead to unproductive thinking and subsequent detrimental behaviors. Once students have identified their stress triggers, they can learn to diagnose their hot buttons and understand how to avoid them or how to cope when they cannot avoid them. The goal is for students to proactively decide how to approach situations when there is a disagreement.

After reflecting on the different personality types presented by the Myers-Briggs test, students meet with others who have similar "personality types" and list their common strengths and areas of potential conflict. Next students repeat the process by joining mixed personality groups to continue their comparisons of strengths and stresses in a more diverse set of perspectives.

Personality Diagnostic ILeva

Identifying Triggers to Unproductive Behaviors to Self-Assess and Self-Manage

Steps	Rationale
1. **Individual Work:** *Teacher Facing: Students begin by individually completing the <u>Myers-Briggs Personality</u> test to obtain their four-letter combination.* Students quietly read their personality results description and annotate. *(Note: Read the questions out loud to pre-readers)* *(What do I **Agree** with? What do I want to **Argue** with? What do I want to **Act** upon?)*	**Reflection Phase.** Ensures that every student has an opportunity to process their personality description and annotate in a journal or notebook to display their thinking using the 3A's protocol as guiding questions.
2. **Small Groups Work:** Separate students based on their personality test results in the following *groups* to compare reactions and notes to their results: <ul><li>ESTJs & ENTJs</li><li>ESFJs & ENFJs</li><li>ENTPs & ENFPs</li><li>ESTPs & ESFPs</li></ul><ul><li>ISTJs & ISFJs</li><li>INTJs & INFJs</li><li>INFPs & ISFPs</li><li>INTPs & ISTPs</li></ul>*Note: If a group is too big, divide that group to ensure that no group is larger than 3-4 students.*	**Discovery Phase.** Facilitates students sharing their opinions and annotations of their personality descriptions with their *groups*. This is an opportunity to find commonalities/differences to share lived experiences. In their groupings, students will form relationships with people who have similar views as they do. This is important as they learn to work together in future projects. This is a fun event, and students will find it easy to open up and share with their peers.
3. **Small Group Work** Students will work in their same groups to complete a structured task. Students will answer their slide of questions on the SEL <u>Personality Diagnostic</u> conversations.	**Discussion Phase.** Recognize and manage their unproductive emotional behaviors from the collective answers to the *Personality Diagnostic* conversations. Perceive these behaviors in others. In order to grow progressively autonomous, students must manage negative emotions so they do not become unproductive behaviors.
4. **Individual Work** Allow students to describe themselves in writing using these two sentence stems:<ul><li>This is how I roll: *(for example: I am....I prefer...I usually....)*</li><li>This is how I manage how I roll: (for example: When I feel...I manage by...)*</li></ul>	**Reflection Phase.** Provides every student the opportunity to process the small group discussion and write a description of "the way they roll" and 'the way they manage how they roll" without interruptions or influence from others.
5. **Mixed Small Group or Whole Group Discussion** *Case study:* Students analyze scenarios to sort out how best to work with or help the person resolve the issues provided in each case study.	**Discussion Phase.** Allows students to verbalize their thinking and pit their opinion against others. Providing a third person scenario will allow the students to speak comfortably and share their honest opinions.

SEL Outcomes:
- Self-examination enriches students' own conclusions about how to identify their personality triggers and manage stressors that may contribute to unproductive behaviors.
- The conclusions can be used throughout the year or brought up when there is a current school or world event to analyze.

Assessment Recommendations:
Determine if students can accurately describe their traits and stressors and can complete a self-reflection follow up (in writing or video) based on the questions:
- o *Why is this learning experience important and how will it affect my friendships, my family, and my school year?*
- o *How will I apply the lessons learned through this activity?*
- o *How can I teach others the lessons that I learned about myself?*

Note: Matinga and Mike do not use the Myers-Briggs personality test to determine or predict behavior; they simply use it as a starting point to determine and describe student group types.[50]

We use the student reflection process from the Personality Diagnostic ILeva to complete Group Contracts for each team. This part of the process will be explained in the Project Management section of Chapter 5. To encourage Self-Awareness, each student grasps their unique identity and brings their particular skill sets to the project challenge. It is essential that students recognize the potential of their role in each project because it is misguided to require every student in a group to show evidence that they have completed the same exact list of tasks. In reality, when assembling a work team, the goal is to select and hire people who bring different skill sets to the table. True collaborative groups are interdependent, with each member bringing their talents to complete the final product. When students contribute their best skills to a project, they are more apt to engage in high quality, collective work.

Student Identity

Teachers often use introductory activities to start off the year to get to know their students and build classroom community. Instead, students could begin building Self-Awareness through personal projects. Try a selfie mini project (see PulseofPBL.com for template) to launch the year. In this short project, each student takes a selfie and presents a set of slides to talk about their strengths and passions. It creates community as students get to know one another, and it encourages them to recognize their strengths. This information then informs how the teacher designs future projects and what roles students might perform inside their teams.

Another option for students to explore Self-Awareness is to perform an Identity Inventory, an exploration of what factors shape who they are. First, students draw or find an image that represents themselves and place it in the middle rectangle. Next students list descriptors they consider to be key aspects of their identity. Conclude the Identity Inventory by reflecting on how their identity factors influence who they perceive themselves to be:

- What identity factors most shape your worldview?
- How do you resolve conflicts when others have opinions diametrically opposed to your perspective?
- How do your identity factors influence your choices and your actions?

Matinga's Identity Inventory

Immigrant

West African

Cis Black Female

American Citizen

Boy Mom

Wife

Have a terminal degree

Award winning educator

Love world foods

Human Rights advocate

My Identity Factors

Messy-Hair-Don't-Care Club

Name:
Dr. Abigail Madua Matinga Ebuka Morgades de Ragatz...at your service!

Oldest Sibling

Middle aged

Homeowner (suburbs)

Multi-lingual

World Traveler

innovator

Author

Korean Drama buff

Dyslexic

How much does my identity inspire my actions and views?

Early in the year, invite students to tell the story of their lives. First share your identity story, modeling vulnerability with personal details that shape how you became who you are. To keep your story on track, use the Identity Inventory. After connecting with your story, students will be inspired to tell their own. Divide students into small groups and use the Identity ILeva along with the Identity Inventory to structure students sharing their stories. The goal is for students to find connections with each other through their peer's experiences. Compassionate empathy is easier to practice when young people know more about their peer's lives, circumstances, and outlooks. This personal knowledge changes the way students interact with each other.

Identity Factors ILeva

Exploring Identity Factors to Recognize Students' Strengths and Promote Self-Awareness

Steps	Rationale
1. **Teacher Story**: Using the Identity Factor Inventory, the teacher shares their story showing vulnerability.	Connects students with you in personal ways as they learn things about you that they do not know. Modeles the process, inspiring students to share.
2. **Complete Identity Factors Inventory**: Each student fills out their own Identity Factors Inventory with the understanding that they will be sharing out descriptors of their choice.	Ponders the different aspects of their identity and the sources of it during silent reflection time. Respects the privacy of what they choose to share.
3. **Role of Audience:** Review with students the actions of an effective listener: body language, verbal and non-verbal cues, and eye contact.	Clearly defines the role of the audience and expected listening behaviors for triads.
4. **Small Group Triads**: In groups of three, give each student 5-8 minutes to share their identity story, picking which factors of their identity they choose to share. Audience practices listening skills. Complete confidentiality.	Practices listening skills and finding connections with their classmates, building compassionate empathy.
5. **Whole Class Debrief**: Discuss their level of listening skills in the triads. Debrief how this experience made them feel. Focus on the process and avoid sharing any personal stories.	Provides positive reinforcement of empathetic listening. Strengthens classroom community and builds trust.

SEL Outcomes:
- Reflection on Self-Awareness skills of integrating personal and social identities; identifying personal, cultural, and linguistic assets; and linking feelings, values, and thoughts.
- Practicing Social Awareness competencies of taking others' perspectives; recognizing strengths in others; and demonstrating empathy and compassion.

Assessment Recommendations:
- This is primarily a self and peer assessed activity. Students could journal the impact of *sharing triad* discussions both as a speaker vs. as a listener.
- Use a Fist to 5 or Exit ticket to reflect on their listening skills used during the activity.

For a different identity exploration, Shana V. White has her students draw identity self-portraits. She advocates for this practice because it builds trust, allowing students to feel safe to be their true selves. First, she has students draw an outline of their head and shoulders on a piece of paper with colored marker, pencils, or crayons. Next students draw a line down the middle of the paper. On the left side, they color their face and clothing. On the right side, students list the identity markers that they wish to share with the class.

It is important for students to understand up front that the self-portraits will be publicly displayed on the classroom wall so that they only reveal what they are comfortable sharing. One of the big takeaways from identity self-portraits is that students learn the difference between visible and invisible identity traits. Most young people initially focus on visible identity traits, but many of our most important identity markers are internal and not easily seen.[51]

In the middle of the year, after students have had the opportunity to work together and know each other well, conduct a follow-up to the Identity Inventory, the Human Gallery Walk. While the Identity Inventory is designed for student reflection on factors that compose their personal identity, the Human Gallery Walk is designed to invite descriptors from others. The results from this experience are surprising, inspiring, and often emotional.

Ask five to ten student volunteers to stand in front of a blank wall or window. Give each member of the rest of the class (audience) fifteen to twenty sticky notes and divide them into equal-sized groups in front of each volunteer. Invite the audience to think of a positive descriptor for each volunteer, write it on a sticky note, and place it on the wall around the volunteer. The descriptors are meant to celebrate accomplishments, character traits, aspirations, growth, inspirations, and positive qualities. Discourage students from fixating on physical characteristics unless it is a positive trait that the person is known for or is obviously proud of. For example: amazing hair, athletic, beautiful inside and out, fashionista, kind eyes, etc.

After everyone has contributed a descriptor, rotate the audience groups to the next volunteer in a clockwise direction. Repeat this process until everyone has added sticky notes to each volunteer student standing by the wall. Then take a quality photo of each of the volunteers surrounded by their sticky notes, making sure that all of their descriptors are legible. Allow students to make funny poses if they choose or to opt out of the photo. The following days, repeat with a different set of volunteers until you have collected photos of all your students. For a lasting surprise, print each of the photos, place them into dollar-store frames, and gift them to each student.

Mike's Human Gallery Walk

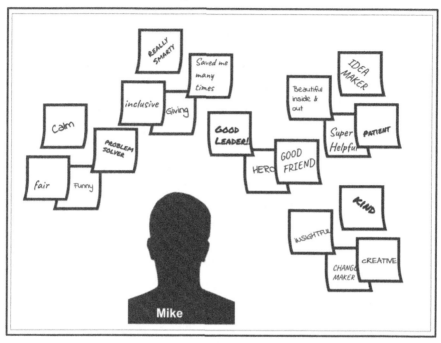

Identity work aligns with Transformative Self-Awareness, especially for BIPOC children because it honors their unique cultural strengths, providing a buffer against the historical racism that they may have internalized through social norms. Reflecting on the strength and value of their identity gives these students confidence to find positive solutions to current-day injustices they may encounter.[52]

Furthermore, when students are immersed in a project that focuses on self-exploration, they learn to identify their emo-tions and gain an accurate self-perception of themselves. One approach that instinctively leads to this introspection is a project with a strong literature component.

Whether looking at memoirs, classic texts, graphic novels, or picture books (they are great for kids of all ages!), students can explore topics such as personal character, identity, and theme.

For example, elementary students could explore the DQ "What makes me unique?" with whole class read-alouds of pic-ture books exploring identity and characters from diverse cultures. While reading *Night* by Elie Wiesel or *The Diary of Anne Frank*, middle school students might reflect and answer the DQ "What would I do if confronted with injustice?" or "How do I handle tough situations?" After reading various memoirs and biographies, high school students could compose and perform slam poetry addressing the DQ "What makes me, me?"

Voice and Choice

One of the hallmarks of PBL is that students have voice and choice throughout the project process, honoring each one's unique abilities. Then they utilize their strengths to create per-sonalized final products. Unfortunately, one of the shortcomings of traditional teaching is that students don't get a say on how they show evidence of their learning because most assessment is collected in writing. Students who are weaker writers lose confidence and "feel stupid." Sometimes the issue is not that the students have trouble with written expression. Matinga and Mike have had special education students who seemed to struggle with writing, but in reality they simply needed more time to process their thoughts, so they buckled under the constraints of timed written assessments. A real-world example is that Matinga's writing-processing time is slower than molasses in a harsh Michigan winter. Lucky for Matinga, Mike is a patient PBL expert, so no one was hurt in the development of this project.

In child development courses, teachers learn that children develop and process in unique ways, yet we often administer assessments in a singular way. To mitigate this inconsistency, Mike and Matinga allowed all students to demonstrate their learning through various methods beyond writing. Sometimes students would draw comics, perform skits, or give verbal presentations. Many students experienced academic success for the first time by showcasing their knowledge and skill set in alternative ways. To the students, these options revealed new ways that they were successful learners (Self-Awareness), boost-ing their self-esteem. Matinga and Mike were then able to build on their students' content knowledge and newfound confi-dence to develop their writing skills.

First and second graders in Melissa Riggs and Tracy Saylor's class in rural Necedah, Wisconsin, went to the local cranberry marsh to learn about the life cycle of the cranberry plants. This was an authentic experience for students because not only had Saylor worked there before becoming a teacher but one-third of the students had parents or other family members who worked at the cranberry farm. Students were engaged because they got to see the entire process of cranberry farming—from growing the tiny fruit, to harvesting, to packaging, to shipping. It demystified the Craisins® that they loved in their lunchboxes and showed that their food came from other sources than their local grocery store. Students learned firsthand the importance of their local economy in the larger food supply chain of the country.

Next students chose a fruit or vegetable to research as part of a larger project, exploring the question "How does a plant go from seed to table?" Most students picked a plant they were familiar with from their garden or the farmer's market. The teachers found relevant websites and books and then taught students how to pull pertinent information from the texts. Students determined how their plant grows, how it is harvested, and its important uses. They were familiar with "harvesting" from their home gardens but were amazed at the machinery of mass harvesting on commercial farms that they watched on YouTube.

Even though it was the students first time researching, they were engrossed in inquiry throughout the project because of the choices they were given. They continuously wanted to know more about their selected plant and were proud to share their learning with teachers and classmates. All of the students could explain the details from their research and grew in confidence! Tracy commented that Brendan, a low-level reader, "needed lots of support, but let me tell you, he could tell you about a plum." Students of all reading abilities were successful in research and in communicating their learning verbally. PBL provides students of all ability levels universal access to content, recognizing their strengths and building self-confidence.

On the other hand, when students are new to PBL, too much choice can be overwhelming.

During the inaugural year at Mike's PBL lab school, he was enthusiastic to turn the learning over to students! In world history, he designed an open-ended project where the students would create minidocumentaries on genocide. It had all kinds of voice and choice options, but no support or clarity of what he wanted students to do. Quickly his students came to him begging for some structure because they were confused and lost. Mike had to pivot and provide more guidance in the form of study guides with key terms and events to research.

Then he prepared a rubric that outlined the requirements for the documentary videos, intentionally leaving the style of the product undefined. After Mike reviewed the rubric with the class, Paul raised his hand. "We understand the content of what we have to do for the videos, but we just don't get what you want them to look like."

"I don't know what they should look like" was his response. Mike paused as students stared at him with apprehension. "If I showed you an example or told you my idea, then they would all turn out the same. I want you to be creative with formats and storytelling techniques. This is your chance to own this project and make it yours."

Mike literally saw the light bulbs coming on in their heads. For the first time, his students realized that they had some control in their learning, and there was a tangible excitement in the room. Students created Ken Burns–style videos, Common Craft–style videos, silent films with text, and sketchbook drawing videos. They were all unique, reflecting the strengths and styles of individual students. Mike learned an important lesson through this project: teachers need to provide the appropriate scaffolding as students new to PBL get comfortable.

Students need to be gradually released[53] into voice and choice as they gain confidence and are ready.

Reflection

CASEL places *reflection* as a subcategory under Responsible Decision Making (see Chapter 8). In practice, reflection is intermixed in all the five competencies which is why we are introducing it here in "Self-Awareness" chapter.

Harvard professors, David Perkins and Gavriel Salomon found that reflection created the conditions that led to what they call high road transfer, the ability to transfer learning skills to new situations.[54] Oftentimes reflection is reserved for the end of a project, but reflection throughout the PBL process is vital to helping students see their personal development. Self-Awareness increases when students reflect on their emotions, strengths, and progress during the project, not just when it is finished. We love what PBL expert and fifth grade teacher at Foulks Ranch Elementary School Jim Bentley says:

"Reflection creates the Velcro® moments where learning sticks."

Part of the ethos of Project Based Learning is that students are on a path of inquiry, testing, and discovering as they go. As a result, students are going to make mistakes along the way.

That's what learning is! In design thinking, the mantra "fail fast and fail often"[55] and "failing forward" is followed by "go back to the drawing board to make improvements where you failed" to encourage multiple prototypes and iterations. In education, the word *fail* almost always has a negative connotation, so it takes a culture and mindset shift to get students comfortable with the idea of failing in order to improve.

PBL teacher Nate Langel's science students design their own experiments. When they do not get their predicted results, he gives them high-fives. "You failed and it was awesome!" he loudly proclaims, quoting from the cartoon movie *Meet the Robinsons.*[56] "Now we know one way that doesn't work. What are you going to change in your next experiment?" Langel shows the movie clip to his students to create a culture that failure in his class is expected and celebrated.

In PBL, students are in a cycle of first draft, fail, feedback, and fix. Students perform their best first draft and then subject their work to a feedback protocol (see Chapter 7) with classmates or outside experts. No one, including adults, accomplishes their best work on the first try, so students reflect on their peers' feedback and fix their work to make it better. This shift in thinking encourages students to take risks, knowing that they will have the opportunity to improve on their initial efforts.

Another way to embed reflection is to give each student a reflection card based on their assigned SEL group role (see Chapter 5). Students journal daily or weekly, reflecting on how their group functioned during project work time and on their SEL strengths and weaknesses. Younger students can use the turn-and-talk discussion protocol to share their thoughts with a partner from a different group. Students develop a sharper Self-Awareness by reflecting and improving their work and skills continuously.

Public Presentations

Once students have refined their work based on their classmates' feedback, they are ready to share it publicly. In order to have a successful public presentation, students must have workable communication skills. Communication is one of the most fundamental skills developed and displayed in PBL. Public presentation of student work creates a positive self-perception (Self-Awareness) because they see their work reflected through the eyes of their target audience. In PBL, students develop a deep level of content knowledge because they are exploring real-life problems requiring real life solutions. Their solutions matter because their work is meant to shift the needle in positive ways.

When students proudly present meaningful work to others, their self-confidence swells exponentially!

In traditional classrooms, students often listen passively most of the time. In PBL, not only are students constantly communicating in their project teams, but they are giving professional-level presentations to their class and the community around them. This is an experience most high school students rarely get the opportunity to do. They may only present a few times in front of their peers over the course of their four years. Younger students in middle and elementary school may present to the public even less. In a comprehensive PBL classroom, students will likely present their work ten to twenty times a year in one class alone. This verbal practice leads to great improvements in their oracy and public speaking skills. The preparation and delivery of presentations requires students to have a deep understanding of their content. Positive evaluations from experts in the field who can gauge, challenge, and assess students' content knowledge provides legitimate feedback on project work which builds students' faith in themselves.

Public speaking is one of the areas that we have seen the greatest progress in students. Remember Chris, the shy, special-education student in chapter introduction who became a confident public speaker? The trajectory of his transformation into a confident scholar is not a special case, but the norm of our PBL experience as students consistently present their learning to classmates and the public. Chris shifted from a shy student with no confidence to a poised speaker leading public tours and speaking on issues that he was passionate about. No longer does he sit silently in the corner feeling insecure; instead, he bravely advocates for himself and others.

Mike's PBL school was a lab school for the county and a demonstration site for New Tech Network, with visitors from all over the country constantly touring the building. The school featured a set of students who were school ambassadors leading tours and participating in student Q&A panels for guests. The school did not handpick the strongest academic students for this role. On the contrary, they often chose students who showed potential but needed a confidence boost. Dozens of students excelled in this role. Afterward, comments from guests were always the same: "Is this a magnet school for gifted and talented kids? Your students communicate so well." Oftentimes the students those guests were referring to were labeled for special education services or struggled academically in class. PBL is not magic, but students give so many oral presentations that they see enormous growth in their public relations skills, especially compared to students who spend most of their time in class passively listening to a teacher lecture. This boost in confidence leads students to tackle their academic responsibilities with new purpose.

Public Presentation Prep ILeva

Practicing Presentations to Build Confidence and Effective Communications Skills

Steps	Rationale
1. **Observe**: Watch videos of presentations such as *Shark Tank*, spoken word poetry, or historic speeches. Have students take notes of what makes them noteworthy or fall flat.	Inspects presentations of varying quality as examples that parallel their final product so students see what both good and poor presentations look like.
2. **Analyze**: Break down the key components of the style of presentation that students will be performing.	Examines the structures and design behind different types of presentations.
3. **Co-create a Rubric**: Use a Talking Circle to co-create a rubric for a high-quality presentation of their product	Creates student buy-in and keeps the key qualities in the front of their mind from the onset.
4. **Prepare**: Complete any notes, slides, outline, or writing. Check the rubric to guarantee they are meeting content requirements.	Produces high quality presentations based on project research, rather than improvisation
5. **Practice**: Allot class time for teams to practice their presentations, initially independently and then with other groups for feedback. Have them video record and critique themselves.	Improves confidence through practice. Low stakes feedback from other students sharpens performance.

SEL Outcomes:
- Students will display higher proficiency in Relationship Skills by communicating more effectively.
- Increase in Responsible Decision-Making as students share their work with the community.

Assessment Recommendations:
- Encourage peer and self-reflection on the co-created rubric to evaluate effectiveness
- Provide a 'final presentation' feedback protocol for audience members using the project rubric then observe how students apply audience feedback to their final product before final submissions.

Self-Directed Learning

Some students seem unable to complete any task without continual guidance and affirmation from the teacher or other adult. We have all had the student who constantly asks, "Is this right?" Rather than functioning as an answer key, the teacher's role is to be an ally to students on their journey to independent learning. PBL trains students to advocate for themselves since they are given options on how they learn, how they are assessed, and where they go deep in the content. The PBL framework directs students to learn through personal inquiry so they develop the skills to pursue any topic that they are passionate about on their own.

"Learned helplessness is just another form of hopelessness."
Zaretta Hammond[57]

Kurt and Mark were two of Mike's students who loved nature conservation and wanted to be forest rangers. They would be "off task" in his history class because they were reading college-level botany texts and watching YouTube videos of people living off the grid in the wilderness. Kurt had built a full-size wigwam at his house for fun. With PBL, Mike was able to harness their passion by having them consider Native American perspectives on nature conservation and how different events such as industrialization and the Dust Bowl affected the environment. In PBL, the teacher's job is to find every way possible to connect students to their content.

Not all students have learned the skills of independent research. As you will see in the coming chapters, the PBL process teaches them skills of how to research, organize themselves, and manage their project. All students can shift from dependence to independence by increasing these SEL abilities. Traditionally, when they're stuck, the so-called "smart" students ask questions and refuse to let the teacher continue with the lesson until they understand. The "struggling" students often just coast and passively watch the teacher move on even when they still have more questions. They are so used to being lost that they expect it. "Normal" for them is checking out and giving up.

Teachers can jump in and change this mindset by creating a culture where students ask for a student-led or teacher-led workshop about the topic they're stuck on. They can request a workshop at any time, but it may not be given immediately depending on the day's schedule and especially if time is needed for the teacher to prepare. We define a workshop as a peripheral mini-informational session that usually happens during project work time. Workshops can take place in a quiet corner of the classroom while other students are working individually or in their project groups.

When offering a workshop, students choose whether or not to attend the session. At the beginning of the year, there may be students that, based on observations and formative assessments, need the assistance of a workshop but choose not to show up. Run the workshop without them. As soon as it is completed, check in on each student who should have attended but didn't.

Give them this spiel:

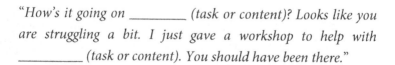

"How's it going on _____ (task or content)? Looks like you are struggling a bit. I just gave a workshop to help with _____ (task or content). You should have been there."

Then quickly turn and walk away to the next student. After repeating this spiel with all of the students that should have attended, announce to the class, "I have decided to repeat the workshop in case anyone missed it." If any of the students that you just checked in on don't move to attend the workshop, give them the teacher stink eye until they come on over.

Matinga is especially fond of student-led workshops. In her classroom, she encouraged volunteer students to run a workshop after they had demonstrated mastery of required tasks or new academic content. While working the room during project work time, she might approach a student and quietly ask something like: *"Hey Femi, your thesis statement was really, really good. You included all the elements that make a powerful hook for the reader, would you mind doing a five- to ten-minute workshop to demonstrate your process?"* Students love to showcase their knowledge and love to help their peers. In turn, many students choose to attend because workshops replace repetitive general review sessions from the front of the classroom by their teacher with a ten-minute exercise addressing a specific concern. Soon students ask for workshops organically, and this becomes an unintrusive scaffold for all involved.

Teach students to advocate for themselves when they need help and then give them the tools to be independent.

Self-Awareness is the first SEL competency because it is the lifeblood of learning.

The heartbeat is vital for life. Without a discernible pulse, your body cannot perform even the simplest task. Without Self-Awareness skills, students will struggle internalizing the rest of the SEL competencies. PBL is the perfect vehicle to build a strong sense of self in ways that traditional approaches often ignore. When students see the value of their authentic work reflected in the eyes of their community, it awakens their Self-Awareness.

Reflection Questions

- How will you check in with each student daily to gauge their emotional state?
- How will you teach students to self-assess their emotions?
- How will you help students see how their identities influence their group interactions?
- In what areas of your curriculum could you launch a project where students explore their identity?
- How can you use voice and choice to build on students' strengths?
- When in your project plans will you reserve time for intentional student reflection?
- How will your students practice effective communication with each other and in presentations?
- How will you develop students' confidence so that they become self-directed learners?

Chapter 5

Building Self-Management

Self-Management skills create high performing groups where each member understands how to manage their time, tasks, and team.

- Norms and Routines
- Need to Knows
- Project Management for Students
- Self-Assessment

Fifteen-year-old Sofia was not excited about starting her second year at Brooklyn International High School (BIHS) in New York City. Last fall, her family had moved to the United States from Central America, and at BIHS, she saw herself as an average student who struggled as an English Learner (EL). BIHS is primarily composed of EL students like Sofia, who make up 75 percent of the student body, including many who are recent immigrants to the US.

Sofia was particularly unhappy about having the same science teacher, Mr. Derian, because she knew his class constantly utilized group projects. Sofia had a reputation with her classmates of being rude, mean, and controlling, so other students did not want to work with her. In fact, Sofia liked doing things her own way and often refused to work with students who didn't speak Spanish. The first day of school she trudged into class with her head down, dreading every minute.

Her teacher, John Derian, is an experienced PBL educator who taught a combined ninth and tenth grade science class. Admittedly the previous year had been a struggle as he felt the students in his classroom did not feel a sense of community. His ninth grade students were all recent immigrants from around the world who preferred to stay within their language groups, creating cliques and refusing to mix with students who spoke other languages. All group work was met with resistance. Derian was surprised because his school's culture emphasized student collaboration in interdisciplinary projects. He tried creating group contracts from a cookie-cutter form, but since they didn't originate from his students, the agreements carried no weight or meaning. Every day there was constant arguing. Single students monopolized the entire project while other students did not contribute at all. The students preferred to sit in traditional rows and work by themselves.

Over the summer, Derian knew that he would be looped back with the same group of students the following year, so he reflected on how to build a better classroom community. At the same time, he was taking a workshop focusing on the Indigenous practice of Talking Circles.[58] In many cultures, Talking Circles are used to ensure everyone in the circle is heard and that those speakers are not interrupted. Derian had an epiphany that he could use Talking Circles to create group contracts. He invited some former students to model the concept of Talking Circles with his new class (See Ch. 6 for an explanation of how to use Talking Circles). Privately Derian targeted some tenth graders to be future circle keepers (students who would facilitate the Talking Circle) and asked them to pay particular attention to the format and structure of the Talking Circle protocol. Derian knew Sofia could fulfill this role with some encouragement.

When Derian challenged Sofia to observe how Talking Circles worked so she could become a circle keeper, she rose to the occasion. There was a dramatic shift in her attitude and behavior as Sofia now self-identified as a leader in the class. Through the conversations within the Talking Circles, students began to reflect on the commonalities in their stories of personal struggles and feel more empathy toward those they did not consider to be part of their language groups. Sofia's visible acceptance of the Talking Circle process and her willingness to lead it played an important role in the whole class transformation. Students began to appreciate the purpose of working together toward a common good and started enjoying group work time.

Derian credits the change in the students' dispositions to the consistent practice of specific collaboration skills and moments of reflection.

Through the positive experience of collaborating on projects, the sense of community in his classroom grew stronger. At the end of each project, students enthusiastically asked, "What are we going to do next?" The best part is that Sofia exhibited leadership skills for the rest of her high school career.

Self-Management is the ability to regulate oneself in a variety of situations to set and achieve goals. Coping with stress is a vital skill for healthy bodies and minds. In PBL students develop project management skills using business tools to practice Self-Management competencies daily. Investigating real life problems provides an authentic setting to fully develop Self-Management skills.

Self-Management skills matter for the sake of the learner, not the teacher. Instead of a top-down approach to control behavior, PBL builds important life skills by applying them to problem-solving opportunities. PBL encourages students to bring their unique backgrounds and cultures to their work, rather than only drawing knowledge from white, middle-class points of view that encourage assimilation.

Norms and Routines

Every classroom has norms and routines that keep it running smoothly. Setting norms allows students to understand the real purpose of your class. By using relevant norms and routines, students will comprehend the impact of class culture on their learning experiences and, in turn, will impact their world. Class norms should aim to progressively make students take more responsibility, become more self-directed, and practice more autonomy. A PBL classroom is no different.

Contrary to a popular misconception, PBL is not a student free-for-all without teacher-provided structure. It is actually quite the opposite. The PBL framework provides the structure for successful student-centered learning.

"Teachers who maintain a learner-centered environment must take time to establish norms and routines that create a classroom culture where students develop independence, confidence, and competence."

Sara Lev[59]

At the beginning of the year, it is critical that PBL teachers establish certain norms and routines, especially around group dynamics. One advantage of PBL is that the norms and routines are focused on students building their Self-Management skills through the project cycle. Remember that a group's time, tasks, and teamwork are often co-opted by students who lack Self-Management skills.

Your first goal is to establish a responsive classroom culture from the beginning. Everyone knows the power of first impressions. For example, on day one, a traditional secondary class often starts with a review of the syllabus, with the teacher establishing rules and consequences. This "rules and regulations first" approach communicates a veiled message of mistrust for students. It presents the teacher as the center of power who assumes that children will behave poorly. In a PBL environment, it is important to start the year with team building activities and develop a social contract with students instead.

Spending the first day on syllabus rules is not helpful. By simply reading these rules, you assume that ALL students, no matter their background and disposition, have a crystal-clear understanding of your interpretation of said rules. During the first week of school, most students are focused on creating their own social connections and may not internalize the content of the syllabus. Instead use that first week to adopt common class culture agreements.

Class norms should aim to progressively make students take more responsibility, become more self-directed, and practice more autonomy.

Jon Ives, math teacher in Farmington, New Mexico, has only one rule, "Nothing -that can hurt another student." Everything else in his class is just procedures. If a procedure is "broken" then students try again tomorrow. Other schools use the mantra "We don't do that here; that's not who we are" to redirect students from off-task or unproductive behavior.

Create a culture of self-discipline where learning to manage one's emotions is more important than legalistic guidelines.

In his classroom, Mike posted the words *Trust, Respect*, and *Responsibility* on the wall and that was how actions were judged. After discussing the three-word mantra, he informed the class that he only had one rule. Sternly he commanded, "Do not, under any circumstances, ask me to use the bathroom or get a drink."

Mike paused for dramatic effect, keeping a straight face as they stared back at him in horror.

"Just get up and go. You are old enough to monitor your own bodily functions without my permission."

Now, Mike does not suggest this particular rule for every classroom. You must know your school climate and follow your school's expectations. But this approach assumes, from the onset, that students will be responsible and not need a babysitter. Rather than take this example as prescriptive advice, think about your students, and consider how you can show them that you trust them. In order for students to learn self-discipline, they need to understand what it means and be given the opportunity to practice upholding the appropriate classroom culture.

Need to Knows

One of the biggest challenges that teachers face is when students lack self-motivation to participate in learning experiences at school. Some students *appear* to be apathetic about everything. A 2020 Gallup poll made up of the voices of over six million students showed that the longer students are in school, the less engaged they become.[60] Some of this disengagement is developmental; older students often develop interests in things not emphasized in school and tend to be more focused on self-discovery and friendships during adolescence. However, a large contributor to their lack of motivation is the coercive and controlling nature of traditional schooling. The school system dictates to students what classes to take, what content to learn, and when. This approach is antithetical to many of the notions we teach students. For example, students cannot practice autonomy when teachers control every aspect of their learning.

> **"Management is great if you want compliance. But if you want engagement . . . then self-direction is better."**
> **Daniel Pink[61]**

Daniel Pink, in his bestselling book *Drive*, asserts that intrinsic motivation comes from three elements: autonomy, mastery, and purpose.[62] While agreeing with his overall argument, the order in which these three elements are introduced in the school environment matters. In other words, students who have been conditioned by years of a controlled environment cannot just be handed full **autonomy**. That will lead to the feared chaos that many educators perceive PBL to be.

Many academic problems can be simmered down to a lack of student engagement due to a stale, often irrelevant curriculum. It is imperative for student motivation to start with the element of **purpose**. This is the reason PBL begins with a dynamic entry event and a motivating DQ. Once students have bought into the "why" of what they will be doing, then they can focus on developing **mastery** in the skill areas needed to perform the tasks at hand. Then teachers can gradually hand over **autonomy** by providing more choices. Autonomy without purpose leaves students feeling rudderless, leading to frustration for both students and teachers alike. This, in turn, leads to no **mastery** at all. The table below demonstrates the relationship between the initial phases of a project and Pink's motivation drivers.

PBL "DRIVE" MOTIVATION

PBL ELEMENTS	RATIONALE	INTRINSIC MOTIVATION
Entry Event	Captures students' heads and hearts	Purpose
DQ	Defines the why of the project	Purpose
N2Ks	Drives project inquiry through student-generated questions	Autonomy, Mastery, & Purpose
Next Steps	Plots inquiry path as students and teachers collaboratively plan research and product development	Autonomy & Purpose
Pulse of PBL		

From the beginning, PBL puts students in charge of their own learning, increasing self-motivation and practicing self-discipline. Launching a project with an entry event, Driving Question, and Need to Knows puts the students' interests at the center. When students feel connected from the start, they will ask higher-order questions related to the topic in the N2K process. These questions become the foundation for the learning throughout the rest of the project.

In the initial PBL experience, students may not know what to ask. Frame N2Ks with the following prompt:

"Given the experience of the entry event, your background knowledge about the topic, and the requirements in the entry document, if I told you to start working on the project right now, where would you get stuck? What help would you need?"

Younger learners may need this process broken down into simpler questions, but the concept is the same: "What do you **need to know** to accomplish this task?" The Need to Know 1Leva reveals some considerations for a successful N2K process.

Need To Know ILeva

Creating Insightful Student Questions to Fuel Deeper Inquiry

Steps	Rationale
1. **Individual Work**: Students silently write their questions on sticky notes, in a journal, or on a shared document.	Ensures that every student gets wait time to process their own questions without the influence of others.
2. **Small Group Work**: Working in small groups of four to five, students explain their questions and select their group's best 3 questions.	Tests their assertions in small groups, comparing questions and sharing knowledge in a safe space.
3. **Whole Class Share Out:** Each group shares out their top three questions to the whole class.	Builds confidence as students notice that other students have similar questions to their own. Weeds out less relevant questions, limiting the class list to an achievable amount to zero in on
4. **N2K List:** One student writes questions on butcher paper that is posted in the classroom in a highly visible location	Keeps student questions as a focal point throughout the project. Groups develop Next Steps based off from the N2K list
5. **Daily Check-Ins:** Teacher connects class activities (research, labs, readings, etc.) to the N2K list and students add new questions as they arise during inquiry	Demonstrates how students are driving the inquiry process through their queries. Cross off questions as students answer them.

SEL Outcomes:
- Rich and productive whole class discussions that are inclusive of all students' processing speeds
- Opportunities for students to demonstrate their thinking by first reflecting individually, then practicing or role playing their questions in a small group to enrich the Whole Class Share out.
- Observable displays of self-discipline and self-motivation
- Observable demonstrations of personal and collective agency

Assessment Recommendations:
- Evaluate how often students use closed vs. opened-ended questions.
- Analyze who is doing the majority of the talking.
- Consider how many questions lead to deeper inquiry.
- Assess observable student connection to more productive(self-directed and self-motivated) behaviors.
- Assess and annotate group dynamic to later bring back for group evaluation, and possible norm adjustment.

Another option for N2Ks is the Question Formulation Technique (QFT) from the Right Question Institute. This structured protocol teaches students to ask better questions. More specifically, it illustrates the difference between open-ended and closed-ended questions. In a PBL version of the QFT, step one of the Question Focus is the Driving Question after an entry event. Step two is the normal N2K process of writing down questions privately. The third step of the QFT is the core of the protocol where small groups of students define open- and closed-ended questions, sort their questions, and convert between the two types.[63] Then follow the rest of the Need to Know ILeva. [64]

The QFT, on one slide...

1) **Question Focus**

2) **Produce Your Questions**
   - ✓ Follow the rules
   - ✓ Number your questions

3) **Improve Your Questions**
   - ✓ Categorize questions as Closed or Open-ended
   - ✓ Change questions from one type to another

4) **Prioritize Your Questions**

5) **Share & Discuss Next Steps**

6) **Reflect**

1. Ask as many questions as you can
2. Do not stop to discuss, judge or answer
3. Record *exactly* as stated
4. Change statements into questions

Closed-Ended: Answered with "yes," "no" or one word

Open-Ended: Require longer explanation

RQI

Mike has found that after experiencing the QFT protocol, students can readily convert closed-ended questions to open-ended ones and vice-versa. When a student asks a closed-ended question in class, he asks them to convert it to an open-ended one. Other times he would specifically ask students for open-ended questions only.

The N2K list is a living document. Mark off questions as they are answered and add new questions to the N2K list throughout the project as they arise. Depending on their background knowledge around the project topic, students will often ask better questions once they have done some preliminary research, interviews, or explorations. The **autonomy** in the N2K process builds student ownership throughout the project. Matinga encourages individual project groups to start and manage their own N2Ks on sticky poster paper or sticky notes on the walls or windows. Students are encouraged to peruse other groups' N2K brainstorms for inspiration and cross-pollination.

After the N2K process, the students and their teacher collaboratively determine where the project will go, creating Next Steps based on the N2K list. As a class, they determine what tasks the project calls for and in what order to tackle them. The older and more experienced in PBL that your students are, the more these processes can be turned over to them. Students become self-motivated when they exercise their voice to direct their learning as they explore their passions in the N2Ks and Next Steps processes.

Project Management for Students

Many of our students struggle in school due to their lack of organizational skills, which greatly affects their academic performance. These may be students who do their homework but never turn it in because it is probably "lost" somewhere in their backpack. Or at the end of the year during locker cleanout, they find assignments that may not have been graded.

Lack of organization is not a permanent character trait but a skill set that all students can develop to improve their academic performance.

Procrastination is another common occurrence among students (and adults!). In PBL, procrastination often occurs when a student feels adrift or lacks clarity about the project scope and sequence. Sometimes they may simply be confused about their role within their group. This leads to a predictable domino effect where the student waits until the last minute to start a large project, and subsequently diminishes the quality of their work. Another subset of students might feel so stressed out by school or events in their personal lives that they shut down completely and are unable to find the strength to even start thinking about a possible solution to a complex world problem. More and more students report that they feel overwhelmed by school, which is contributing to the rise of reports of mental health issues in school-aged young people. School stress leads to distraction and decreased academic output. Explicitly teaching students how to manage their stress and themselves brings improvement to their physical and mental health.[65]

Project management is the ability to see a deliverable from beginning to end in a timely matter. It is the same skill set that a contractor uses to successfully build a backyard deck. Students must be taught how to properly manage the three Ts: tasks, time, and teams. PBL uses several different tools in conjunction, enabling students to complete high-quality work collaboratively and efficiently.

3 T'S OF PROJECT MANAGEMENT

MANAGE PBL TOOLS

TASK
DRIVING QUESTION,
NEED TO KNOW'S,
NEXT STEPS,
SCRUM BOARD

TIME
SCRUM BOARD,
TRELLO,
PROJECT WALL

TEAM
SEL GROUP
ROLES, GROUP
CONTRACTS,
KARE GAP

Pulse of PBL

Effective project management skills help students manage their stress, their work, and their relationships with each other in healthy ways for maximum success. Students might know how to complete a typical classroom assignment, but they might not always understand the steps necessary to bring a complex final product to fruition. It is vital for students to learn the skills to manage the project themselves.

As noted previously, a critical element of PBL is turning more responsibility over to the students through voice and choice. Autonomy does not mean random chaos. Teachers should preplan extensively but be prepared to "call an audible" and alter the project whenever student interests are worthy of a shift. The teacher should intentionally leave chunks of the project plan open for students to fill in with their background knowledge and experiences. In other words, if the teacher is doing all the project planning, then they are stealing away from students the opportunity to practice their planning and organizing skills. What better way for students to learn Self-Management than to manage their own projects?

Everyone who has ever been a part of a group project knows how rare it is to have an equal amount of participation and an equal distribution of labor among the group members. You have probably had group experiences where you were the workhorse who got things done. Worse yet, you may have been on the receiving end of a phone call from an angry parent who believes their student is doing all the work while the rest of the group slacks off. So how do you create a safe environment where all students develop the skills to contribute in meaningful ways?

One way for students to learn Self-Management is to directly teach the SEL competencies through the introduction of group roles. Print off a set of SEL Group Role Cards on colored paper for each group in your class. Assign each member one of the SEL roles and have students self-assess daily and evaluate their group's practice of that competency. They can also add responsibilities to their Group Role Card to customize each card to the needs of their group. Check out the SEL Group Role Cards ILeva below for alternative ways to implement the cards and look for a complete set of printable SEL Group Role Cards on our website, **PulseofPBL.com.**

Sample Elementary SEL Group Role Card:

Responsible Decision Designer
- Asks questions
- Looks carefully and pays attention to details
- Tries new ideas
- Takes risks
- Keeps a growth mindset
- Makes positive choices

Reflection: How did my group solve problems?

Sample Secondary SEL Group Role Card:

Self-Awareness Supporter

- Monitors each group member's dispositions
- Ensures team is an emotionally safe space
- Encourages teammates
- Identifies member's strengths and matches to project tasks

Reflection: How did my group maximize their strengths?

SEL Group Role Cards ILeva

Integrating SEL Competencies into Daily Project Tasks to Practice, Reflect and Develop Each Skills

Options	Rationale
1. **Laminate**: Print on colored paper and laminate one set of SEL Group Role Cards for each group in your class	Enables students to write pluses and deltas on the cards with erasable markers, reflecting on their group's daily practice.
2. **Jigsaw**: Each group member chooses a different card and monitors that competency for the duration of the project	Empowers all members with different leadership positions. Students lead from their strengths while improving their growth areas.
3. **Whole Class Focus**: For younger students, introduce one SEL competency at a time, giving every group the same card. Rotate student leaders daily.	Allows younger children to focus on one competency at a time. Leadership and responsibility are shared.
4. **Role of the Day**: Assign an SEL role for each day of the week (for example Relationship Skills Thursday). Each group circles one bullet point to practice and reflect on.	Permits the entire class to concentrate on one competency daily, addressing all five of them weekly.
5. **Goal Setting**: Students create group goals around their competencies and answer their SEL card reflection question daily or weekly.	Centers reflection as an essential practice, keeping SEL skills the focal point of all learning.
6. **Daily Check-Ins**: Use quick formative assessments such as thumbs up/down or fist to five for students to communicate their practice of the competency.	Normalizes self-assessment with SEL as a consistent part of the routines and culture of the classroom.

SEL Outcomes:
- Students will understand and display the SEL competencies since they are embedded into the daily fabric of the project.
- Students will continually reflect on their personal and group goals to monitor the progress of their project, keeping it on track to meet deadlines.

Assessment Recommendations:
- Provide opportunities for students to describe their individual understanding of each SEL group role.
- Observe and discuss displays of each SEL group role responsibility.
- Use quick check-ins such as fist to five, thumbs tp/down, or exit tickets for self and group reflection.

145

Students should set goals as a team to hold each other accountable for the completion of the project. In PBL, group contracts facilitate students working together productively. After dividing students into their project teams, have every group fill out a copy of the Group Contract Template. Each student should select one SEL strength and one SEL goal from the list of SEL Learning Targets (see "Planning" in Chapter 9). The group determines which SEL role each member will fulfill from the SEL Group Role Cards (above). At this point, students should engage in a group discussion about their learning approaches and productivity triggers. If you haven't done so yet, this might be a relevant time to introduce the Personality Diagnostic ILeva (Chapter 4, "Group Roles" section) for students to share their "how I roll and how I manage how I role" observations. This might seem like a long and drawn-out process, but it is an essential step to teaching students to understand their value and constructive contributions to their projects. This onboarding process will avoid many project management issues throughout the school year.

After the students have had time to share and discuss the SEL traits that they bring to their work, they draft agreements for how they will work together, what expectations for work completion will be, and what restrictions they propose for the group. All these steps open up communication and set up the team with realistic conflict resolutions strategies BEFORE they engage in the project.

Group Contract

Student Name	SEL Area of Strength	SEL Area for Im- provement	SEL Role	How I roll	How I manage

Agreements:

- I agree to complete on time, all tasks assigned to me on the scrum board: _____(link to your copy)
- I agree to give 100% effort to our group and not be off task watching gaming, or on social media.
- I agree to treat all members of our group in a polite, respectful manner.
- I agree to listen, support, and help my group members.

Accountability:

1. Verbal Warning -documented with teacher
2. Second Warning -with teacher intervention with the group
3. Fired -must start project over by yourself

Signatures:

When introducing group contracts for the first time, explain the purpose of the contract in great detail. Mike always tells the story about the student who volunteered to write the contract for his group. The document ended up being thirty pages long, and everyone in the group signed it. When the project was complete, the teacher told this group that they had done such a good job keeping the project on schedule and collaborated so well as a group that they were awarded additional points. The contract writer immediately interrupted, "I get all of the additional points. The rule is on page 23 of the contract." To the students' astonishment, the teacher honored the contract. This is a fabricated story, but Mike tells it to make the point that students need to take the process of creating a group contract seriously.

Starting in upper elementary school, students who don't pull their weight or fail to uphold the contractual agreements with the group can be "fired" from their team. Students do not fire their teammates but must present a documented case to the teacher, who acts as the ombudsman and ensures that the group has given all three steps of the process a fair chance. The contract has a minimum three-step process before a team member can be fired:

1. **Formal Verbal Warning** (documented with no teacher involvement): Working in groups often elicits informal verbal reminders or warnings done in passing. Team members can remind each other to stay on task or to remember to bring important project as-sets next time without consequence. However, they should not need to resort to nagging each other. If an

unproductive student misses an essential deadline or step, team members must agree that the action deserves a formal verbal warning. The team should then approach the student(s) in question, inform them of the group decision, and review the expectations and responsibilities outlined in the Group Role Cards or agreed upon in the group contract. At this point, the student in question can verbally recommit to the group contract and repair the damage (finish a project asset, etc.). This event is documented in writing on a log or on the scrum board. The group must present this documentation to the teacher before any future steps can be enacted. Remember that your students are experiencing the value of their contributions to a project and the importance of self-management and goal completion to the project process.

2. **Second Formal Verbal Warning and Teacher Conference** (documented with teacher involvement): As in step 1, the team must agree about an undesired behavior before involving their teacher. If an unproductive student chooses to forget or ignore the first formal verbal warning, the team can decide to present the previously documented behaviors to the teacher. The offending student(s) must meet one-on-one with the teacher to present their case. Sometimes there may be circumstances that a student might want to share with their teacher but not in front of their peers. The goal here is to have the student explain where they are in their journey, ensure that they understand their role

and the group contract, and not to wag a finger at them. There is not much the teacher can say that the team members have not already mentioned. The teacher ends the teacher-student conference by reviewing the Group Role Card assigned to this student and the group contract. This is the final warning.

3. **Fired:** This final step need not be dramatic, personal, nor be a big surprise to anyone. A student that has breached the group contract for the third time should know and expect the consequences of their dereliction of their responsibilities. Once the team has decided to turn in all documentation based on a third formal misstep, the teacher takes the student aside, informing them that they will no longer be working with their group. The teacher should review the project description and outcome to the student because they will now be working alone or closely supervised. Fired students are not allowed to take any resources from their team but must start from scratch. Some teachers use a "re-hiring" process, where students can earn their way back into the group by completing missing assignments and restoring broken relationships. Another option is to allow the student to join another team. The goal here is not to create a culture of firing, but for students to learn how to motivate and hold each other accountable in respectful ways. In reality, students rarely get fired. What normally occurs after an initial warning is that students begin contributing productively to their group.

PBL teachers have a daily opportunity to work the room like a restaurant waitstaff and connect with individuals or groups of students. During project worktime, you watch out for or even predict unproductive behavior before it gets to step 1 of the firing process. Remember that negative behaviors commonly occur when the student is not connecting with the task at hand. Consider the following:

Scenario

It is the second week of the project. Students are researching, and you have planned a guided work session. Student groups have a deliverable due by the end of the week. As you are working the room, you once again spot a group that is goofing off and not using their time wisely. You notice that they are not self-correcting or working to meet the coming deadline. Okay, it's time to step in:

Strategy #1:	Strategy #2:
You go to the group's table to point out their unproductive behavior. You calmly remind them of the stakes of this project, their responsibilities, and the consequences of their current behaviors. You paint a clear picture of how they might feel on showcase night if their project is subpar. The students feel bad and	You think to yourself, *The students understand their group contract, they understand the behavior that gets the results they want/need. So, hmmm, there must be a gap elsewhere.* You approach the group and pull up a chair to join their table, engaging them in a seemingly casual conversation with the KARE Gap ILeva in hand (pg

...continued　　　*...continued*

apologize, become quiet, and begin pulling out work materials from their backpacks. A few minutes later, you notice that, although they are quiet, they are not really collaborating but simply shuffling resources around and pretending to read materials.	154). You remind the students to use the KARE Gap ILeva to discover what is keeping them from being productive. Together, and through a series of questions, you find and bridge the correct gap, helping the students refocus their efforts.

In strategy #1, what exactly did you tell them that they did not already know to do?

NAGGING DOES NOT WORK! If it did, you would not have to keep repeating yourself. When giving students a directive, you are presenting them with two options: follow the directive or ignore it. If they choose to ignore all or parts of your directive, chances are they will perceive it as your fault, while you will see it as a consequence of their poor choice. The inability to resolve this impasse without blame results in failure for the student and frustration for you. This is the kind of dance that discourages students in the long run and even pushes them out of school. The KARE Gap ILeva takes a potentially negative encounter with your students and makes it a personable opportunity to get to the root of the problem. You can make specific recommendations, further developing the students' Social and Emotional skills while managing academic requirements. The KARE Gap ILeva contains diagnostic questions and sentence stems that direct your students toward self-assessment of their own gaps. Eventually you can release this gap diagnostic to the students to help them practice self-correction. (See online resources for a student version.) Note, however, that the questions are meant to be used to create a free-flowing conversation and not to interrogate the student.

KARE Gap ILeva

Find the Gap: Probing Questions

Knowledge/Skills Gap

- Can you explain the project description?
- Summarize the requirements for me.
- What do you need to accomplish today?
- What is your role in this group?
- How do you want to start working today?
- Do you think you have overestimated your own skills when choosing your project topic? Explain.

Authenticity Gap

- What is the purpose of this project?
- How do you feel this knowledge applies to you?
- How is this topic relevant to you and your audience?
- Who is your audience?
- How will you connect with your audience?
- What are the audience's expectations of your topic?

Resource Gap

- What resources or strategies are you contemplating?
- How did you choose appropriate resources for the job?
- How are you using the resources you have?
- Do you know how and where to find the resources you do not have?
- Do you need my network to find better resources?

Effort Gap

- Are you overwhelmed?
- What is the division of labor within your group?
- Are you delivering what you planned?
- Are your expectations clearly connected to your actions?
- Are you the right group member to tackle this task?
- Are your deadlines realistic?

Bridging the Gap: Strategy Recommendations

Knowledge/Skills Gap

- Review the project description, purpose, outcomes, and specifically the role students need to play.
- Brainstorm a to-do list or create a scrum board.
- Remind them how to use the scrum board to chop the work into manageable pieces, prioritizing tasks.
- Determine whether the group has distributed roles to each member and reference the SEL Group Role cards to refresh their responsibilities.
- Recommend starting points when students vacillate.
- Use your expertise and lived experiences to evaluate whether the size of the students' plans aligns with the time allotted.

Authenticity Gap

- Reiterate the purpose of the project (it is your role to ensure clarity and understanding in what you need the students to deliver).
- Explain the current real world application of the benchmark experiences of this project. Avoid using future scenarios but instead show how this knowledge is applicable for the student presently.
- Brainstorm different types of audiences with your students and point out how they may want to determine their audience and connect their topic to their audience type.
- Refer back to their N2K experience and allow the student to list N2K questions their audience may have.

Resource Gap

- Suggest alternative resources or strategies that are compatible with the information the group needs.
- Showcase quick searching hacks to help maximize their time online.
- Offer the use of your network and make suggestions of the types of people they might want to reach out to as well as how people in your network might help. Be prepared to share contact information.
- Sketch an example of how you would use a specific resource.
- Reveal your favorite resource and the best places to find great resources for the topic they have chosen.

Effort Gap

- Use a scrum board to break down the work into manageable bites or help the student trim their project to discard unnecessary aspects.
- Designate individual responsibility in the scrum board.
- Reference the SEL Group Role cards to refresh the responsibilities of each role.
- Evaluate deadlines for plausibility and suggest a new approach.
- Create a daily work plan with built in breaks.
- Establish accountability partners to keep each member focused.

SEL Outcomes:
- After one round of the KARE Gap strategies, you should be able to identify the gap(s) that halt your students' progress. Often students begin a project with the same negative tendencies. However, as you teach your students how to use the KARE Gap strategy to self-correct, they will practice SEL higher level skills in tackling progressively difficult, and complicated tasks.
- Students will use the KARE Gap strategies organically; identifying and diagnosing gaps in their progress and that of their peers.
- Students will suggest pre-emptive recommendations before unproductive behavior occurs.

Assessment Recommendations: Use these questions to evaluate the impact of the KARE GAP
- How long does it take a 'problematic' group to self-correct unproductive behavior?
- How much more self-directed are the students than previously? (in other words, do you hear less of the "I don't even know what I am doing" song?)

In John Derian's science class, a generic group contract template didn't work. Let's look in depth at how he used Talking Circles to create personalized contracts instead. First of all, each student wrote on an index card a word or phrase describing what successful collaboration looks like. Since the class was full of English Learners, they did a "turn and talk" to practice sharing with a partner before starting the whole group Talking Circle. As the talking piece (any object that is used to indicate who has the floor to speak) was passed around the circle, students shared their word(s) and placed their index cards in the middle of the circle.

Next students responded to the question "What are common team challenges during project collaboration?" While students shared, Derian made a list of the example scenarios they were sharing on the board for all to see. Then, after dividing into groups of four, they selected one example scenario to create and perform a short "Do and Don't" skit that, in one scene, showed how not to handle the scenario and, in the other scene, showed how to productively fix the scenario. Students had fun and, regardless of their English skills, were able to participate in the exercise.

The following day, students were given a Group Agreement Form (Figure 1) with a table full of the words and phrases that they had generated on the index cards (Derian stapled all the index cards onto a bulletin board). After forming groups, students highlighted three boxes to focus on and then reflected on what specific actions they would perform to accomplish them (Figure 2). Finally, they responded to some "what to do and not do" scenarios (Figure 3). Derian found that by taking the time to develop group contracts from student input, they were more meaningful and impactful. He followed up with a giant class scrum board on a grid that he created with painter's tape on his whiteboard to help groups track their daily progress. He found that the public nature of the scrum board built collective agency, motivating all students to stay on track during the project. Additionally, Derian conferenced with each group and used the scrum board and team contracts to coach teams through collaboration issues when they surfaced.[66]

Figure 1
John Derian Group Agreement Example
With your group, highlight three SEL skills that will propel your project.

John Derian Group Agreement Example		
With your group, highlight three SEL skills that will propel your project.		
What do you need to do to be successful?		
Actively participate	Collaborate with each other	Be tolerant and patient
Be positive	Focus	Work together to solve problems
Use teamwork	Be present at school everyday	Be serious about the work
Be respectful	Try your best	Finish your work on time
Communicate clearly	Set up goals and follow them	Have fun
Share ideas	Challenge ourselves	Listen to everyone's ideas
Help each other	Ask each other questions	Be creative
Trust each other	Be organized	Use our resources

We agree to do our best to achieve these as a group:

Digital Signature	Date	Digital Signature	Date
Yusuf	09/13/21	DongXiu	09/13/21
ZhouCan	09/13/21	Abdul	09/13/21

Adapted from John Derian

Figure 2

2.

Copy and paste one of the things you highlighted	
Why is this important to your group?	
What are ACTIONS that will help you achieve this?	

Adapted from John Derian

Figure 3
Common Group Challenges

Someone is absent for multiple days.	
What should you do?	
What should you **not** do?	

Someone doesn't do their work on time.	
What should you do?	
What should you **not** do?	

You disagree about an important decision.	
What should you do?	
What should you **not** do?	

Someone tries to take over and do all the work alone.	
What should you do?	
What should you **not** do?	

Adapted from John Derian

Scrum boards (also known as Kanban boards) teach students to plan and organize their work in a visible way. They are a professional project management tool used in Agile methodology. Agile methodology in the business world breaks a project into several phases to make it more manageable. Scrum boards may take on many forms depending on the age of the students and the technology available. The basic format has three main columns: To Do, Doing, and Done. Initially tasks from next steps are added to the To Do column and assigned to group members, and due dates are negotiated. (See the Need to Know ILeva at the beginning of this chapter.) As students engage in a task, they move it over to the appropriate column to track progress.

	Civil Rights Podcast			Class:	American History	
Group Members:	Luke, Nia, Javier, Emma					
Group Member	**Task**	**To Do**	**In Progress**	**Done**	**Due Date**	**Completion Date**
All	Research local civil rights topics		x		3/15	
Luke	Research sitins			x	3/12	3/11
Nia	Research Freedom Riders		x		3/12	
Emma	Research Children's March			x	3/12	3/10
Javier	Research KKK			x	3/12	3/12
All	Choose local topic	x				
Emma	Interview community members	x			3/25	
Javier, Nia	Write script		x		3/25	
All	Practice speaking	x			3/26	
Luke, Emma	Record	x			3/27	
Luke	Edit	x			3/29	
Nia	Add sound effects	x			3/29	
Javier	Add buffer music	x			3/29	
Emma	Publish to Soundcloud	x			3/29	

Scrum boards can be created online with a business tool such as Trello or on a shared spreadsheet (above and also available on our website). This way everyone, including the teacher, can monitor progress. For younger students, or as a no-tech option, students can use sticky notes with the columns on poster paper or on a wall. Another option is to create a scrum board chart on a bulletin board or hallway wall. No matter which format you choose, scrum boards are a great tool to teach students how to manage both their work and themselves. They give a visible structure to goal setting and help students manage stress by creating a realistic timeline, instead of cramming in all their work at the last minute.

Self-Assessment

The most compelling form of evaluation is self-assessment. When a student honestly and accurately analyzes the progress of their own learning, it is powerful! We are not talking about comparisons to other students but looking at their own progress compared to a rubric. Students should be reflecting on their academic knowledge and SEL skills. They can check in on their group contracts and SEL Group Role Cards to determine whether or not they are being an effective team member. Students can start the day with a scrum meeting to track and assess their progress on their self-selected timeline.

Students demonstrate personal agency when they choose the appropriate scaffolding and tools that they need to complete their work. The term *scaffolding* is borrowed from the construction field and refers to the use of temporary supports, particularly to reach high altitudes. In education, scaffolding refers to any support given to students to help them master specific skills or content. Traditionally scaffoldings are mandated (and accommodations still need to be followed in PBL) for labeled students: special education, English Learners, those with 504 plans or Individual Education Plans (IEPs), etc. Students that are not on the list of labeled students are commonly treated as if they are a homogeneous group or "at grade level" (whatever that means). Most teachers know that this is an outdated and debunked teaching approach.

Limiting scaffolding to a certain few students and labeling children are both harmful practices.

First of all, students who are "behind" set grade-level stand-ards are stigmatized.[67] These students are often labeled with a disability (although they might not necessarily be disabled but simply have limited resources), suffer from mental health is-sues, have less academic support at home, or other social issues outside of their control. These students may be targeted for teasing or bullying. It can affect their self-perception, leading to doubt, low expectations, and low self-esteem. Secondly all clas-ses have students who, for whatever reason, fall through the cracks without labels, who truly need extra support and scaf-folding. In our experience, universal scaffolding (teaching scaffolding strategies to all students, not just ones with man-dated plans) benefits all learners.

In PBL, the teacher gives menus of scaffolding opportuni-ties to all students. The scaffolding might include sentence stems, outlines, different reading levels, audio books, content videos, visual models, concept maps, sketchnotes, or individual and small group workshops. PBL scaffolds are actually the same strategies that most teachers are already using. The difference is that all students are taught the different strategies and given support as needed, and then they get to choose what works for them. Sometimes the highest-achieving students need scaffold-ing too and benefit from access to new learning strategies. The teacher's role is to coach students to choose the appropriate support and then to release themselves when the scaffolding is no longer required. There is a flashback scene in the movie *Forrest Gump*[68] where the main character, Forrest, who wears leg braces, is being chased by bullies. As he runs, his braces break away from his suddenly healed legs. He no longer needs the leg braces because he discovers what becomes one of Forrest's greatest abilities: running. The same applies to scaffolding used to develop students' learning. Students should cast it aside when no longer necessary. An encouragement from a teacher that "you got this on your own" affirms students' growth.

Visualize a host of scaffolds sitting on a shelf. After introducing the scaffold to the entire class, they are placed where students can easily find and retrieve them (in a course learning management system, on a website, on literal classroom shelves, or in a file cabinet). Students are encouraged to use the scaffold whenever they need it. This way, the use of scaffolds becomes an autonomy strategy rather than a crutch.

Beware, though, that scaffolds can easily become busywork when assigned to the entire class. For example, a math assignment is a scaffold. It is a tool that will help the students master specific math skills. So, the teacher assigns fifteen math problems as an assignment due tomorrow. However, there are students in the class who have proven that they have mastered the task presented in the assignment after they have done five to six problems, making the rest of the problems just busywork.

Instead, be more proactive and use scaffolds to support individual or specific groups of students as needed. Scaffolds should not be graded, but instead the outcome of the use of that tool should be assessed and evaluated. In other words, it should not matter how many math problems the student has completed. What should matter is that the student can demonstrate that they fully understand the content standard and demonstrate the process you ask for. Another act of self-assessment is when students choose to attend in-class workshops as discussed in the previous chapter. After students reflect on their learning, they should be expected to accurately assess where they need help and ask for it or organically attend an offered workshop for assistance. The requested workshop is then offered to any students who would like to come, or the teacher can offer workshops with specific targets based on observation of student progress.

With a weak Self-Management pulse, you end up managing your students rather than the students managing the project.

A debilitating symptom of a weak pulse is vertigo, which makes one feel dizzy and off balance. This lack of equilibrium makes you want to close your eyes or even shut down. Self-Management is like a pulse. Without teaching Self-Management structures, students will lack focus or stray off track. When students lack the ability to manage themselves, they may shut down and quit the project in frustration. SEL group roles, group contracts, scrum boards, and the KARE gap ILeva are useful tools to manage their time, task, and team. Strong Self-Management skills lead to high-performing teams in which each member understands how to manage their output.

Reflection Questions

- What ways will you use norms and routines to establish a culture of trust?
- How will you adapt PBL protocols such as N2Ks and Next Steps to motivate your students?
- How can you use group roles to teach and practice SEL competencies?
- What tools will you borrow from business project management for students to set goals and organize themselves and the project?
- How will you adapt Indigenous practices such as Talking Circles to customize structures for your students of all backgrounds, cultures, and abilities?
- Self-assessment is powerful. How will you use it to promote goal setting?

Chapter 6

Sharpening Social Awareness

We need students who comprehend diverse perspectives in their community and the world so they approach complex problems with empathy.

- Oracy
- Discussion Protocols
- Dialogue Over Debate
- Multi-faceted Driving Questions
- Connections with the Community
- Empathy in PBL

Toward the end of the first year at his comprehensive PBL high school, Mike observed that his students were ready to add more of their voices into the project design process. He invited any interested students to join a project design team for the following year's American Studies class, which integrated tenth grade ELA and post–Civil War US history. The project design team brainstormed project ideas for the next year's class including themes, product ideas, and community partnerships. Mike printed out the state standards for US History and cut them into individual strips. The student design team sorted the standard strips into different themes. Finally, students brainstormed project ideas, final products, and community partners around each cluster of standards.

The students were drawn to a collection of modern standards around the September 11 Twin Tower attack in New York City and wanted to build memorials to commemorate the horrible terrorist acts. Mike agreed, but secretly added a twist because he didn't want his students only focusing on the tragedy itself or simply honoring the victims (as important as that is). The following year, he launched the Monument Project with the Driving Question "Who is a terrorist?" After defining terrorism, students investigated the past one hundred years of United States' foreign policy.

Students analyzed key foreign policy decisions, determining in each case if the United States' international relations were motivated by altruistic moral values of helping others and spreading democracy or by a desire for economic advantages. Students analyzed how the United States' decisions were perceived from other countries' perspectives. Mike pushed students to scrutinize how our past actions may have inadvertently created new terrorists and contributed to the reasons why some countries around the world consider the United States to be the aggressor.

For the literature component of the project, students read *Ender's Game* by Orson Scott Card, a science fiction story about a six-year-old prodigy, Ender Wiggins who "saves" the world. Ender attends a special academy called Battle School, where he masters training simulations against the Buggers, an alien species who had previously attacked earth. One of the major themes of the book is the contrast between Ender and his older brother, Peter, and whether people should be judged by their actions or intentions. Ender is an empathetic child with the purest intentions in everything he does but ends up killing a classmate in self-defense. As it turns out, the battle "simulations" that Ender and his peers train on are actual military engagements with the Buggers, and the adult leaders of Battle School manipulate Ender into unknowingly committing genocide, wiping out the entire Bugger species. In contrast to Ender's innocent disposition is that of his brother, Peter, a narcissistic, power-hungry character who tortures Ender and his sister. Peter has selfish ambitions in all that he does but ends up preventing a major world war and negotiating a lasting world peace on earth.[69]

Using the theme from *Ender's Game* as a backdrop, each student group researched a different US foreign policy event and shared their findings with the class. For their final product, students designed a monument to represent the patterns they

168

observed in the entire story of US diplomatic relations from multiple perspectives. Students grappled with whether the United States should be judged by its good intentions or the results of its actions in the world. Throughout this project, students reflected on the Driving Question, "Who is a terrorist?" and organically realized that this seemingly simple question was too complex to answer by labeling an entire group of people for the actions of a few. Their research, readings, and work with community partners had challenged their thinking. The students wanted their final products to reflect the complexity of international diplomacy in relation to the historical and current weight of US policy decisions abroad.

Ultimately students designed monuments to US foreign policy composed of complex symbolism showing the competing vantage points in United States history. One of Mike's favorite designs had a fountain with four hands inside. Here is the students' description:

"Our proposed location will be in the Ellipse Circle, in front of the White House, where it can be a reminder to future presidents of **both the triumphs and mistakes** of their predecessors. The hands in the fountain represent the US foreign policy, a fist for brutality, an offering hand for kindness, a thief's hand for greed, and a hand holding a flag representing the peoples' sense of nationalism. The fountain is symbolism for the **US having equal parts of both the good and bad things we've done as a country**." (emphasis ours).

The Monument Project sharpened students' Social Awareness by explicitly asking them to consider others' perspectives and having empathy for people from diverse backgrounds and standpoints. Today's public discourse is polarized with people shouting over each other on TV and constantly trolling on social media, rather than listening and working toward compromise. The Transformative SEL prerequisites braided into the Monument Project design compelled students to consider the dangers of telling a story from single perspective by examining the ramifications of US foreign policy through multiple viewpoints. Project Based Learning sharpens Social Awareness skills by requiring students to listen to varied opinions and reflect on contrasting points of view before negotiating solutions.

While the previous chapter focused on Self-Management methods for students, this chapter highlights Social Awareness strategies for the teacher to pivot their practice for more productive results.

If we cannot find time to develop Social Awareness skills, then we will be wasting time dealing with the consequences for the rest of the school year.

Oracy

Imagine overhearing a fascinating ideological conversation while you are sipping your favorite hot drink at your local coffee shop. The people at the next table are discussing issues that you have strong opinions about. One of them notices you leaning in to listen better and invites your thoughts. But before you can open your mouth to speak, you are asked for a list of peer-reviewed references you have read and whether you can produce five pieces of your own writing on the subject. What? Ridiculous! Who needs that with their morning latte?

As disconcerting as this scene would be, reading and writing are often the only ways that educators ensure that students can prove an informed opinion or present a cohesive argument. Schools might offer a one-semester public speaking course or debate club, but there is little expectation that oral communication skills are transferable from level to level the way that reading and writing are. One of the most salient physical elements that people use to create a first impression is the way one speaks. Surprisingly the ability to express oneself verbally in the classroom and in the public at large is not an academic focus. Somehow, especially in the United States, educators tend to spend little time on the third member of the communication trio: reading, writing, and oracy. After all, oracy is not a tested concept. However, everyone uses oracy all day, every day, and people are more likely to ask you for a verbal opinion than for a piece you have authored on a topic.

Sometimes knowing how to speak is more important than the message itself.

Oracy is the ability to speak well and to structure thoughts verbally, in a way that makes sense to others.[70] Teaching oracy skills does not mean teaching literacy, changing a student's accent, colloquial habits, cultural dialect, or even expecting a level of diction. Oracy refers to the intentional cultivation of speaking behaviors and language skills that students need to develop an oral dexterity for effective communication and collaboration.

Explicitly teaching oracy skills by embedding them in your classroom culture or project design creates a shared common language expectation (not language assimilation) and a more elevated verbal academic expression. Oral language is one of the first skills a human learns, so it is a prerequisite for literacy in later years. Developing strong oracy skills gives your students more equitable opportunities for full participation in the democratic process. Students must be taught to use their voices in effective ways so that what they say matters.

As students practice oracy in PBL, they will

- communicate fluidly with community stakeholders,
- ask better questions of guest experts,
- listen to arguments with intention,
- provide practical feedback,
- present themselves professionally,
- use more descriptive words,
- partake in substantial discussions,
- enhance the engagement in their presentations, and
- witness the impact of their voice.

Establishing norms around oral communication helps ensure a more impartial speaking space for students who are extroverted and outspoken, introverted, and quiet, or anywhere in between. The purpose of your speaking norms must be rec-ognizable by students from every background. To do that, students must be explicitly taught and given opportunities to routinely practice oracy. Before the deep dive into dialogue and discussion protocols later in this chapter, let's establish a basic beginner's guide to help students develop basic but effective spoken language skills.

Using oracy strands help your students consider a set of markers to gauge and evaluate their speaking. Your project design should provide your student opportunities to practice these protocols daily. Conversation activities such as Socratic seminars, peer-review, and critique protocols, small- and whole-group discussions, interviews with experts, and simple academic discourse can be enhanced when students are made to consider their oral communication expression in these four different strands:

Voice and Body Language (Physical)

- Talk at a speed that gives listeners time to process.
- Speak with varied levels of volume and pitch to enhance meaning.
- Use facial expressions and gestures to enhance meaning and engage the listener.
- Use socially acceptable facial expressions, eye contact, and gestures to match recognized cultural and local norms, especially in public presentations.
- Speak clearly without mumbling or slurring words (regardless of accent, dialect, or use of colloquialisms).

Oral Language (Linguistic)

- Adapt language to be appropriate for the social situation and to the listener (code switching).
- Select and organize content to make it relevant and clear to the listener.

Thinking Language (Cognitive)

- Listen and draw upon what others say to enrich their contributions.
- Use questions to seek and clarify information.
- Organize thoughts before speaking to maintain control of what is said.
- Manage available time and ensure not to dominate discussions.
- Clearly explain and justify points of view effectively using words.
- Use language to test ideas and opinions in ways which are constructive and not aggressive.
- Keep account of the listener's understanding.

Pathos Language (Emotional)

- Expand a conversation or discussion by encouraging others to contribute.
- Take turns when speaking to allow others sufficient opportunity to speak.
- Listen actively and respond appropriately.
- Listen to learn.
- Listen to understand other perspectives.
- Listen to make others feel they are heard.
- Cope when questioned, interrogated, or heckled; deal with disputes, emotional conflicts, lack of cooperation, etc.
- Show enthusiasm and use imagination to enhance the discussion or presentation message.

Based on the Oracy Cambridge framework.[71]

Code Switching

Code switching is a common way of adjusting language and be-havior to optimize the comfort of others. Everyone code switches habitually. You don't talk to your grandma as you talk to your friends. However, BIPOC use this term as an acknowl-edgement of an intentional tactic taught and used to switch speaking style, appearance, and expression to assimilate and gain acceptance in white spaces.

Code switching in the academic space is not about assimilation but about empathetic deference. Empathetic deference is a mannerism used to show understanding, regard, and humility to others. In secondary school, when students are most likely to test the "social waters," they adopt expressions that they feel are true to the identity they are trying to portray. These expressions are often categorized as respectful or disrespectful. Instead, we propose that these so-called "disrespectful" expressions are signs of an inadequate understanding of Social Awareness.

Explicitly teaching code switching in oracy practice is not about teaching respect or robbing the students of self-expression. It is about replacing the word *disrespect* with *empathetic deference* to hone a skill that is essential in navigating an ever-changing, multifaceted world.

The following tables can be used as cheat sheets for students to consider when elevating their communications skills. Please remember that the tables are meant to be learning tools and not evaluation tools. Students can be encouraged to record themselves in conversations or while they practice their presentation and then use the cheat sheets to assess their progress. The classroom oracy cheat sheet can be posted on the wall or on table tents as a way to nudge the students to utilize them. Presentation oracy cheat sheets can be used as a practice rubric during peer feedback protocols (Chapter 7).

Classroom Oracy Framework

Voice and Body Language	Pathos Language (Emotional)	Thinking Language (Cognitive)	Oral Language (Emotional)
• How are you using your face to convey your message? • How are you using your voice to enhance your message? • What gestures are you making? • Does your body language and your gestures support (enhance) what you are saying and hearing?	• How are you connecting with your listeners? • Are you able to take turns and allow others sufficient opportunity to speak? • How are you signaling to a speaker that you are actively listening? • How are you able to handle difficult questions or comments from the listeners? • What attitude are you presenting when you speak?	• What do you want the listeners (peers) to know? • How is your narrative transporting your listeners? • What is the quality of the info that you are giving your peers? • Are you making a strong argument? • Have you presented a complex argument clearly?	• Who is your listener? • Are you speaking formally or informally? • Do you need to code switch? • Are you using technical vocabulary and/or new vocabulary used in your research?

Presentation Oracy Cheatsheet

Voice and Body Language	Pathos Language (Emotional)	Thinking Language (Cognitive)	Oral Language (Emotional)
• Is the pitch, tone, and rhythm of our voice varying throughout your presentation? • Are your gestures big enough to be seen throughout the room?	• Is the presentation given with energy and 100% commitment? • Are you connecting with your audience?	• Have you presented a complex argument clearly? • What do you want the audience to know? • Where is your narrative taking your audience?	• Who is your audience? • Do you need to code switch? Are you using the appropriate vocabulary? • Are you using technical vocabulary and/or new vocabulary used in your research?

Adapted from School 21 Oracy Framework[72]

Discussion Protocols

Before diving into controversial content, some discussion boundaries need to be established. Don't assume that students will naturally get along and dialogue civilly or even understand the rules of productive discussion protocols. The showing concern for the perspectives of others aspect of Social Awareness begins in the classroom. Every teacher begins the year by establishing classroom norms. In a collaborative PBL environment, these norms are focused on acknowledging and respecting each other, especially when students disagree. These norms should be collaboratively developed and reinforced over time using specific discussion protocols.

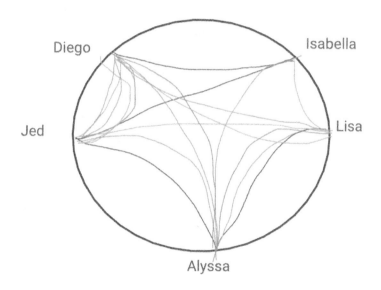

Harkness Discussion Conversation Map

Begin by establishing a culture of respect, safety, and openness with specific discussion protocols. Socratic seminars, fishbowls, Talking Circles, and Harkness Discussions[73] are ways to teach oracy skills such as listening, paraphrasing, pausing before speaking, sharing the "space" in a conversation, and encouraging all students to participate. Begin your chosen protocol by giving the class a specific goal and skill to practice. For example, during a Harkness Discussion, the **goal** might be for all students to contribute equally to the conversation. A Harkness Discussion is a circle discussion protocol that requires the students to take the lead and manage the arch of the discussion without the teacher. To illustrate the progress of the discussion, the moderator maps who speaks by charting the conversation in a visible way (see Graphic and Harkness Discussion ILeva below). The **skill** the students would learn in the Harkness Discussion would be for students to notice who is not speaking and invite them into the conversation. Give students sentence stems to stimulate the conversation and to help them include everyone. The purpose of a Harkness Discussion is not to shame anyone, but to make both assertive and shy students self-aware of how much or how little they are contributing to the conversation. High-quality PBL honors all students' voices, not just the loud ones.

Harkness Discussion ILeva

Communicating Equitably so Students are Active and Empathetic Listeners

Steps	Rationale
1. **Circle Up:** Students sit or stand in a circle. Teacher remains outside as a non-participant. Remind students of the rules and expectations.	Represents equality without hierarchy. Promotes student discussion while the teacher is a silent observer.
2. **Discussion:** Students talk about the selected topic or text with a goal of equal participation. Provide sentence stems: *"I am wondering how _____(name) feels about that point?"* *"_____(name), do you agree/disagree that ..."* *"_____(name) found some research on .... Could you summarize for the group?"* *"_____ (name), what is your perspective on ..."* *"Does everyone agree or does someone have a different opinion?"*	Develops the skill of civil and inclusive conversation.
3. **Rules:** • Conversation flows freely without order. • Stay on topic when given. • Critique ideas, not people. • Let 3 others speak before speaking again. • Encourage everyone in the circle to participate by inviting others in.	Establishes expectations for civility and goals of inclusion. Teaches students to self-correct and return to the topic at hand without teacher intervention.
4. **Charting:** Teacher maps out the path of who is speaking in a weblike fashion on butcher paper or whiteboard. Switch the colors when the conversation topics change.	Creates a visual reference for students of how balanced the conversation is or isn't.
5. **Reflection:** Wrap up with a reflective conversation evaluating the goal of equal participation.	Provides opportunities for students to reflect and evaluate themselves without judgment.

SEL Outcomes:
- Assertive students learn to step back and listen to others. Shy students find their voice to share their thoughts.
- Actively listening to others' perspectives during the discussion.
- Demonstrating empathy and compassion.
- Showing concern for the plight of others.

Assessment Recommendations:
- Evaluate the balance of the conversation map and use inconsistencies as norms for the next discussion.
- Observe how often students invite others into the conversation.
- Use symbols such as '?" for asking questions, "I" for inviting others into conversation, "P" for paraphrasing, "V" for using unit vocabulary or SEL stems, "R" for redirecting or changing topic rather than answering question.

179

Another discussion protocol that is effective in building So-cial Awareness is the previously mentioned Talking Circles. At its core, PBL is about student-centered learning and Talking Circles are compatible with that goal: building community, es-tablishing norms, and giving space for students to solve problems as they come up. Once students are comfortable us-ing Talking Circles, variations can be added that are appropriate for their age and maturity level. In PBL, Talking Circles can be used in a variety of ways, including discussing content, reflecting on group interactions, resolving conflicts, and evaluating classroom behavior.

Don't expect perfection the first time you use any of these protocols. Rather think of them as practice sessions where students focus on developing specific skills. Choose an entertaining or scandalous topic the first time that you introduce a protocol to help the students learn the process. The brain has limited processing ability, and some students may struggle to understand the protocol process and new academic content at the same time. By initially using a fun topic, students first learn how the protocol works, then they are ready to use this new skill to discuss academic content. Remember that the purpose of the protocols is to give students a predictable experience and safe place to practice and learn skills that are new to them. Protocols create a vital SEL culture where students learn respect for one another before diving deep into potentially controversial PBL content.

Talking Circle ILeva
Creating the Conditions for Equitable Conversations

Steps	Rationale
1. **Circle Up:** Students sit or stand in a circle. Explain the cultural origin of Talking Circles as an Indigenous practice around the world.	Represents equality without hierarchy as a circle has no "front" or head position.
2. **Talking Stick:** An object is passed around the circle signifying who has the floor to speak. Students may choose to pass their turn.	Develops the skill of civil and inclusive conversation.
3. **Rules:** · Respect the talking stick · Speak from your heart · Listen with your heart · Speak with respect · Listen with respect · Remain in the circle · Honor confidentiality	Establishes a culture of safety and respect. Develop a caring community.
4. **Rounds:** Multiple rounds can be completed with different questions, topics, or reflections.	Begin with inviting questions before moving to more complex topics.

SEL Outcomes:
- Students will develop and practice the core components of Social Awareness of perspective taking, empathy, compassion, and identifying diverse social norms.
- Students will engage in deep, Transformative discussions.

Assessment Recommendations:
- Reflect on how well students followed the rules and norms.
- Pay attention to students who share more or less than usual.
- Follow up with individual students who share personal or passionate opinions.

Dialogue over Debate

Student debates can be engaging ways to have students engage in higher-order thinking, but sometimes they can lead to strong emotions and hurt feelings. For this reason, many teachers avoid hot-button topics. Instead of sidestepping controversy, direct students to unpack complex issues in ways that lead to more constructive outcomes. Ryan Sprott, San Antonio teacher and founder of the Borderland Collective, a long-term art and education project focusing on immigration and other complex social issues, advises that dialogue rather than debate is more effective when dealing with controversial issues. Sprott warns that debate can lead students into thinking that complex issues have only two sides, leading to an "us vs. them" mentality that is in direct opposition to collaboration.[74] One only needs to look at the United States' two-party political system to see how problematic that can be!

Dialogue is based on mutual respect by honoring everyone's voice. It leaves room for nuance and presents issues as multifaceted.

One technique is to make the discussion question more open ended by starting with the phrase "To what extent . . . ."[75] For example, a binary question such as "Are genetically engineered foods safe to eat?" becomes "To what extent are genetically engineered foods safe to eat?" This slight twist of phrasing gives space for more than a rigid yes/no response.

Rephrasing the opening question will not be enough to change a debate into a dialogue. The teacher must frame the purpose of any dialogue as gathering as many perspectives as possible on a topic. The goal is not to "win" with your opinion, but to figure out why someone else might see things differently. It should not be the teacher's goal to change any student's opinion. This approach frees students to thoughtfully consider different points of view without the pressure of being right.

Discourage students from sharing their own opinions initially. Instead ask them to share other viewpoints. Some great sentence stems are the following:

- What is everything that you have heard about . . . (the topic)?
- Others might say . . .
- Who would disagree with you and what would they say?
- What might be another side's strongest counterpoint?

During closing reflection, you might ask these questions:

- What is something that you heard someone else say that increased your understanding of . . . (the topic)?
- What is a strong point that you heard from a counter point of view?

It is not the case that students will not or should not have opinions on controversial topics, but rather they should be steered to articulate other viewpoints. Again, this is not about trying to change their minds, but about training students to appreciate nuance in a complex topic. They should consider multiple points of view as having legitimacy, even when they strongly disagree. When presented with vastly opposing views, this skill prompts your students to see the humanity of the person speaking rather than fixate on their emotional reaction to the topic.

At the same time, articulating various viewpoints is an opportunity to normalize conversations around identity. In delicate conversations, students should be encouraged to preface their comment by reminding themselves and their listeners through what specific lens they are describing the world:

- from a white, cis-gendered, male point of view
- from a person that lives in the suburbs
- from an LGBTQ+ perspective
- from a person that has never experienced poverty
- from a BIPOC

To include identity in an elementary setting, students might say the following:

- "From a third grader's point of view . . ."
- "From a person that finds school easy . . ."
- "From a white person's point of view . . ."
- "From a bullied person's point of view . . ."

Instruct students only to share if they have experience or evidence about the topic. Otherwise, it is their job to be a listener and ask questions. Listening to each perspective can lead to collaborative solutions that represent all viewpoints. Sometimes consensus does not happen and may even be an unreasonable expectation. What ultimately matters is that students learn to listen and appreciate diverse perspectives, especially when they disagree. Civility is the direct result of Social Awareness skills practiced in PBL.

What if a student makes an outrageous assertion? If a statement made is offensive to any group of people, rude, inappropriate, or demeaning, stop the conversation immediately and remind the student of class agreements regarding respect and deference. There can be no toleration of that kind of comment. If the assertion is simply controversial or baseless, then table the topic for a future Talking Circle discussion. Remember the Talking Circle already has established rules. During class discussions, the teacher's job is to redirect the conversation where the burden of proof is placed on the student making the assertion. If a student makes an outlandish claim or contentious statement from a specific, narrow viewpoint, then they should be required to back it up with legitimate evidence. For example, Matinga discourages circular arguments. She tells her students, "If you make an assertion based on your religious beliefs, then the support for that statement cannot be based on your religious texts because there are students in class that do not follow the teachings of that religion." If a student becomes agitated, defensive, or angry while continuing to advocate their opinion, then the teacher pauses and refocuses the discussion by encouraging the student to preface their statement through an identity lens—for example, "From the view of my religious beliefs . . . ." Students are entitled to their opinions but must follow the Talking Circle and discussion protocol agreements about respect and civility.

In Mike's US History class, students created their own political parties in the #MyParty Election Project. A core requirement was drafting a party platform addressing at least four political issues. This project was ripe with potential for heated debate, but that was not the goal. To prepare for the project launch, Mike rolled out a piece of butcher paper as long as his room and numbered it from 1 to 5. Next, he wrote up five positions on the topic of who should pay for healthcare. Mike intentionally made the number 1 position the most liberal position on the political "left" end of the spectrum and the 5 position the most conservative on the "right" end of the paper.

Healthcare Spectrum on Butcher Paper

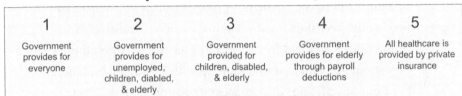

1	2	3	4	5
Government provides for everyone	Government provides for unemployed, children, diabled, & elderly	Government provided for children, disabled, & elderly	Government provides for elderly through payroll deductions	All healthcare is provided by private insurance

For the entry event, Mike unrolled the butcher paper in the hallway and explained the spectrum of different positions on who should pay for healthcare. He intentionally avoided terms such as *right* or *left* and *conservative* or *liberal*. Mike wanted students to focus on the issues written on the butcher paper and not their perceived political alignments. Each student wrote their initials on the butcher paper in the spot that best matched their personal views. The rest of the class period, student pairs chose their own political issue, researched it, and wrote a spectrum of five positions on their issue in a similar fashion.

After school, Mike hung the butcher paper on the wall like a banner. The following day, each student pair presented their chosen political issue with its five positions to the class. Then the class got up out of their seats and stood under the number of the position that best represented their personal views on that particular issue. As he did the day before, Mike framed the spectrum of their positions so that the liberal position was always a "left" 1 and the conservative position was a "right" 5 but didn't reveal that secret to students until later in the project. He took pictures to document how students were standing in different places for each issue.

This entry event accomplished two goals. First, as Ryan Sprott asserts, it was not a two-sided debate between the extremes on each issue. Instead, students could see that every issue had complicated shades of nuance. Secondly, the day after student presentations, Mike used the pictures of the students standing below the butcher paper numbers in a slideshow to demonstrate that no one was consistently standing in the same place for every topic. That in fact, students were all independent thinkers when it came to individual issues. Most of his students fell into the "moderate middle" the majority of the time. Of course, there were always a few students at the extreme positions in each case, but they were outliers and were not the same students for every issue.

The political issues on butcher paper established a couple of powerful ideas when students dove deep into the project. First of all, the class was tasked with creating a civility rubric. They used this rubric throughout the project to evaluate each other and the current politicians who were running for office. The students watched and critiqued the presidential debates. To satisfy the civility rubric, students were required to share the issues that they were passionate about in respectful ways.

Secondly, students recognized that political issues are as complex as the diversity of the people living in the United States. Each student was grouped with similarly minded classmates to create their own political party complete with slogan, logo, platform, and thirty-second commercial. Based on the diverse viewpoints demonstrated in the entry event, it was crystal clear that if groups wanted to win votes for their party, that they would have to respect and appeal to a wide variety of perspectives along the political spectrum.

The Exploding Atom is another dialogue protocol where students can reflect on the various opinions in the class.[76] To begin, mark the center of the room with an "X" or an object and make a strong statement about the discussion topic: for example, "The electoral college should be abolished." Students then stand up and position themselves in relationship to how much they agree with the statement. Those who agree move toward the center, and those who disagree move away to the outside edges of the room. The students should now be spread throughout the room like the electrons of an atom. Next students in different areas of the room share their viewpoints. Other students can take a step closer or further from the center as their opinions are swayed or challenged by their classmates.

Projects like the #MyParty Election Project are the perfect vehicle for students to practice Social Awareness. Through dialogue, Mike's students learned to identify diverse social norms, including unjust ones. They researched the power structures in the United States, analyzing concepts of rights, equality, and the common good. Social Awareness led to more constructive policy recommendations in their party platforms. They practiced respect for one another and self-assessed using the civility rubric. Ultimately the dialogue throughout the project led to the Responsible Decision-Making skills that will be explored in detail in Chapter 8.

Multi-Faceted Driving Questions

High-quality PBL focuses on a local or global problem that is messy and complex. The very reason that a problem is worthy of students' time is that it has multiple solutions and potentially unexplored approaches. Age-appropriate and authentic topics are extensive and could be chosen from current events, community resources, student observations and interests, or targeted academic standards. At an elementary level, the topic might be designing a zoo in the school playground, covering math, science, and language arts. A middle school team might focus on cafeteria food economics to include financial math, environmental impact, food science, research and data analysis, and writing. A high school geometry class may team up with the shop class to design and build an emergency tiny house to mass-deliver after a natural disaster. The Driving Question frames the issue so that students can pursue multiple avenues toward a solution, rather than one clear path.

The Driving Question is vital for sharpening students' Social Awareness by urging them to appreciate contending positions, varying access to resources, and circles of influence. The best DQs are philosophical in nature, requiring students to consider complex issues from multiple viewpoints. At first, students might be tempted to immediately jump to conclusions and pick a side based on their personal values. They need to be taught to "hold their truth with an open hand, rather than a closed fist." The goal is to teach the skills of researching, interviewing, analyzing, and formulating conclusions based on observation and data. This approach requires students to acknowledge their limited knowledge (N2Ks) and embark on a

189

journey where they consult experts, make observations, collect evidence, and use their imagination to redesign their world. The answers to a good Driving Question might confirm or challenges students' beliefs as they gain background knowledge from people with conflicting opinions.

A rewarding aspect for the PBL teacher is learning alongside students as part of the PBL process, modeling life-long learning. Your students will ask questions and listen to understand, observe, research, and experiment BEFORE arriving at any conclusions. More importantly, students will identify this investigative approach in methodologies like the scientific method and design thinking used by scientists and engineers. If teachers create a safe culture of "failing forward," then students won't have to worry about quickly picking the "right" side but will view each failure as a closer step to success.

Examples of Multi-Faceted DQs by Academic Level

Elementary	Middle School	High School
• Can a lizard live in the trees? • What is the world's healthiest food? • Should we eat genetically engineered foods? • Should humans travel to Mars? • Can you keep your family safe in a fire?	• Which forms of energy are truly "green"? • When do the ends justify the means? • How do you select the best soccer players based on your budget?	• Are unions beneficial? Prove mathematically. • Should we clone people? • How do different cultures deal with death? • How much is a "livable" wage? • What one adjustment would have the largest impact on climate change?

A common concern that teachers have about Driving Questions is the feeling that their students lack adequate background knowledge to answer them. The temptation is to pre-teach content before launching the project. But this thinking misses a vital point: the purpose of the DQ, and the PBL process in general, is to motivate students to *want* to learn the academic content standards and understand their purpose. If you pre-teach required content before launching a project with an open-ended DQ, then students are still stuck in "Why are we learning this?" mode.

The faulty logic of the need to pre-teach content is a misinterpretation of the pyramid shape of Bloom's Taxonomy. Once Matinga asked a group of teachers to describe the skill sets of the Ideal Graduate of their school as described in Chapter 1. A high school teacher opined, "I'd be happy if my students are able to write a complete sentence by the end of the lesson." Of course educators would be failing if students couldn't complete basic skills, but the implication of comments like this is that "you don't know my students. They are so low ability that I could never do a PBL project without teaching them a long list of basic skills first." This is "pyramid" thinking, and it is damaging to students by setting low expectations of them.

Bloom himself did not construct the pyramid image so often associated with his taxonomy, nor does it accurately display his ideas.[77] Bloom's Taxonomy has been revised[78] and in-verted, but many educators still misunderstand its purpose. The original intention of the diagram was for teachers to reflect on what students were doing and to make sure that their lessons were not stuck in basic knowledge level all the time. Bloom's Taxonomy is a reflection tool for teacher planning, not student learning. It was never meant to be hierarchical nor sequential. In other words, one does not HAVE to remember and under-stand basic knowledge BEFORE they can analyze or create. Let us say it louder for those in the back:

Bloom's Taxonomy was never intended to be a hierarchy for how students learn!

Bloom's Taxonomy should not be viewed as steps to be completed in sequence as knowledge and skills are mastered like leveling up in a video game. A better analogy for Bloom's Taxonomy would be a ladder where students are using multiple rungs at the same time. Think of each student with their feet on one rung and their hands holding another as they lean their body against the other rungs. Students are constantly moving up and down Bloom's Ladder as needed in the moment. Teachers can ask students to analyze, evaluate, and create before they have basic knowledge and comprehension on a given subject. That is what a great Driving Question does! It invites students into complex problems through curiosity. PBL starts by getting students excited about the top rungs of the ladder. Now students are motivated to research the web, read books, watch videos, or interview experts to build up their knowledge and comprehension. Next, during the Need to Know process, students ask questions about what they don't know so they can successfully complete the project and address the DQ. They are identifying the missing rungs at the bottom of the ladder, the ones they need to make it to the top.

Throughout the middle of the project cycle, students move up and down the ladder, evaluating and analyzing the problem and researching their own questions to fill in what they need to remember and understand. Every project ends with students demonstrating their learning. Oftentimes they create a physical object such as an art piece, prototype, or model. On other projects, they write a plan or essay analyzing the problem and presenting solutions. Whatever the final artifact of their

learning looks like, it provides evidence that students have arrived at the top rungs of the ladder.

Here's the kicker, what is the purpose of a ladder? A ladder
is a tool to climb to an area out of reach, oftentimes to do important work. Hence if one thinks of the higher rungs of
Bloom's Taxonomy as where students should function the majority of the time, then the ladder analogy works. One does not
grab a ladder unless they have a desire to reach a higher place
for a specific purpose. PBL launches by showing students what
is waiting at the top of the ladder. With engagement, motivation, and a purpose for the learning, students are eager to grab
onto the ladder, moving up and down, developing skills as
needed until they reach their goal of a creative solution at the
top.

In Mike's Monument Project, students had minimal background knowledge of American foreign policy of the past one
hundred years. They had some knowledge about the World
Wars and Vietnam War but had limited grasp of the hundreds
of smaller, more common interactions between the United
States and other countries. Initially most students viewed the
United States as a constant force for good in the world, so they
had no idea why terrorists hate their country. The DQ invited
them to research our foreign policy through the eyes of the people from numerous other countries to examine outside
perspectives of the United States.

Voice and choice (one of the secret sauces of PBL) flows out
of an open-ended DQ. Instead of every student traveling down
the same path to a planned destination, the DQ invites students
to explore a topic using the paths of their choice. Along the way,

they gain different insights about the topic that they then share with other students who chose other paths. A good project always assumes that there are multiple paths and solutions. For the Monument Project, each group chose to research a different American foreign policy. Students shared their findings to the class and then synthesized the patterns. In the #MyParty Election Project students chose which issues they were passionate about to build their party platform. Their choice became voice when they presented their positions to local politicians and lawmakers. After showing campaign commercials and giving stump speeches, students were stampeded by the guest politicians who specifically wanted to know more about their opinions on LGBTQ+ rights. The predominantly conservative leaders were shocked to hear that students who were conservative on other issues supported marriage equality for the LGBTQ+ community. Mike credits the student's disposition to the strong community of acceptance cultivated within their school.

Driving Questions invite students to practice Transformative Social Awareness throughout the project. Students start with an attitude of compassion and empathy for others as they investigate various angles of the chosen problem without judgment. All options are sought out and evaluated independently. Systemic forces, dominant culture, and specific situations are evaluated for equity and justice. Students contemplate the perspectives of all sides of the issue and consider each for its merit before working toward a solution compatible for all involved.

Connections with the Community

Project Based Learning moves students outside of the traditional classroom into the local community and beyond. In Chapter 3, we mentioned that community connections are one of the secret sauces of PBL. While investigating authentic problems, students should consult community members from a wide variety of backgrounds and experiences. Guest speakers add the real-time knowledge a teacher might lack in specific areas, and they might come from racial, economic, and cultural backgrounds underrepresented within the confines of a school or even a community. By interacting with a variety of people from multiple perspectives, students sharpen their Social Awareness, discovering that complex problems require a combination of multi-faceted solutions.

Educators may be wary about the safety of students, especially younger ones, interacting with the community. Since the birth of the nationwide Stranger Danger panic of the 1980s, children in the United States have been taught that every adult they do not know could be a potential danger to them. Horrific headlines in the twenty-four-hour news cycles and newspapers exposed parents to stories of kidnappings and murders. These sensationalized stories, which continue today on the internet, make it difficult for parents to align what they hear and see in the media with their own safe and free roaming childhoods. Although it is important to teach children to be vigilant, especially around schools and playgrounds, it is essential that teachers do not use the Stranger Danger narrative to separate children from their community.

On the one hand, we teach children to reach out to an adult for help when they need it, but on the other hand, we tell them that every adult could be a danger.

The current disconnect between schools and the neighborhoods that surround them is not only a disservice to the community but a squandered opportunity for our students to understand their potential role as valuable community members. Interacting with local residents in informative and productive ways is a crucial Social and Emotional Learning skill because it allows students to prepare to enter said community. It is not sufficient to prepare students to successfully enter society as adults, but they should navigate their own community as children to help them understand their personal and often symbiotic connection with their immediate world.

Community members share a wealth of life experiences and how they use their own skills to cope in difficult situations. Guest speakers can transport your students to unimaginable worlds, contributing to students' background knowledge. If young children do not seem to care about the community around them, it is not for lack of empathy but because they simply lack a relevant connection to the people, places, and events in which they live. Projects seated in the community give life to student work, an important part of the Pulse of PBL.

Before opening up your classroom to guests from the community, set up clear expectations for their role. One of the challenges in recent times has been inviting members of the community who want to challenge school policies or disrupt school proceedings to advance their uncompromising opinions. Noneducators may not understand the boundaries required by student's cognitive and emotional development or the school's legal obligations. Consider screening guests and setting norms for their interactions with children before inviting them to your class.

Matinga had a habit of inviting captivating community members to Grand Ledge High School to draw connections between the students' projects and their neighbors. Her high school Global Studies class was notorious for a constant parade of visitors often bedecked in traditional clothing from all over the world. One of the most impactful guest speakers was a young alumnus of the school, Brian Daniels, who had recently completed boot camp in the US army. Standing six feet tall, Brian cut an impressive figure in full uniform, wearing samples of his tactical gear. Students who knew him before he graduated from high school were shocked at his transformation into a commanding military asset. Brian shared his difficult journey through high school and how army discipline helped him overcome aspects of his troubled background. In 2005, a few weeks after his visit, he flew to Baghdad to serve his first deployment in the Iraq War.

Months later, while on patrol in Iraq, Brian's Humvee detonated an improvised explosive device (IED). The explosion killed all the soldiers in the caravan except for Brian, who was ejected forcibly from his vehicle by the blast causing severe injury to his legs. After he flew back to the US, he asked if he could return to the Global Studies class to add to his story. The students were shocked to see the once statuesque Brian reduced to an emaciated young man sitting in a wheelchair.

Brian talked about innocence lost in his personal trauma and the deaths of his best friends and brothers in the blast. He told of the futility of war, the conflicting empathy, and even kinship he felt for the people who were supposed to be his enemies. Today Brian is a recipient of a Purple Heart and the owner of a popular boxing gym, where he uses his military background to train others suffering from post-traumatic stress to cope using physical fitness. Brian's visit to Matinga's classroom left an indelible experience on her students who became Socially Aware of a new perspective to inspire their writing and conversations about conflicting US government foreign policies.

Sometimes, instead of bringing in guest speakers, teachers guide their students out into the community.

Question: *When do most schools take field trips?*

Answer: *At the end of a project or year, often as a reward or celebration.*

In PBL, flip the script and plan fieldwork at the beginning of the project using it as an entry event or as a research opportunity in the middle of the project. We use the term *fieldwork* instead of field trips because the former implies vocation, while the latter implies recreation. Out students won't be passive spectators, but actively engaged in early research.[79]

Fifth grade students at the diverse Foulks Ranch Elementary School in urban Elk Grove, California, explored the Driving Question of *"How can we prevent marine debris from entering our oceans?"* They produced public service announcements for their city's Waste and Recycling Division about how to properly recycle different kinds of plastic. Teacher Jim Bentley launched the project with a multi-stage entry event. First students interviewed via video a National Geographic explorer stationed in Newfoundland studying plastics digested by seabirds. Next, they used the Notice and Wonder routine to analyze graphic pictures of birds' and sea turtles' intestines that had died from eating plastic. Next, a freshwater ecologist talked to students about food webs in the Sacramento River, and students discussed places where plastic could enter the food chain.

Originally, Bentley had scheduled fieldwork at a material recovery facility to observe how a recycling operation works but had to cancel due to COVID-19 pandemic restrictions. The students would have recorded observations and questions related to the investigation they were conducting on recycling rates of different types of plastics. This active experience would have continued the research—fieldwork—as compared to a passive experience as tourists—field trip.

The culmination of this expansive entry event was a student fishing expedition. Students harvested fish guts and sent them to a lab to test for how much plastic the fish had ingested. The fishing expedition was not a reward at the end of the project, but a vital early step of their authentic research to give data to their community concerning the need to properly recycle.[80]

Whether through fieldwork or a guest speaker, community connections are a vital part of the PBL process that increase Social Awareness. No matter how diverse or isolated your community is, technology easily connects us to experts and regular people across the globe. PBL transforms these outside interactions from "fun enrichment" to integral parts of the learning process by requiring community viewpoints to be implemented into student project solutions.

Empathy in PBL

The highest level of Social Awareness is when students empathize with others organically. However, teaching empathy can be a nebulous term. In the context of SEL, empathy is the ability to understand and share the feelings of others or the capability to "feel with" someone. In order for students to practice and recognize empathy, we use the different elements of empathy as defined by CASEL cofounder Daniel Goleman and psychologist Paul Ekman:

1. Cognitive empathy: the ability to put oneself into someone else's place and see their perspective
2. Emotional empathy: the ability to feel someone else's emotions alongside them
3. Compassionate empathy: the ability to feel someone else's pain and be compelled to take action to help[81]

Breaking the concept of empathy down this way makes inserting this SEL skill more relevant to students. PBL requires students to empathize at different levels and to design solutions to the problems posed to them. Specificity about types of empathy helps students understand when it is appropriate to take action, when an empathetic interaction requires simple emotional support, or when skills are needed to build stronger and healthier relationships.

Cognitive Empathy

Framing a project with cognitive empathy compels students to clearly see or experience the perspective of others. Understanding cognitive empathy makes our students better communicators because they relay information in ways that best reach their audience. Consider the following question and project example:

Do wealthy company owners have the cognitive empathy to provide support for their employees?

When studying industrialization and the rise of monopolies and unions, Mike's students participated in a simulation of the Pullman Strike of 1894. The Pullman Strike was caused by a rigid lack of empathy by George Pullman, owner of Pullman Palace Car Company, toward the laborers who built his custom railroad coaches. After the depression of 1893, he cut wages but refused to lower rent in Pullman, Chicago, the company town where his employees were forced to live. To make themselves heard, the workers led a widespread railroad boycott that undermined rail traffic across the entire western United States. Ultimately President Grover Cleveland brought in the army to break up the strike and shut down the union. This action shaped national labor policy in the United States.

The majority of the students in Mike's class were assigned the role of unhappy railway workers, with a list of historical demands and options such as strikes and protests. A few students were designated to be the wealthy owners and were given historically accurate responses but were strictly instructed not to concede to any employee demands. As in real history, it quickly escalated to (simulated) violence. When debriefing, students were able to understand how the harsh restrictions that owners placed on workers led to the formation of labor unions and strikes.

Simulations can be emotionally powerful experiences, but a word of caution: Teacher discretion must be used. Not everything is appropriate to be simulated. Students could never truly experience the many horrible atrocities of history, and it is disrespectful to even attempt simulations of them. Events such as slavery, Native American removals to reservations, the Holocaust and other genocides, refugee camps, etc. should NEVER be simulated in the classroom. Many teachers want their students to feel empathy for historical events, but some traumatic, historic events are not appropriate or fair for the classroom. Furthermore, these events may trigger trauma responses in some students. A more respectful way to build empathy for victims of historical tragedies is by examining primary source pictures and reading diaries or memoirs.

Topics like the Pullman Strike simulation are perfect opportunities to build cognitive empathy. Demonstrating cognitive empathy is simply the act of considering what you know about a person and what you are willing to know about them before you engage with them. Using the Pullman Strike simulation as a backdrop, a teacher could divide the students into small groups. Each team could create a list of administrative decisions, school rules, and requirements they consider unfair, irrelevant, or even oppressive. Students are always enthusiastic to point out what is not working in their school.

Each group would develop a rationale, evidence, outcomes, and solution of each item on their list. Then students would explain their list to the class. After all groups have shared, students would vote for the top three rules or requirements that should be changed. This is a great opportunity for the students to investigate why certain school rules and requirements were put in place and, better yet, who created them. Most importantly, are those rules and requirements keeping up with the times? Are they actually helpful? Do the rules and regulations contribute to academic success, or are they hindering student progress? Consider inviting a panel of administrators, teachers, and community members to hear the students' rationale and solutions.

These types of exchanges have inspired teachers and administrators throughout the United States to shadow their students for a day or two to understand what it is like to attend school these days. Some administrators allow students to spend a day in their office, shadowing their complex jobs to understand how and why some decisions are made.[82] These experiences align with the plight of the Pullman railroad employees and whether the trigger to their strike could have been avoided by exercising cognitive empathy.

The dream result of these SEL exercises would be that the administrators would consider their students' positions and adopt plausible student solutions. Imagine how empowered students would feel if they took part in ridding their school of an unpopular regulation. However, any results will make for a deep Social Awareness debriefing with the students and food for thought for the administrators.

Emotional Empathy

The ability to feel for someone's emotion is a trait that humans practice from the cradle. Babies reciprocate a mother's smile while adults get caught up in contagious giggles at a formal event. Emotional empathy can be fine-tuned as a powerful Social Awareness skill that sharpens the way students connect the topic of their project and the humanity behind it. To teach students to understand empathy in this way requires teachers to push their thinking to form deeper connections. In other words, it is not enough to simply feel another's pain, but the students must be taught to resist judging a person or situation, resist the urge to make recommendations or suggestions, and resist the telling of one's own personal experiences.

During Mike's Monument Project, Mo Shamali, a Palestinian American, and his niece recounted the prejudice and harassment that they experienced after the September 11 terrorist attacks. Mr. Shamali told of how he was profiled and verbally assaulted by a stranger in a restaurant because he "looked" Muslim. He described his frustration of being profiled even though he considered himself a loyal American citizen. The niece, who was visiting from Jordan, explained the tradition and meaning of the hijab, the modesty headdress that some Muslim women wear publicly. She invited a couple of female students to try some of her extra scarves and showed them how to wear a hijab properly. She challenged them to a social experiment where female students would opt to wear a hijab for twenty-four hours to observe how they were treated by others. A few girls chose to participate in each class and came in the next day with powerful stories about feeling judged in ways that they had never experienced.

The Monument Project forced students to consider other perspectives beyond the dominant media narrative and memory of the time. Most of Mike's students had never thought about how the terrorist attacks of September 11 and the subsequent reporting felt for American Muslims. Instead of being a time of national unity against a common enemy, many practicing Muslims, Sikhs, and Americans with Middle Eastern physical traits were treated as enemies in their own country. Through the experiences of the two guests that day, Mike's students were able to see past their own perspective and practice empathy toward others.

Guest visits should be followed by debriefing exercises where, through guided questions, students can reflect on their learning in journal entries, conversations with a partner, or in whole group discussions. After a reflection stage, it is appropriate for students to draw lines to when they might have experienced similar issues using a protocol like "I used to think, but now I know"[83] and then even propose viable solutions.

Emotional empathy overload is often responsible for much of the drama that happens in school because of poor self-regulation or self-control skills. Listening to other's stories, observing their situation without a rush to judgement, and reserving emotional reactions to a more controlled reflection session teaches students to connect after they have a more complete picture of the situation.

If you can't find an appropriate guest speaker, one of the most powerful ways to teach empathy in PBL is through literature.[84] Stories build empathy by lighting up neurons in the action regions of our brains when we listen or tell stories as if we were experiencing the adventure ourselves. Our brains are wired to use stories as a way to imagine things outside of the realm of our personal experience.[85] As mentioned in Chapter 4 under Self-Awareness, stories can shape our students' identities and building empathy is an essential ingredient of our Profile of a Graduate. Students can interact with stories through picture books, graphic novels, short stories, and even YouTube videos. The reason stories are so powerful is that the audience puts itself into the role of the protagonist and other characters. People literally live vicariously through them. Stories invite us outside of our own existence and into the experiences of others.

Literature shouldn't be limited to English class either. In the Monument Project, *Ender's Game* provided the philosophical question to evaluate American foreign policy: Should people (or a nation) be judged for their actions or intentions? In biology, students can read *The Immortal Life of Henrietta Lacks* in a project that looks at the intersection of racism, ethics, and human genetics. In math class, they can explore *Hidden Figures* to investigate how Black female mathematicians propelled the US position in the Space Race against the Soviet

Union. Transformative SEL empowers students to reflect on the experience of diverse people and the emotions they have felt in challenging circumstances.

Elementary teachers often use read-alouds. In PBL, teachers choose a book related to the theme of the project to reinforce the project dilemma in a narrative form. Next students reflect with partners and in writing about how the characters relate to the project that they are studying. One should include a variety of author voices throughout the year, reflecting the diversity of society and showing students that characters from all backgrounds and perspectives matter.

Compassionate Empathy

Taking action as a gesture of empathy is what is universally understood as compassionate empathy. Students can be taught to ask others what they can do to help rather than taking uninvited actions. A first step in creating a culture of compassionate empathy is to use the Identity ILeva. As students develop deeper relationships with each other through honest sharing, they will be less likely to hurt one another with their actions and words.

Another wonderful way of teaching compassionate empathy in PBL is narrative writing as the final product. After a tragic suicide by a former student in their community, some fifth grade girls in Lisa Yau's class in South Philadelphia began cutting themselves as a way to cope. Yau's school, Eliza B. Kirkbride School, is 50 percent Hispanic and 30 percent Asian; half of the students are English Learners, and all of them are economically disadvantaged. When Yau launched a project through Need in Deed, a local organization that connects schools to the community through service learning, her class told her that they wanted to do a project on depression. Initially Yau was hesitant to take on the topic with fifth graders, but she agreed when she learned that children in low income and minority communities are at a higher risk for depression. Yau brought in a mental health expert who had attempted suicide when he was eighteen by jumping off from a nine-story building. After learning about how he sought and found help for his depression, students wanted to inform others that there was help and a way out. After months of research, the students came together to write *Demystifying Depression: 29 Voices to Normalize Crazy Goodness*, a book of poems to encourage others who are struggling with mental health issues.

Yau declared,

"The most important thing students learned from this project is that it's OK to ask for help. All of them now feel this compassion for other people, as well as forgiveness for themselves."[86]

Yau was surprised that some of the best writing came from students who struggled in traditional, structured writing assignments. As a result of this project, students began to stick up when someone was being picked on and speaking out for themselves with confidence.

PBL has no pulse at all when it is "dead" to the diverse viewpoints of others.

Without Transformative Social Awareness, projects can be cold and heartless. The foundation of sharpening Social Aware-ness is choosing a project and framing a Driving Question that invites students to explore a complex problem from multiple perspectives. Protocols build a culture of respect and acceptance of differing viewpoints, while dialogue teaches students that few issues are limited to two opposite extremes but are full of nuance. Connecting to the community through guests and fieldwork exposes students to points of view that they may not have considered. Literature offers rich encounters with characters from broad backgrounds. The end result of Transformative Social Awareness is a genuine empathy toward others, creating citizens who look for solutions that respect everyone affected.

Reflection Questions

- How will you explicitly teach oracy skills for differing social contexts?
- How will you build a school/class culture of mutual respect for all students?
- What protocols will you use to practice civil dialogue?
- What type of project and driving question will you design so that students are required to consider diverse perspectives?
- What fieldwork will you plan to enrich students' views on a topic?

- What organizations or community members will you contact to give your students varied perspectives on their project?
- What literature will students read to build empathy on their project topic?
- How can you sharpen your students' Social Awareness toward Transformative SEL?

Chapter 7

Forging Relationship Skills

Coaching effective communication and collaboration skills builds strong leaders.

- Teacher-Student Relationship
- Group Contracts
- Peer Feedback
- Outside Collaboration
- Student Leadership

Mike's all-time favorite project began when he heard about the dreams of Grand Rapids Whitewater (GRWW), a Michigan nonprofit organization dedicated to removing and lowering dams in the Grand River, to bring back the original river rapids for ecological, economic, and recreational purposes. As the GRWW's efforts became a reality with the help of federal backing, Mike and his colleagues realized that they HAD to get students involved in the most impactful change that their city had seen in decades.

The geometry teacher and Mike participated in a public forum hosted by GRWW about what redesigning the city, with the Grand River as the focal point, might look like. They met with city officials and tried to connect them to a student project idea but failed. As the end of the school year approached, Mike and his colleagues still had no community connections for the proposed project. It was time to decide. Should they scrap it or go forward? Ultimately the teachers decided to launch the Water Project and figure it out as they went. This seemingly reckless decision was key to the project's eventual success.

On the third day of the project, students went downtown for fieldwork to explore the Grand River in person. Students chose to join one of three teams: design, ecology, or public relations (PR). The design team took pictures along the river, spotting areas with abandoned buildings, empty lots, and some homeless tents. The ecology team ran tests to measure how high and fast the river was running. Mike worked with the PR team, who administered a survey to obtain data of the public's feedback on the proposed changes to the river. Students were answering one of their N2K questions: "What would be the community's future vision of Grand Rapids?"

Unfortunately, the trip to the Grand River was early in the morning, and the students were only able to interview about a dozen people in the nearly empty sidewalks and paths along the river. One student, Kylie, asked if she could post the survey questions on social media to get more community feedback. Mike told her to go for it, without giving it much thought. She posted it on her Facebook page and tagged local media, who in turn reposted it. The post went viral locally, and Kylie became the leader of a newly created social media team that managed a Facebook page, Twitter, and Instagram accounts for the project. By the end of the week, the survey had over eight hundred responses! Kylie started thinking about a career in marketing, a field that she had never considered before. The students had made the local connections that the teachers failed to accomplish!

Just like Kylie, each of the three teams had students who stepped up and chose themselves as leaders. A group of boys, who truthfully scuffled through the year without much motivation, excitedly created a Google Maps tour overlayed on downtown Grand Rapids displaying where the students' proposed changes were located. When in the middle of the project work ground to a halt due to a lack of communication between the different teams, the student leaders called a meeting to workshop a plan to get the teams out of the weeds. On the day of the student organized meeting, a couple of teachers stopped in to observe or maybe facilitate. Suddenly one of the students, Brad, said to them, "We don't need you guys here; we've got this." There were grunts and nods of agreement among the students and the teachers realized that this was a defining moment as students took total ownership of the project. The teachers had created a project opportunity that gave space for students to demonstrate their SEL strengths rather than tightly managing the teams.

The design team created a twenty-five-foot-long, 3D miniature replica of a future downtown Grand Rapids out of cardboard. They color-coded the model by spray painting existing structures white and their new ideas in red. The replica was placed in the center of the large common space in the hall for easy access. There were posters on the wall showing prototypes in the design process, computer stations displaying their website and social media presence, and the Google Maps tour of the area. Truth be told, the physical product of painted cardboard was basic and not that fancy. The power of this project came from the students' collaboration, creative ideas, and passionate explanations of their design.

When the day came for the student-initiated showcase of their model, students sent out invitations via their social media platforms. Everyone waited anxiously to see who would show up. Students were surprised and excited to see guests from the Michigan Department of Environmental Quality, a local watershed protection group, the director of the public museum, and one of the cofounders of Grand Rapids Whitewater attend their presentation. When Mike asked each guest how they found out about the showcase, they couldn't name a specific source, but rather the invitation came from the students' viral social media campaign.

Kylie and two other girls gave a tour of the school and their city replica to a guest from the public museum. He was so impressed by the project and how the girls conducted themselves that he offered them a paid internship working on a similar project at the museum that summer. One of the girls, Haley, jumped onto his team and ended up meeting the governor of Michigan later that fall at the museum project showcase. As a result of the student-initiated connection to the local watershed protection group, Kent Innovation High began a long-term partnership that has continued with various projects over the years.

Relationship Skills are the ability to maintain healthy relationships with diverse people through communication and cooperation. Since PBL involves significant time spent working in groups, it is the perfect structure to forge Relationship Skills. During the Water Project, students engaged with the community through the surveys, the social media campaign, and the final showcase. They demonstrated excellent communication skills when leading tours of the project and the school during the showcase. Students showed teamwork by dividing the many aspects of this project between the three teams and organizing meetings to facilitate clearer communication. They cemented relationships with each other and made new connections with the community for future project partnerships.

Teacher-Student Relationship

Any pedagogy, including PBL, is built on the teacher-student relationship. This is the bedrock of students learning to forge appropriate Relationship Skills with others outside of their family. There is a strong relationship between feeling a sense of belonging and the evolution of Social Awareness.[87] This is especially vital for students of color, English Learners, and our most vulnerable students. As James Baldwin states, "A child cannot be taught by anyone who despises him, and a child cannot afford to be fooled. A child cannot be taught by anyone whose demand, essentially, is that the child repudiate his experience, and all that gives him sustenance."[88] Classrooms must be centers of caring where the culture and backgrounds of all learners are respected. Students can learn deference for the space, their peers, and their teachers in an environment free of fear. True respect is not built on fear, but on meaningful connections built with trusting adults. Trust gives the brain space for higher-level thinking, leading to creativity.[89] Without a trusting relationship, students literally cannot give us their full selves.

PBL thrives in a culture where the teacher knows what productive Social and Emotional skills the students have and works to create the conditions to promote an arch for the student to develop skills they lack.

The SEL skill of Relationship Building starts with adult modeling for students. As educator Paul Bogush asserts in his blog subtitle, "kids will be who you are, not who you want them to be."[90] That is why it is essential to launch your school year by establishing a position of trust, as discussed in Chapter 5. The most important "learning objective" that every teacher has at the beginning of the school year is creating the conditions to foster deep relationships with their students to discover their SEL strengths to expand upon. As a teacher, one builds trust by showing vulnerability, sharing your own shortcomings, and how you slew each dragon in your path. This might seem a bit personal and indulging, but we now understand that being distant and strict might demand obedience but simply does not inspire students to follow your lead. The old adage "Don't let them see you smile before Christmas" is as ridiculous as it is unproductive, punitive, and petty. Strong relationships are at the core of all learning.

One natural occurrence in the classroom, especially for secondary teachers with multiple classes of students, is that you get to know some students better than others. Often the more extroverted kids demand more attention from the start. If you are struggling to start relationships with all of your students, we developed a simple spreadsheet called "Student Relationship Data" to track what you know about each kid. The advantage of the chart is twofold. At a glance, you can see students who have mostly blanks, and you can commit to spending more time in conversation with them. Secondly you can use this data to customize projects and SEL group roles around student strengths and interests.

Student Relationship Data Chart

Student Name	Family	Languages	Traditions	Pets	Favorite Animal	Hobbies	Talents	Heroes	Food	Candy	Music

Having strong teacher-student relationships does not mean that there are no consequences when students are off track. Students will get off task because they are young and do not always understand how their lack of self-management affects the learning environment. Teachers can relate to students while building a cooperative climate and still hold high behavior expectations. The difference is that instead of punishing students, the focus is on improving Social and Emotional skills through redirection and feedback. When a student is disruptive in class, you now have set up an environment where the student can reflect on how their actions affect others. For students who struggle with repeat unproductive behaviors, it is an appropriate time to codesign a plan to help them be successful. Remember that the PBL approach does not require you to be in the front of the room the entire class time, so you have the bandwidth to develop important skills in your students.

PBL teachers realize that unproductive behavior may actually reflect poor instructional design. If students are restless due to sitting for prolonged periods of explicit instruction, the cure is not punishment but more options for movement that are developmentally appropriate. In PBL, students spend more time working with each other in their teams than listening to the teacher.

One time Mike made a time lapse film of his two-hour class period condensed down to one minute. It was amazing to watch the amount of natural movement there was in the room as students worked on their project. When students are restless, shift to a protocol with movement or away from whole group discussion to smaller groups activities. PBL teachers use their solid relationships with students to encourage and motivate them for the duration of the project.

Group Contracts

With a strong foundational relationship with the teacher, students begin to forge relationships with each other as they learn new SEL skills, protocols, and ways to collaborate to solve problems. As you add more SEL skill-building into your PBL practice, coaching students how to function in groups becomes one of your primary roles in the classroom. Students and, let's be honest, adults don't just naturally get along all of the time. Sibling and family relationships are proof. Everyone is unique, with strengths and shortcomings that play out in interpersonal relationships. SEL skills of relationships and teamwork must be taught, practiced, and assessed consistently.

The majority of the school year is spent coaching students how to use these SEL strategies and tools effectively to collaborate.

As mentioned previously in Chapter 5 under Self-Management, SEL group role cards, group contracts, and scrum boards help students learn how to interact with each other in productive ways and invoke teamwork for successful completion of their goals. By the time you launch your second project of the year, very little time should be spent on creating new group contracts. Lawyers do not write contracts from scratch. They adapt and update previous documents. In a similar manner, students should reflect on the last project about what did and didn't work in their teams. Then they can modify their previous contract based on their reflection. From here on out, students will discover how worthless the contract is if they don't use it. This is the challenging but rewarding work of the PBL teacher. Forging Relationship Skills is a critical part of the pulse of PBL.

Applying Group Contracts ILeva

Implementing Team Agreements so Students Manage their Time, Team, and Tasks.

Steps	Rationale
1. **Create**: After the N2K process, form teams and have each group fill out a Group Contract template. They should customize as needed based on their previous group experiences.	Sets clear expectations for how the group will work. Communicates SEL strengths and goals with each other.
2. **SEL Roles:** Give each group a set of laminated SEL Group Role Cards and have them pick roles for themselves.	Establishes the SEL focus for the group and individual students. Determines SEL responsibilities of each student toward the group and the tasks.
3. **Scrum board:** Each group completes a scrum board from the N2Ks with tasks, personal assignments, and due dates.	Organizes the project process so that students can self-manage.
4. **Warnings:** Any warnings should be based on failure to complete assigned tasks in the scrum board, not on personality conflicts.	Holds all team members accountable for completing their part of the work in a fair and equitable way.

5. **Roleplay**: Practice handling persistent student issues in class. Divide into triads rotating roles for three separate scenarios from the Group Contract Scenarios
    o Contract breaker
    o Contract enforcer
    o Observer
	Practices how to give specific, helpful, and kind feedback to support or redirect a team member who is distracted or off-task.

6. **Sentence Stems:** Contract enforcers should practice using the sentence stems on the Group Contract Scenarios sheet.	Facilitates for students who do not know how to communicate when someone is not fulfilling their responsibilities.
7. **Emotions:** Have students explain how they feel: *"We're friends, but we all committed to having this task done by today and your part isn't completed. I am sorry, but I am giving you a verbal warning. And just so you know, it is really stressing me out because I care about this project and want to do well."*	Creates positive peer-pressure to contribute and not let their teammate down when students share their emotions (Self-Awareness).
8. **Modeling:** Another option is to have a couple of teachers or other adults come into your classroom and model the scenarios and sentence stems for students.	Provides non-threatening examples of productive communication and feedback.

SEL Outcomes:
- All students learn leadership and how to effectively resolve group conflicts.
- Gives students the language to help a struggling team member without judgment.
- Builds positive relationships for collaborative problem-solving.

Assessment Recommendations:
- Observe role plays for students who are uncomfortable giving or receiving feedback.
- Provide opportunities for students to explain how comfortable they are giving and receiving peer feedback.
- Circle back in a few days and have students reflect on whether or not their group is more effective.

Let's consider how these group contracts and scrum boards work together. Combine them to make student warnings based on work completion rather than personality conflicts. Instead of students attacking each other with comments such as "You are annoying. I can't stand you, so I am giving you a warning," teach students that the warnings should be given when a group member does not meet agreed upon work deadlines on the scrum board.

Modeling is just as important for SEL skills as it is for content.

Another strategy is roleplaying with sentence stems. Sentence stems are an excellent strategy for English Learners, helping make content universally accessible for all. Students rehearse how they would handle situations by acting out scenes based on persistent issues in class. This is a safe way for them to practice and feel comfortable using effective communication to share their state of mind and solve group conflicts. Use a triad, where one student takes the role of contract breaker, one student enforces the contract, while the third student observes and gives feedback afterward. Choose three common situations from your class and rotate roles so everyone has a chance to practice using the sentence stems with their group contract. Another variation is to have another teacher or two visit your class and have the adults role-play for students. This does not have to be focused on behavior. Some of our colleagues role-played how to have an academic discussion so that students could see how to build upon other people's comments and opinions.

Group Contract Scenarios

Reenact the following scenarios using a contract to help a
member of your group:

- Member is constantly on Snapchat, Instagram, Twitter, or other social media.
- Member is constantly playing games on their phone.
- Member is not completing their assigned tasks.
- Member is wandering/not staying with the group.
- Member is talking disrespectfully to other members.
- Member does not accept groups' request to change behavior.

Some sentence frames to use:

- I noticed that you are on _____, could you please close that tab and help us by _____?
- Our end product relies on each of us knowing the content, so could you stop _____and begin participating with the group by _____?
- We are feeling _____ (stressed, frustrated, angry) about this project. We really want to do well on this project, and we need your help. Could you _____?
- We are behind on our project, and I am feeling overwhelmed. Could you please help me by completing_____ (fill in a specific task)?

...continued

- According to our group contract, we are not supposed to be
  _____ (fill in off task choice). Can you please stop and
  help me with _____?
- You agreed on the scrum board to complete _____
  (list task) by _____ (list time frame) and you did not, so
  I am giving you a warning.
- Are you confused about our project? Can I help you get started on
  _____?
- We have asked you to stop _____ many times and you have
  not yet. Would it help if we give you a specific task? Great! Please
  note that this counts as one of your warnings.
- Your task today was _____; can you share with us
  what you have accomplished?
- According to our group contract you are not supposed to be
  _____. I am giving you a warning. Please get back on track.

Peer Feedback

It is insufficient to focus on students merely getting along.
Students should push and encourage each other to perform
their best work. Receiving feedback is one of the most powerful
tools to improve learning.[91] PBL provides the ideal opportunity
to teach the communication skill of peer feedback and refinement to elevate projects to their highest potential. The vast
majority of students have not learned how to give or receive
feedback in productive ways. Feedback protocols teach

students to both give and accept peer critiques on their products in a healthy way that leads to refinement. Once students experience the protocols and realize that the goal of the feedback is to help them unlock their full potential, not to cut them down, they will enthusiastically seek constructive feedback.

Before introducing a feedback protocol, you should establish some ground rules for healthy communication. This might be a review of classroom social agreements, or you might use a Talking Circle focused on how it feels to receive both positive and negative feedback. Here are some helpful prompts:

- Think about a time that you received constructive criticism that led to growth. It might be in your family, at a job, as part of a sports team, or in the arts.
- How did it feel initially?
- How did you feel after you had made refinements?
- Did the tone of the delivery affect your willingness to listen?

Students of all ages would benefit from Ron Berger's advice to make sure that feedback is "specific, helpful, and kind."[92] Researcher Brené Brown combines these into the mantra "Clear is kind. Unclear is unkind."[93] It is important for students to learn that by giving specific, clear feedback in a gentle manner, they are always helping others grow and improve. Generic feedback and flattery are totally useless. Teachers should model what explicit feedback looks like in whole class critiques of project examples. They should acknowledge and praise students who offer clear feedback to classmates.

Feedback should be integrated throughout the project cycle. Instead of waiting until the end of the project, feedback needs to happen early and often in the project trajectory. It should be expected that student work is a rough draft or in progress. The purpose of feedback protocols is to improve work in the middle of a project so there is no need for students to stress about how polished their work is at this stage. Let's explore six protocols that can be used at different stages of the project cycle for different purposes. Note that these are all available as slides on the book website (PulseofPBL.com).

1. **Speed Dating**: A favorite feedback strategy for early in the project process is a protocol called Speed Dating.[94] It is great for brainstorming or short feedback on a small part of the project.

Speed Dating

Share	• Students stand in two lines facing each other. • Left side shares their project idea for 1 minute while the right side listens. May choose to end with a specific question for feedback. • Right side gives feedback for 1 minute. • Consider giving students specific items to comment on based on your rubric.	2 minutes
Switch	• Right side shares their project idea for 1 minute while the left side listens. • Left side gives feedback for 1 minute.	2 minutes
Rotate	• One or more students from the right line move to the opposite end of the same line and everyone	1 minute

shifts down to new partners.
- Repeat both partners sharing as above.
- Complete 3-4 rotations as time allows.
- Adaptation: instead of two lines, form concentric circles with the inside circle facing out and have the outside circle rotate.

Total: 5 minutes/round

2. **Gallery Walk:** The Gallery Walk[95] is a helpful protocol once students have committed to a plan of attack in their project. To begin this activity, provide the students with sticky notes or a way for them to leave helpful comments on the work they are about to review. Some teachers share specific prompts or focal points they would like their students to consider. Students display some kind of artifact to demonstrate their thinking, such as a poster describing their project, a storyboard, a sketch, or a rough draft. A Gallery Walk is similar to a stroll through an art gallery so there is no talking. As they ponder each artifact, students can leave comments on sticky notes or write directly on the sketch.

Upon completion of a Gallery Walk, students quietly read each note and reflect on the feedback they have received. Remind students that no one understands their project as well as they do, so they have permission to throw away and ignore any feedback that is not helpful. Instruct them to pay special attention to any feedback that is similar. This is strong evidence that part of their project was explained poorly or needs development.

Gallery Walk

Set up	Options	5 minutes
	• Hang a poster defining your solution on the wall in a hallway • Set up 3D items such as artifact, storyboard, sketch, model, or prototype on tables around the room	
Student Directions	• Every student has sticky notes and rubric • Write on the **back** of the sticky notes so when placed on poster they are anonymous • Leave feedback that is helpful, specific, and kind based on the rubric Options: • "I like" for things done well • "I wonder" for things that are missing or need improvement • Silent activity like at an Art Gallery	5 minutes
Gallery Walk	• Students leave feedback on as many posters as possible • Play classical music quietly in the background	15 minutes
Follow Up	• Each group reads their feedback • Give permission to ignore feedback that is not helpful • Modify your project and Next Steps based on helpful feedback	10 minutes

Total: 25 minutes

3. <u>3A's:</u> This protocol is frequently used to have students analyze a text, but it is flexible and can be useful for peer feedback. Matinga uses it during the research phase of a project to have students analyze each other's sources. One student shares a summary of a source and their opinion based on newfound evidence. The audience then shares if they **Agree** or **Argue** with it. During the final, crucial step the audience tells the presenter what their next steps should be: what would you **Act upon**?[96] Furthermore, 3As can be used to give feedback on any artifact throughout the project process.

3 A's

Share	<ul><li>Place students in small groups (2-4) dividing up project teams</li><li>Presenter shares one of the following:<ul><li>Project summary</li><li>Presentation</li><li>Prototype</li><li>Written piece</li></ul></li><li>Audience silently takes notes for feedback</li></ul>	3 minutes
3A's	<ul><li>Audience responds to the 3 prompts in order for 1 minute each:<ul><li>What do you Agree with?</li><li>What would you Argue about?</li><li>What should we Act upon?</li></ul></li><li>Presenter silently takes notes on feedback</li></ul>	3 minutes
Discussion	<ul><li>Open discussion framed around the topic or question</li></ul>	2 minutes

Total: 8 minutes/round

4. <u>**ABCD:**</u> The next two protocols are best used in the middle of a project for feedback on the rough draft of a document or artifact. The first is ABCD Feedback, originating from Hugo Award–winning author Mary Robinette Kowal, who designed it for content editors of manuscripts.[97] This protocol can be used for rough drafts of presentations, written pieces, or prototypes. Its simplicity makes it easy to implement, but the questions are specific, leading to helpful observations to improve final products.

ABCD

Share	• Place students in small groups (2-4) dividing up project teams
	• Presenter shares one of the following:
	  ○ Project summary
	  ○ Presentation
	  ○ Prototype
	  ○ Written piece
	• Audience silently takes notes for feedback
		3 minutes

ABCD	• Audience responds to the 4 prompts in order for 1 minute each:
	  ○ What's Awesome?
	  ○ What's Boring?
	  ○ What's Confusing?
	  ○ What Didn't you believe? (Disbelief)
	• Presenter silently takes notes on feedback
		4 minutes

Reflect	• Presenter responds to any part of the feedback that they choose. • Open dialogue is permitted.	2 minutes

...continued

| | • Complete rotations with each group member sharing.
• Adaptation: For digitally written pieces, ABCD can be done individually with comments as a peer review. | |

Total: 9 minutes/round

5. <u>Charrette:</u> When students get stuck in the middle of a project the Charrette Protocol[98] can be helpful. The word *charrette* comes from the 1800s field of architecture meaning "cart" in French. Students at the Paris School of Arts would cram unfinished architectural models "in the cart" as they were loaded up at the turn-in deadline for review.[99] It has since been simplified in education as a small group protocol to promote innovative thinking and provide meaningful feedback.

Charrette

| Story | • Presenter shares the story of their current solution to the proposed problem.
• They explain how they have empathized with those affected by the problem.
• May include prototypes, storyboards, or rough drafts.
• Audience members may not speak.
• Presenter ends with a focus question asking for feedback. Sentence Stems:
   ○ How could I refine…?
   ○ What is my next step?
   ○ What am I missing or forgetting…? | 3 minutes |

…continued

Response	• Audience members respond to focus question with suggestions that are specific, helpful, and kind. 　○ Glows-positive feedback 　○ Grows-constructive criticism • The presenter may not speak, but takes notes.	2 minutes
Discus-sion	• Open discussion with presenter responding to feedback. • Everyone may speak.	2 minutes

Total: 7 minutes/round

6. **Ladder of Feedback:**   The Ladder of Feedback Protocol[100] is most useful a few days before a project is due to make final tweaks to the deliverable. It is an approach that sequences feedback in a specific order. The Ladder of Feedback can be done verbally or in writing. It has no time limits, so adjust as necessary for your students. Sentence stems and examples are helpful modeling for all students.

Ladder of Feedback Sentence Stems

Share	• Presenter gives a detailed explanation of their project.	Presenter
Clarify	• What do you mean by...? • Tell me more about... • How does ... work?	Audience
Value	• This part is effective because... • It is eye-catching because...	Audience

...continued

	• You had a great idea...	
Con-cerns	• I am wondering if... • Is it possible... • I don't understand how... • How might you...	Audience
Suggest	• Have you thought about... • What about adding... • Could you leave out the part where...	Audience
Thanks	• Your ideas made me think of... • I can see ... working in my design. • I learned about ... from your idea.	Presenter

Time: flexible based on student age and project complexity Adapted from Sonya Terborg[101]

A seventh protocol to consider as an alternative to the Lad-der of Feedback is the Tuning Protocol, which we will describe in Chapter 8. Note that it is not necessary to grade students in any of these feedback protocols. In fact, grading may actually be counterproductive.[102] All of these feedback protocols can be used from kindergarten through high school with slight modifications. In addition, feedback protocols are helpful scaffolding for students who are struggling or falling behind. In each protocol, these students get to see quality work from their classmates that can help clarify what they need to do or help redirect an unfocused group, putting them back on track.

Feedback and refinement protocols teach students how to communicate clearly in positive, helpful ways. Feedback builds relationships as students discover that the PBL classroom is a safe place to share their ideas and build trust as they experience the power of their classmates' coaching. Giving and receiving quality feedback is an SEL skill that students will benefit from in all their relationships both personal and professional for the rest of their lives.

Outside Collaboration

A common practice in PBL is to invite community guests as a showcase audience, as seen in the example of the Water Project in the chapter introduction, but why limit community participation to the end of the project? Experts can interact with students during at any stage of a project, giving students the opportunity to forge Relationship Skills with adults in professional ways. One of our favorite impressions from outside collaborations is opening students' perspectives to future roles or careers that they might not have known or understood before.

For instance, at Perry Innovation Center, Karen Cormony's middle school Graphic Design class began their first project with fieldwork at the College of Creative Studies (CCS) in Detroit, Michigan. CCS is a nationally ranked digital and fine arts school with impressive departments in not only graphic design but in animation and digital illustration, industrial and products design, and photography. Students were astonished to learn of the industrial and commercial uses of an art degree beyond painting on a canvas. They were excited to sit in on demonstrations of design machinery and see the student showcase that indicated which projects had earned internships or jobs in businesses like General Motors, Nike, and other large corporate partners.

Cormony's students returned to their classrooms inspired to embark in their project to create graphic design agencies to rebrand small local businesses. Cormony searched the community for potential clients by notifying parents and school colleagues who owned small businesses and asked the students to look for community businesses with outdated or missing websites. Some students volunteered their parents' small businesses as well. Cormony made sure that the list of local businesses owners was diverse and that they offered a wide variety of consumer goods and services. Her students then emailed each business with an offer of a free website and business rebranding.

The community response was overwhelming and enthusiastic. Each student-led graphic design agency was assigned a local business based on their interests. Each local business provided their team of young graphic designers with a company brief, which included the company background, objective, brand voice, requirements, and other specific insights. Students used the company briefs to create their Need to Know questions as well as a list of interview questions to guide their first client intake meetings. During the N2K exercise, students shared their planned client intake questions in a Charrette protocol focused on the purpose and effectiveness of each question. The class discussed the best ways to introduce themselves, how to lead a professional intake meeting, and how to maintain productive communication with the client through role-playing and simulations.

Each local business client met with their graphic design agency and maintained a focused conversation using the company brief and client intake questions. Students sketched logos, drafted websites, and created taglines. Clients gave feedback through email communication and video conferencing at later dates.

After the students completed their client intake call phase, they began to digest the interview information. To assist the process, Cormony invited a local graphic designer, who demonstrated each step of her design process: the client intake interview, the research phase and concept development, the revisions with clients, and the completion with product reveals. The graphic designer facilitated and supported the students via email and video conferencing at each team's request. With her guidance, students created mood boards from their client information and their research. Creating their first mood boards was a bit intimidating to a few of the design teams, so Cormony invited other high school art students to participate in a Gallery Walk to give her students input and feedback on color selection, logos, and presentations. The visit from the high school students assured some students and redirected others as the students prepared for the client revision phase.

Instead of simply bringing in one guest to speak to the entire class, you could encourage your students to reach out to your vetted list of experts and have each group schedule meetings with experts to support their specific questions or research. For example, if one of Cormony's design teams deals specifically with a local clothing store, the students may want to contact an expert in the fashion industry. Local universities, along with colleges and career technology education (CTE) programs, often have students or interns ready and willing to interact with your students.

Through purposeful community connections, students practice SEL competencies with adults on authentic problems. This small step into the "grown-up world" allows them to role-play interactions with adults from the safety and supervision of their school and teachers. Outside experts could teach students in a mini-workshop format on a specific content topic or skill needed. They could point students to resources to guide re-search. Students can collaborate with outside experts in developing experiments and design solutions. Sometimes students perform fieldwork to support ongoing research to broaden the scope of a scientific trial with action research. It doesn't get any more real than this!

In addition to using project management tools like scrum boards on Trello.com or with community partners, students should be taught how to use other business tools. Instruct students the proper etiquette for a cold call or a professional email. Use a template, or better yet, have students create one in their groups. Remember these are useful communication skills that must be taught. Students may understandably be nervous, but with practice their skill and confidence will soar.

How does a teacher find the right experts in the community? An important business skill is networking, but education has underemphasized it. Many teachers just "shut their door and teach." Networking can feel intimidating, making one feel uncomfortable and self-conscious. We have definitely felt this way. By pushing ourselves out of our comfort zones, we have improved our networking abilities, reaping the benefits of building a broader community of knowledge. The community partners you introduce to your students become vetted members of your students' first professional networks. The Community Connections ILeva outlines practical suggestions for a successful partnership.

Community Connections ILeva

Mastering the Real Application of their Work by Connecting Projects to the World

Steps	Rationale
1. Connect: Find community partners (CP) who are "experts" on or have interest in content relevant to your project. Ask colleagues, business organizations such as the Rotary Club or Chamber of Commerce, non-profits, relevant social media group members, and parents if they are willing to be a part of your project.	Establishes a new network of influence outside of students' school that can vet their skills and knowledge. Allows CP first-hand knowledge of what students are studying and the nature of learning in their community schools. Encourages students to upgrade the quality of their work.
2. Clear Expectations: Explain to CP the purpose and possible outcomes of the project, a brief synopsis of PBL, and their role in the process. Set clear expectation of their commitment: • How much time in hours? How frequently are they needed? • In what aspects of the project will their participation be needed? (Entry Event, feedback, mentoring, final audience, etc.) • Benefits to CP and to the student? Virtual or in-person attendance? • Types of resources, materials, and manipulatives they might bring? • Perimeters of their participation including a review of expected social behaviors, tone, and language.	Establishes what the CP role will be from the onset and set guidelines to avoid wasting time or unintended setbacks. Allows students to observe and practice adult professional behaviors. Promotes delivery of simultaneous small group CP presentations where everyone is on the same page with little teacher involvement. Ensures CP an engaging but professional/academic presentation.
3. Student Preparation: Research subject matter and brainstorm a list of questions so that students are prepared to interact with CP. Create a graphic organizer for all students to take field notes during the conversation. Discuss proper etiquette with a guest whether virtual or in-person.	Prepares all students to participate and engage with CP. Creates an expectation of learning through dialogue.
4. Debrief: Use a Talking Circle or Harkness Discussion to talk about both the learning and the communication skills practiced during the interactions with CP. Use the sentence frame: *I used to think… but now I know…*	Cements learning through reflection and metacognitive analysis of SEL skills used. Carries knowledge beyond one presentation and allows verbal group processing.
5. Alternatives: Provide sentence stems for elementary children or English Learners as needed. Have students practice asking questions in front of the room or with a microphone. Record questions on a tool such as Flipgrid and have CP answer asynchronously.	Provides extra support for younger learners or students with weaker speaking skills. Provides informal oracy practice. Allows for individual processing through writing.

SEL Outcomes:
- Students consider multiple viewpoints from experts, building empathy and developing problem-solving skills.
- Students test their knowledge of the real-world application of what they are learning.
- Students practice professional speaking (oracy) with adults gaining confidence and self-efficacy
- Students practice self-management to adjust their behavior and speaking codes to align with expected formal CP presentations.

Assessment Recommendations:
- Use student graphic organizers notes to understand how students apply feedback and recommendations.
- Provide opportunities for students to self-reflect on etiquette, professionalism, and quality of their questions.
- Observe students' disposition and contributions that create more dynamic and engaging conversations with the CP (asking questions, commenting on interesting points, challenging the groups' thinking, sharing lived experiences, etc)

To find collaborative partners, an easy way to start networking is by reaching out to your own network of colleagues, family, friends, and your students' parents. For example, every year, toward the end of the Monument Project, Mike sent home an email to parents asking for volunteers who were architects, engineers of any kind, interior designers, or any similar career to come in and give critical feedback. He always found four to five people, including his uncle, willing to participate. If your whole school is practicing PBL, consider creating a survey and spreadsheet of willing volunteers at the beginning of the year of experts willing to come in. Consider the following:

- What businesses or organizations are active in your community?
- What professionals do you know who are doing something unique in business, education, or community service?
- Who outside of your area might you connect with via videoconference?

When the distance is too great, guest schedules are too busy, or there is no budget for fieldwork, videoconferencing is an excellent alternative, especially in a post COVID-19 world. In many ways, it is easier than ever to get community members to join your class virtually for an hour or less. They no longer need to take off work, complete a background check, or arrange their entire day around a school visit. They only need to block off an hour of their busy schedule. With today's ubiquitous technology, students can connect with experts from anywhere in the world to learn with them and communicate their own discoveries. When conflicting time zones are an issue or when you do not want to overwhelm a guest by asking them to present in multiple classes, consider exchanging recorded messages with community partners. Students can send video questions and the partner can record responses at their conven-ience for students to watch later. This is another way to teach students relevant etiquette of modern business communication through the project.

As demonstrated in the Water Project, another powerful approach to networking is for your students to make the community connections. Not only will they be learning important communication and networking skills, but it is extremely effec-tive! Sometimes people and organizations will say "no" or ignore a request from an adult but will jump on board when it comes from students. This isn't a fake simulation of business communication; students are actively networking for a profes-sional purpose.

Student Leadership

As students build Relationship Skills with adults in the community, we want to develop leadership skills in our students. Our children don't need to wait for the future but can be leaders right now! Student leadership is a skill that is not talked about enough in education. In fact, it was only recently added to the CASEL framework. In schools, leadership is often praised in athletics and extracurricular activities, but rarely in the class-room setting. When it does come up, it is usually assumed that the honor roll students who excel on every content standard are leadership material. In reality, the high achievers are oftentimes the best followers. When put in leadership roles, they may try to take over their project team in pursuit of higher grades and often struggle to work with others.

Leadership is the ability of a person or group to influence and guide others in a common cause. The beauty of the concept of leadership is that it is a skill that all students can develop. In a traditional classroom, leadership is unnecessary because the emphasis is on compliance to the teacher and the standardized curriculum. But in PBL, the concept of student voice means students will engage with the world harnessing opportunities to lead the charge in meaningful, self-directing ways. Not every-one desires official leadership roles. In fact, a student may not actively seek to lead or influence others, but the quality and consistency of their work inspires others to follow them. Lead-ership is also the ability to recognize their influence, provide helpful feedback, and contribute to the growth of others.

Rebecca Lovelace teaches US History in Farmington, New Mexico, to predominantly Native American and Hispanic students who have struggled in the traditional high school. One day some of her students came to class distraught and incon-solable because close family members had been taken by US Immigration and Customs Enforcement (ICE) or forced into hiding. Lovelace understood that for her students to feel em-powered, they needed to know more about the immigration process in the US, especially regarding the immediate predica-ment of their family members. This situation demanded a project centered on immigration rights. Students brainstormed and decided that they should organize a panel with people rep-resenting both sides of the immigration issue to discuss the topic.

The first step was to get the city mayor on board. They wrote scripts to use for phone calls and emails. The students called and asked if he would participate in a panel to help local immigrants and to consider making Farmington a sanctuary city. Once the mayor agreed to visit, the students contacted and secured the commissioners of Farmington and Aztec (a connected city), Farmington's chief of police, and the San Juan County Sheriff-elect.

Excitedly students prepared questions for the panel. They decorated tables with painted flags from Mexico and South American countries to show solidarity with the immigrants in their community. Student greeters escorted all guests from the parking lot to check in at a depot station. One of Lovelace's students was an "Explorer," a student in a local cadet police-training program. The student organized the depot at the entrance with other Explorer volunteers to check ID's and made sure no one (including officers of ICE) came to the school except those on the invitation list. Students gave everyone a hand-colored picture of different races shaking hands to pin on their lapels, and all of the students wore one. Lovelace connected one of her students to a college radio host who coached her student on how to emcee the event.

The local government and law enforcement officials sat on one side of the panel. On the other side of the panel sat the head of ENLACE (ENgaging LAtino Communities for Education), a Hispanic student organization at the local community college, and the director of Somos un Pueblo Unido, an organization that supports immigrants, arranges legal representation for them, and lobbies to change New Mexico immigration laws.

Somos un Pueblo Unido brought two immigrant women who shared stories in Spanish of how they had been arrested and detained based on mistaken identity. The police chief explained that the ICE raids were focused on people with felonies, not on undocumented people in general. He admitted mistakes had been made, and he apologized. One of the things that was revealed during the panel was that the local police had been assisting ICE raids and even given them free office space without the knowledge of the mayor.

Afterwards, as a result of this panel, the Chief of Police arranged an open panel for the whole community. There was a recognition of the need for better communication and understanding between the immigrant community, the local government, and law enforcement. A student named Jose did not attend the panel even though he wanted to. He was one of several students afraid that ICE officers might show up. Lovelace saw him recently, and he said "Thank God for you. We need someone one to care about us."

Students forged Transformative Relationship Skills as they demanded ethical responsibility from their community, modeled empathy, and respectfully considered multiple perspectives.

The students were proud of their work. Undoubtedly the most important thing that Lovelace did was give her students permission to pursue this project and then get out of their way. She coached them behind the scenes, but students led the charge for an open discussion on immigration in their community. They exercised the Responsible Decision-Making skills of identifying, analyzing, evaluating, and working toward solutions on a community problem that affected them personally. During the project process, her students honed their Relationship Skills bringing together seemingly opposing viewpoints for a civil discussion.

A weak pulse of Relationship Skills leaves students feeling cold and disconnected from their peers.

A weak pulse in the body can lead to poor circulation causing cold hands and feet. Weak Relationship Skills evoke poor circulation of communication and collaboration between group members. There needs to be a clear current between each individual and their group members. Gaps between Self and Social Awareness may lead to narcissistic behavior as students only look inward leaving Collaborative and Transformative SEL out of reach. On the other hand, strong Relationship Skills connect students to their community and each other. They become passionate leaders who listen first and act for the greater good.

Reflection Questions

- How will you intentionally build strong relationships with every student in your class?
- How will you scaffold group contracts to teach teamwork?

- What protocols will students use to provide clear and kind feedback to each other?
- How will your students connect with the community to build social engagement and collaboratively solve problems?
- How does SEL and PBL develop leadership skills?

Chapter 8

Exercising Responsible Decision-Making

The messy middle of the project is where Responsible Decision-Making intersects with Self-Management.

- Student Generated DQ
- Structured Inquiry
- Feedback and Refinement
- Service Projects
- Reflection

Carmen and Teresa were surprised when they arrived at their classroom. There were green streamers and strips of green plastic all over the place. It covered the desks, chairs, bookshelves, and it was even on some trash items scattered on the floor. "What happened?" they wondered while excitedly discussing with their classmates.

Carmen and Teresa were fifth graders in Heather Creelman's class at Goshen Post Elementary, an elite comprehensive PBL school in Loudoun County Public Schools, Virginia. It was launch day for a new project focused on food webs, oceans, and photosynthesis. The "green" streamers represented algae that was out of control at Virginia Beach, located three hours away from their school. Students had many questions:

- Why was there so much algae?
- What caused it to spread?
- What are the uses of algae?
- What are the results of over production of algae?
- Does it matter if there is so much algae?

Students were already familiar with the PBL process and started generating Need to Know questions. The discussion on the causes and effects of massive algae growth led to how problems in the food chain resulted in an overpopulation of algae, due to a lack of oxygen produced by plankton. Students researched the food chain from plankton to sharks and realized that a shortage of sharks created a trickle-down effect. At this point, Creelman showed a video about how the overfishing of sharks was approaching endangerment of this creature. She then asked the Driving Question: "How can we, as stewards of the ocean, advocate for the protection of sharks?"

Creelman and her colleagues planned this project to focus on an authentic problem that matched fifth grade standards in science, technology, and English Language Arts. They knew that sharks would be the focus and that students would create a website of their learning along with an oral presentation as a final product. However, they didn't know what direction students would take the project or who their audience would be. They left that up to the students to decide.

Through research, students soon discovered that sharks are often hunted specifically for their dorsal fin. Fishermen harvest the fins to be sold to restaurants for shark fin soup and throw the rest of the shark back into the ocean. Students were not happy about this practice! Carmen looked into the law and discovered that the state of Virginia already had a law prohibiting shark fishing, but it had a loophole: restaurants could still buy shark fins harvested elsewhere. Teresa discovered that there was a restaurant an hour away from their school that actually served shark fin soup.

Students were outraged because they understood the domino effects of the declining shark population and decided to take action. They wanted to educate the public and eliminate the loophole in the law. Students discussed who the authentic audience should be, and they immediately decided that the President of the United States must act! The teachers redirected them to contact local officials. Students researched and found their State Representative Jennifer Wexton and sent an email inviting her to their classroom to hear about the sale of shark fins in their state. A few days later, Representative Wexton accepted their invitation, and a date was set for her visit.

Carmen and Teresa were so excited! They knew that their work on sharks would be shared with an actual government official. This wasn't a make-believe project. Carmen and Teresa worked hard on their website and elevator pitch. They gave and received feedback with their classmates through a Tuning Protocol. They refined their work so that they could present a factual and persuasive presentation on why shark products should not be sold in their state.

On the day of Representative Wexton's visit, Carmen and Teresa were nervous but confident—because they believed in the urgency of their pitch and were well prepared. When it was their turn, they shook Representative Wexton's hand and delivered their elevator pitch. It was a proud day for Goshen Post Elementary School!

Rep. Jennifer Wexton ✔ @RepWexton · Nov 20, 2019   •••
Hey @GoshenPostES—we just passed the **Shark** Fin Sales Elimination Act!

With this bill, we will ban the commercial sale of **shark fins** and products containing **shark fins**.

Thank you for bringing this important issue to my attention!

Fast forward a year, when out of nowhere, Creelman received a tweet with a video message from now US Congresswoman Wexton announcing that the house of representatives had passed the Shark Fin Sale Elimination Act, a bill banning the commercial sale of shark fins and products containing shark fins in the United States.[103] The students' project had contributed to a national bill! When Creelman shared the news with Carmen and Teresa and the rest of the now sixth grade students, they were overjoyed! They beamed with confidence from what they had achieved.

The Shark Fin Project is an exemplar of how PBL can develop the Transformative SEL Skills implicit in Responsible Decision-Making. Students identified a problem, analyzed the existing data, determined a solution, and evaluated the impact of the entire project. From the entry event onward, students were asking questions and actively investigating the root cause of the excessive amounts of algae near the beach. They were exploring an authentic problem near their community and seeking real-world solutions.

Inquiry milestones throughout the project had them discovering and analyzing the sale of shark fins in their state and concluding that the action needed was to raise awareness and help pass a new law. Through the Tuning Protocol, students evalu-ated each other's work and reflected on changes they needed to make to deliver cohesive and well-developed final presenta-tions. The ultimate result of this project was that students not only learned about ethical responsibility but exercised it in an informed way. They advocated for new legislation to outlaw the sales of shark products. During final reflections, Carmen said, "This made me see that people will actually listen to me even though I am only ten." Teresa agreed, adding, "I am going to vote someday because it does make a difference."

Creelman shared that in her ten years of teaching, students have never been more empowered because they knew they were making a real impact in their community.

Teachers are not only preparing students for the future; young people can make a difference RIGHT NOW if given the opportunity!

Responsible Decision-Making is the act of selecting positive choices based on ethical responsibilities, social norms, and safety. As mentioned in Chapter 2, much of the emphasis by SEL advocates about Responsible Decision Making is focused too narrowly on students' personal behavior. Similarly, to how teachers treat Self-Management, they concentrate primarily on self-discipline and consequences with Responsible Decision-Making for the benefit of teacher classroom management instead of developing the competency in the student. This narrow interpretation is selling the concept of Responsible Decision-Making way too short!

While much of the SEL community emphasizes managing individual student behavior in the classroom, PBL applies the SEL competencies more broadly to issues in the community. The skills are the same in each case, with PBL using Social Awareness to drive this decision-making. In the age of digital information, social and political current events feel precarious and urgent because of ubiquitous clickbait and access to endless news cycles. Our modern society needs students who can expertly detect and unpack complex issues to find viable and equitable solutions.

Climate change, social inequity, racism, poverty, clean water, terrorism, and ethnic wars are serious problems that our students are inheriting from today's adults. In Transformative SEL, Responsible Decision-Making gives kids the opportunity to address these issues right now. They may not be able to solve any of them at a global level, but much like the students in Creelman's class they can make an impact locally that empowers them to speak out for the rest of their lives. At the very least, they can understand and perform the intricate steps involved in practicing civic responsibilities in ways that lead to positive social change.

Student-Generated DQ

The Driving Question launches a project with a focus on an authentic problem, followed by students generating a list of Need to Knows (N2Ks) of information and skills necessary to propose a solution to address the DQ. The entry event provides initial activation of background knowledge, but sometimes students still do not know enough to ask deep questions. Teachers should remind students that the N2K list is a "living" document. Questions should be added to it throughout the inquiry stages of the project. The best N2K questions are often not asked on day one, but in the middle of the project as students increase their background knowledge on the project topic. From the N2Ks, the teacher and students collaboratively plan the next steps of how they will conduct research into the problem. This whole process requires identifying and analyzing the problem at a deep level.

In Chapter 6, on the topic of Social Awareness, we discussed how Driving Questions should elicit multiple viewpoints so that students find value in diversity. It is critical that DQ's focus on an authentic problem. Students have zero investment in the stereotypical math story problem of "Billy is three years older than half of the age of his great aunt's ex-husband's third cousin who is sixty-three. How old is Billy?" because this type of question is so obviously fake. No one uses algebra to figure out how old someone is. "Who cares?" is actually a valid answer to that question. In PBL, students engage by focusing on real situations in the community, not by preparing for a quiz show.

One way to build Responsible Decision-Making skills is for students to create the Driving Question for a project. We do not recommend requiring students to create the DQ for their first PBL experience, but once they are accustomed to the process, students as young as kindergartners can create or co-create the DQ with the teacher. As demonstrated in the shark fin project, teachers should guide students down a path of inquiry from the entry event to the DQ. The reality is that the teacher knows the general direction that the project is headed but permits students to discover and shape the path along the way, rather than just announcing, "We are going to study food chains and sharks."

Another approach is the open-ended project. This is not the popular Genius Hour concept of giving kids a set amount of time each week to pursue their passion (although it works for that situation too). Rather it is an open-ended PBL project that has a broad theme such as "How can we improve our neighborhood?" The teacher provides the overarching topic, and students identify the specific problems that they will explore inside of it. Each student team then generates their own DQ focused on their particular concentration. The theme can be narrowed down for younger students so the scope is not overwhelming: "How can we improve our neighborhood sidewalks?"

Structured Inquiry

According to a 2016 PayScale survey of over sixty thousand managers, critical thinking/problem-solving is the top soft skill missing from college graduates. Sixty percent of managers found it lacking in new hires.[104] The traditional practice of teacher lecture, student notetaking, and regurgitation of facts on a test are a key reason why so many students lack critical thinking and problem-solving skills. The most relevant problem-solving that many students practice is figuring out ways to hack high school! They spend more effort figuring out how to jump through hoops than actually learning. The lucky ones have strong family support systems, trusted mentors, or resources to help them through. To level the playing field for all students, we propose that critical thinking and problem-solving skills be taught in the classroom in tangible and constructive ways rather than expecting students to muddle through problems without support or guidance.

From the start, PBL launches with inquiry. The entry event engages students so that they are full of questions. The Need to Know (N2K) process helps students identify, sort, and prioritize their questions. Within the first few days of the project, students are using the Responsible Decision-Making skills of identifying problems and analyzing situations while planning how they will evaluate and solve them. Once the N2Ks and Next Steps have been determined, students jump into research. Since the process in PBL is driven by student interest, inquiry is embedded as students evaluate both resources and the DQ at every stage. The teacher's role shifts during inquiry. No longer are they viewed by students as the source of all knowledge. Instead of downloading content into students' minds through daily direct instruction, the teacher asks probing questions to encourage deeper thinking. This shift can be difficult for some students who are used to being spoon fed.

Therefore, teachers must use structures to train students how to research rather than expecting them to successfully research on their own. Structured Inquiry is when students engage in methodical rounds of questioning, exploration, data collection and analysis, protocols, and application of findings driven by a powerful Driving Question. There are many methods to choose from depending on the scope and goals of the project. It is critical that the teacher direct students back to the DQ and N2Ks daily as they work through their numerous rounds.

Methodical Rounds of Structured Inquiry

Methodical rounds of Structured Inquiry comprise a sequence of rounds utilizing a combination of the suggested methods below to structure and enhance inquiry based on the DQ and the N2K list.

1. Round 1 - Resource Exploration (Understanding):
fieldwork, observations, interviews, lectures, expert visits, lived experiences, testimonials, noticing and wondering, reading, writing surveys, videos, reflection protocols, pitches and ideation, executive summaries, planning, feedback, discussions protocols

2. Round 2 - Data Collection and Analysis (Defining):
survey results, observation and fieldwork notes, case notes, experiment data, categorizing and testing results, verifying with experts, concept mapping, templates, feedback and discussion protocols, ideation, prototyping, testing

3. Round 2 - Application of Findings (Addressing DQ):
feedback protocols, designing, refining, prototyping, testing to refine prototype, iterations, installations, presentations, demonstrations, teaching, tutorials, workshops, community improvement and engagement in positive social change

The structured inquiry focus in PBL pushes students to learn critical thinking while simultaneously learning essential content. To shift students' dependance away from you, the teacher, consider using Ron Ritchhart's favorite facilitation question "What makes you say that?"[105] to encourage students to reflect and think deeper about their ideas. Answering a student's question with questions challenges them to deepen their thinking. Your class will realize that students are trusted to seek out answers for themselves.

The messy middle of the project is where Responsible Decision-Making intersects with Self-Management.

Student teams use group contracts and scrum boards to manage the analysis, evaluation, and possible solutions of their project. As noted in Chapter 7, work time is not unstructured time. Instead, students follow protocols, use concept maps, and utilize templates to frame both their research and whole group discussions. In addition, many teachers combine PBL with design thinking. This is particularly common in science and STEM classes but is effective in any subject area. Our favorite design thinking framework is the Liberatory Design for Equity Process from the National Equity Project. The words *notice* and *reflect* are located in the center of the diagram, indicating that they are integrated into each step of the circular process. It is a human-centered process beginning with empathy of the end user while focused on analyzing the systems in place for equity or lack thereof.[106]

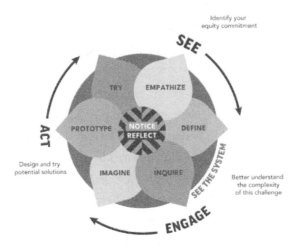

Liberatory Design for Equity Process

Matt McCullough, chief of innovation and PBL designer at Schoolcraft Elementary School in rural Michigan, launched his students into structured inquiry by connecting with local community partners. After watching an entry event video introducing their next project challenge, students were excited to help a local potato farmer decide the next variety of potato that he should plant. The entire student body had a role: Kindergarteners counted the months of storage duration for each potato variety, and first graders mapped the test fields. Second graders graphed the yield per acre, and third graders calculated the amount of fertilizer used. Fourth graders conducted a taste test with the entire school and collected the mathematical results from the other grade levels to make the final recommendation. Each grade had contributed to the inquiry process along the way.

The fourth graders prepared for the final proposal to the farmer. They compiled and computed the data, ranking the varieties of potatoes according to marketable yield, fertilizer efficiency, and taste profiles on a scale system that they had developed. Students created spreadsheets, charts, graphs, and a professional presentation to reveal why the Reveille Russet variety was their strong recommendation based on their evidence. They practiced pitching their findings multiple times, receiving feedback, and perfecting every detail. They were ready to convince the potato farmer that Reveille Russet potatoes should be the next variety to be planted.

The students boarded a bus and headed out to share the culmination of what they had learned, but they were not headed to a small farm. Although it is a family business, Walther Farms has over two hundred employees in farms ranging from the Carolinas to Texas. The students went to the corporate headquarters to present to over one hundred people at their annual shareholder meeting. They stated how their research and data demonstrated that the Reveille Russet variety was superior to the other choices. Mr. Walther then had the shareholders in the audience vote on which potato to grow next. Everyone raised their hands to vote for the student recommendation of Reveille Russet potatoes. The students cheered with joy! To this day, Mr. Walther says it was the best shareholder meeting that they have ever had.

Principal Matt Webster described the school's philosophy as "finding opportunities for learning to be more authentic, so that we no longer have to rely on page 57 followed by page 58 for students to practice and master their skills. But rather, take these real life, authentic problems that their community members are trying to solve, and let our kids master skills and standards as the basis of these projects and partnerships." When asked if the school continues to work with Walther Farms, Webster said that they were pursuing new projects with other local businesses and organizations noting that even though they are a small, rural community there are all kinds of authentic opportunities if one looks for them.

Schoolcraft fourth graders made a difference in their community through their potato research, but the project impacted them as well. Principal Webster noted that the students grew in confidence from the positive reception to their work. They had accurately calculated real story problems instead of the ones previously mentioned on page 58.

It is important to note that a structured inquiry approach does not mean that the teacher never delivers instruction. Direct instruction remains a part of the PBL pedagogical framework but is usually done through the workshop model. Whenever possible, small group instruction is preferable in order to customize content and deepen relationships by talking more directly to students.

Feedback and Refinement

Key aspects of exercising Responsible Decision-Making include analyzing data, applying critical thinking, and scrutinizing potential solutions. After students have completed a prototype in the design thinking process, they are ready to receive feedback in the "try" stage. Students can engage in one of the feedback and refinement protocols explained in the last chapter such as speed dating, gallery walks, the 3A's, ABCD, Charrettes, or the Ladder of Feedback. These are excellent opportunities for students to reflect on their work and evaluate each other's progress. But our favorite feedback protocol is the Tuning Protocol, which is designed to give targeted, detailed responses. It is most beneficial toward the end of a project once the majority of the work or draft of a prototype has been completed.

Introduce the Tuning Protocol three days before the scheduled showcase with your community audience. This gives students a few days to implement the feedback, refining their final products:

Tuning Protocol

Present	Project or product is shared in as much detail as possible. Audience is silent.	5 minutes
Clarifying Questions	Audience asks questions for clarity only; presenter responds. No feedback is given by the audience.	3 minutes
"I likes"	Presenter turns chair around, takes notes, and may not respond. Audience shares strengths.	3 minutes
"I wonders"	Presenter remains turned around and silent.	3 minutes

...continued

	Audience asks questions to provoke thought about improvements.	
Feedback	Presenter turns around, faces audience, and responds to anything of their choosing. Dialogue with all participants	3 minutes

Total: 17 minutes

When introducing the Tuning Protocol for the first time, pick one group of volunteer students who are confident speakers to practice their presentation. Then run the protocol as a fishbowl activity with the whole class as the audience giving feedback. An adaptation that you may consider is to shorten the times for younger students, but don't rush them either. Many times, the presenting student will stop talking before the five minutes is up. Instead of moving on to clarifying questions immediately, remind the students to sit in silence for the rest of the five minutes. This awkward wait time gives presenters more processing time to organize their thinking. Oftentimes the presenters will remember more details and continue sharing. After experiencing the protocol as a whole class through the fishbowl, divide the students into groups of three and have them run it themselves. The teacher should moderate the time limits by displaying an online timer projected on the board, directing students to follow each step.

Tuning Protocol lLeva

Providing Feedback Opportunities to Increase the Quality of Student Work

Steps	Rationale
1. **Setup**: Divide students into groups of 3, breaking up project teams. Teacher acts as strict timekeeper, displaying an online stopwatch. Instruct students to wait rather than moving to next step. Consider using a fishbowl with one group to demonstrate the first time that you implement.	Provides high volume feedback as each group member meets with multiple people. Structures the Tuning Protocol with student wait time for maximum feedback opportunities. Models the protocol for the class.
2. **Present**: Project or product is shared with as much detail as possible. Audience is silent	Grants no pressure chance to share without interruptions.
3. **Clarifying Questions**: Audience asks questions for clarity only and presenter responds. No feedback from audience yet.	Clarifies any confusing aspects before giving feedback.
4. **"I likes"**: Audience shares strengths of the project from the rubric using the sentence stem: I like.... Presenter turns chair around backwards, takes notes, and may not respond.	Allows audience to talk freely. Prevents the temptation to respond by not facing them. Documents feedback for future refinements.
5. **"I wonders"**: Audience asks questions to provoke thought about refinement using the sentence stem: I wonder.... Present remains backwards and silent.	Identifies gaps from the rubric or suggestions the audience has for fine tuning. Documents feedback for future iterations.
6. **Feedback**: Presenter turns chair back around and responds to any feedback in an open discussion with the audience. Thanks audience!	Responds and clarifies any feedback ideas.
7. **Debrief**: Students return to their project team, sharing and comparing feedback that they received from their audience and plot final refinements on scrum board.	Curates diverse feedback since all team members were split into different triads.

SEL Outcomes:
- Students will learn to give and receive constructive feedback.
- Students will practice collaborative problem-solving and empathy.
- Creates a climate where sharing unfinished work is expected because students know that they will continue to improve it.
- Students use the positive feedback language of "likes and wonders" throughout the day, not just during the protocol.

Assessment Recommendations:
- Graphic organizers for "I likes" and "I wonders" both as a presenter and as an audience member.
- Ensure that audience feedback is based on the project rubric.
- Provide a debrief at the end of the project describing adjustments made as a result of this protocol.
- Listen while students reflect on the quality of feedback that they gave.

At the end of any feedback protocol, remind students that they should consider all feedback and divide it into two piles: helpful and unhelpful. Tell them, "You have the right to throw away and ignore any feedback that isn't helpful." Some students, especially perfectionists, need this "permission" to let go. At Mike's school, they run the Tuning Protocol toward the end of every project. He can remember only once that they skipped it due to a time crunch, and the quality of the final products definitely suffered on that singular occasion. Students take the protocol seriously because they quickly realize it greatly improves their work, which in turn makes them look better on presentation day.

An SEL benefit of the Tuning Protocol is a shift in language of how students talk to each other.

"That was so boring" becomes "I wonder if you could add some energy to your voice during the presentation?"

"That sucked" turns into "I wonder if you could add colorful visuals to your slide deck to make it more interesting?"

In actuality, the message is the same, but the courtesy, politeness, and specificity embedded into an "I wonder" question makes it nonconfrontational and pleasant. Students start to talk to each other using "I wonder" language throughout the project, not just during the Tuning Protocol, building their Relationship Skills. It shifts the culture in your class!

The Tuning Protocol works great for teachers to give each other feedback prior to launching a new project. It is never a waste of time; as project ideas are always improved by the advice of colleagues. We highly recommend using a timer and not running the protocol informally. Although teachers might harvest great feedback from their colleagues in a laid-back conversation, using a timer maximizes valuable time and forces both the presenter and audience to be succinct and purposeful. The truth is that after the time is up, if a colleague still has important feedback, they will tell you later, even if it ends up being the next day. Consider setting aside consistent time in staff meetings or during professional development to run the Tuning Protocol with colleagues. It will improve the student experience and build a PBL culture at your school.

Ultimately, feedback and refinement lead to high quality work in students' final solutions to the Driving Question, and that work can be life changing. We have seen countless students find self-confidence as they exercise the power of their voice in Transformative SEL projects that they are passionate about. Once students make this shift, they are no longer bystanders, but instead they embark on a lifetime of advocating for justice and equity. Students strive for excellence in all that they do. Throughout the book, we have argued that the process is more important than the product. However, when feedback and refinement protocols elevate the final product, students grow in confidence, leading to sustained success.

Note: Sometimes the final product is not always shiny and amazing. Often the student solutions are not really feasible, or their performance needs further development. We urge teachers to focus on the students' understanding of the process through their use of Responsible Decision-Making skills. Students may not have the life experience to navigate big world issues, and even their herculean efforts may fall short of good solutions. When teachers focus and show value for the development of SEL skills, it helps onboard students into their role as agents of change.

Service Projects

The most rewarding projects for students and teachers alike are ones focused on community service. The Civil Rights podcasts (Chapter 3), immigration panel (Chapter 7), and the shark fin project in this chapter are examples of service projects. Students were not just learning about local issues for themselves but acting to inform and influence the public. Service projects are not only some of the most authentic projects, but they are also profoundly engaging. Ron Berger argues that they are the most motivating type of project for students. Service projects create a strong connection for students as they connect their personal ethics to practicing civic responsibility in their neighborhoods and beyond.[107]

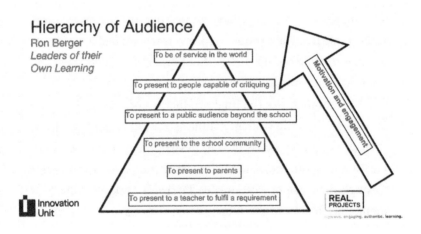

The Poverty Project integrated social studies, ELA, and science curriculum as students investigated the lack of housing in Grand Rapids, Michigan. The project involved the entire freshman class at the Museum School, a diverse, urban, place-based high school located inside the public museum archives. In social studies, students researched the 1920s and '30s, looking at the United States government's role in affecting poverty and homelessness during the Great Depression. For the humanities part of the project, students read *Of Mice and Men* by John Steinbeck and then visited some humanitarian organizations in town and interviewed their patrons. Students considered the Driving Questions, "When does helping help?" and "When does helping hurt?" The final product for the humanities portion was a blog based on their interviews.

In science, students created a variety of products in response to the DQ "How can we use material science to develop food, care, and art products to share with our Heartside neighbors?" Students were challenged to create something in the science lab that demonstrated the polar and nonpolar properties of molecules that they could donate to their community partner, Heartside Ministries, a local homeless organization. Heartside describes itself as a "living room" for underhoused people. They don't offer regular meals or overnight lodging, but a warm, safe space in the daytime to rest and get a cup of coffee. They have a spacious art studio where its patrons produce beautiful pieces, expressing their creativity.

Darius was a struggling student at the Museum School. In fact, he had not completed a project all year. When he learned that the entire freshman class would embark on the Poverty

Project by walking a few blocks to Heartside, Darius was not thrilled. As an introvert, he was nervous about meeting new people and having to talk to strangers. However, after the initial visit to Heartside, Darius admitted that he enjoyed the experience and wanted to make something to help the patrons.

Darius and his group decided to create "Greaterade," a new sports drink. They squeezed out juice from real lemons and oranges. They had researched that a little heat would help an upset stomach, so they put some red pepper flakes in it. They added different electrolytes, vital minerals such as calcium and magnesium, to help with recovery from exercise. Their first batch of Greaterade was a total disaster. It had pulp and seeds in it and tasted horrible from the pepper flakes and too much of the electrolytes. They couldn't even get their peers to participate in their first taste test.

For their second attempt, Darius's group used store-bought lemon and lime juice, decreased the number of electrolytes, and skipped the pepper flakes. The second batch was still too potent because of excessive calcium and magnesium salts. On the third try, they decreased the electrolytes further, and their drink tasted delicious. Now everyone wanted to try it. Darius was proud to bring his new drink to share with Heartside visitors and to explain the health benefits of every ingredient of Greaterade.

Luciana was stressed. She was struggling to create bath bombs for the Poverty Project. In her latest trial, she had forgotten to add cornstarch to her recipe and instead of hardening, the mixture stayed slimy again. She knew better. From previous trials, she understood that cornstarch thickened the compound, but it looked so much like baking soda that she accidently neglected it. Now she had wasted a complete trial and ran out of citric acid, one of the active ingredients that creates the fizz in bathwater. She thought maybe she should give up and just buy some bath bombs at the store. But Luciana persevered, bought more citric acid, and successfully made her bath bombs. They were diamond-shaped from molds that she had designed and 3D printed in the STEM lab.

Luciana had a second problem to solve. Houseless people did not have access to bathtubs, so although her creation of bath bombs met science standards concerning polar and nonpolar molecules, it was not practical to give them to Heartside patrons. She decided to wrap the bath bombs in decorative bags and sell them instead. When her supply exceeded the demand from friends and family, she sold them at her public library. Luciana used the money to purchase art from Heartside patrons, supporting the underhoused people in a dignified way.

Darius and Luciana were not alone in struggling with their experiments. Every student that Mike talked to at the Museum School had generated multiple attempts in the Poverty Project. Sam and Marlene ran fourteen trials attempting to make a healthier toothpaste without the many chemicals in commercial brands. Their sticking point was the nasty flavor of their main active ingredient, baking soda. In the end, they were unsuccessful, but appreciated the freedom to try and fail.

The Poverty Project had an authentic audience of underhoused people and the Heartside staff. It culminated with a return visit by the students to demonstrate their products and explain the science behind them. Students were surprised when the patrons asked many science questions. One patron, who called herself Precise, asked very specific questions and shared life lessons with them. It was eye opening for the students to meet James, who, although houseless himself, was trying to help other houseless people. Students became passionate about finding a solution to the lack of affordable housing in their city.

Science teacher Nate Langel, who designed the Poverty Project shared the following Transformative SEL goals for the Poverty Project: empathy, gratefulness, service, compassion, and social justice. During reflection at the end of the project, a student articulated the analogy of the science concepts of polar and nonpolar properties to our society:

"People are sometimes like oil and water, but they don't have to be. People that have homes are the oil and people who don't are like water. Our school is the soap, an emulsifier that breaks down the separation between them."

Reflection

One of the most important ways to exercise Responsible Decision-Making is to have students reflect on how their work group is functioning. By reflecting throughout the project on their group dynamics, students can identify and solve relationship challenges. Students are going to disagree and have different opinions on how to approach their project difficulties. The teacher is the coach helping students to civilly navigate their conflicts in healthy ways. Reflection helps both successful and struggling groups realize what is happening and how they might adjust if necessary. Group contracts and scrum boards are important, but the truth is that they are ineffective tools unless students actually use them as daily guides.

Reflection rounds need to be embedded throughout the project and not just at the end. It does not have to be time consuming. At the beginning of class, assign a specific SEL learning targets (See Planning in chapter 9) to focus on such as "Listening with my full attention, before responding." When class ends, have students individually reflect on the behavior with a Fist to Five, exit ticket, or have students reflect with their group with a turn and talk.

When groups are not clicking, refrain from rescuing your students. Instead teach them how to get unstuck by working through their difficulties. If students struggled the day before in a specific area, start today's class by reviewing yesterday's issues and having students reflect on what they need to change to be more successful today. When students are languishing in real time, it a great time to pull out the KARE Gap ILeva and have work groups or individuals workshop the gaps in their skill set. The KARE Gap ILeva offers probing questions and strategy recommendations to help your students reflect and self-correct.

Reflection is one of the most effective ways to teach SEL competencies!

Mike's Water Project at the beginning of this chapter was an incredible moment of student leadership and collaboration. Students embraced both the process and their project responsibilities taking the final product to levels that the teachers never thought possible. It was a PBL teacher's dream come true! But it didn't just happen. To fully understand the Water Project, we need to tell you about the Pick Your Path (PYP) Project.

Earlier that year, Mike and his coteacher launched a PYP video project on World War I and World War II in their integrated American history and English Language Arts class. The project married the concept of *Choose Your Own Adventure* books with YouTube videos, where viewers choose what to do next by clicking on one of two links. Rather than have small groups each make their own string of videos, Mike and his coteacher decided to have whole classes of fifty students divide the tasks to create one giant adventure. Students were placed in different teams based on self-identified skills. The roles included writers, actors, directors, prop designers, lighting and camera operators, and video editors.

Each class created a flowchart on a whiteboard wall, plotting all of the paths and choices like the branches of a tree. Groups of students began writing scripts for each scene, including details of the setting and props. When it came time to film, students shot scenes all over campus, both indoors and outside. The students did an excellent job of distributing roles and diagramming the big-picture storyboard, but they struggled with the rest of the project.

The organization and management of a project of this complexity and scale was new to Mike. He underestimated the technology needs of the project and did not devise a clear process for getting footage from the camera's SD cards to the video editors. Footage was lost and had to be reshot. Main actors were absent. Costumes and props were forgotten at home. He had not provided students with tools like scrum boards to organize themselves. After several weeks, students still did not have a final product, and Mike and his coteacher realized that it would still take weeks to complete the videos. (An important side note is that the students had learned the required content standards. They just didn't have the "shiny" product finished). He made the hard choice to kill the project.

Although Mike was disappointed that students never completed their PYP videos, there was a silver lining. At the end of the year, during the final reflection of the Water Project, one of the student leaders told Mike, "Because we failed on the PYP video earlier this year, we learned how to work together and succeed on the Water Project." Using setbacks in projects as learning tools demonstrates for students how challenges can be turned into opportunities. It was a good reminder that students develop SEL skills gradually over the course of a class. Given time, opportunity, and the tools to manage themselves, students will exercise Responsible Decision-Making and become leaders who can work together to make meaningful changes in the classroom and beyond.

A strong pulse of Responsible Decision-Making skills builds endurance to persist to the end of the project.

Congestive heart failure means that your heart cannot pump blood as efficiently as it should, which leads to fatigue and a lack of endurance. Patients may have trouble breathing and need frequent breaks from activities. Similarly, sometimes projects start off with a great entry event, but then fizzle to boring, typical schoolwork. Students become easily tired and off task without structured inquiry to focus them. Exercising Responsible Decision-Making requires students to persevere through the entire project cycle. Feedback and refinement protocols lead to higher-quality final products. Students develop the tenacity to push through challenges when they are reflecting and serving to transform the community.

Reflection Questions

- How can PBL shift Responsible Decision Making beyond personal behavior choices to meaningful problem solving?
- How can students develop or co-develop an authentic Driving Question for projects?
- How will you shift your teacher role to supporting student inquiry?
- What protocols and scaffolding will you use to structure student inquiry?
- How will you consistently use feedback, reflection, and refinement to promote the highest quality of student work?
- What local issues could your students address in service of the community?
- How will you make reflection a consistent ingredient in your classroom culture?

PULSE OF PBL

Chapter 9

Assessing SEL Competencies

Grade less. Assess more. Plan cool stuff for kids.

- Grading vs. Assessment
- Team Building
- Rubrics
- Protocols
- Peers as Experts
- Conferencing and Coaching
- Assessing the Teacher
- Planning

Every teacher knows that Sunday night is not really part of the weekend. There are lesson plans to be completed, learning materials to organize, online links to post, and the class website to update. A ginormous stack of ungraded papers adds to your anxiety. It can feel overwhelming, and you start to question why you gave the assignment in the first place. Maybe you should just quickly give every student credit for completion of that worksheet? Yet you feel guilty because you know the importance of timely feedback.

If one believes that SEL is important in the classroom, then it needs to be assessed. But how can teachers, who are already overwhelmed by too many responsibilities, add assessing SEL competencies to their busy plates? What does assessment of SEL competencies even look like? Should teachers give a letter or percentage grade to them? How do you communicate SEL competency levels with students and their parents?

Grading vs. Assessment

The word assessment has been co-opted to conjure up notions of standardized tests, grading, and report cards. But grading is such a small segment of the practice of assessment. Grading in K–12 spaces is about categorizing students to harvest numerical data and contemplate cut scores. Although we use grades to evaluate students' academic performance, the practice of grading is not always reliable since they often include criteria that do not directly measure learning. Moreover, we have an unequal and unjust system where a letter in the alphabet defines a child's value, character, and future.

A–F grading is ultimately about competitive ranking. The high achievers battle for awards and recognition, falsely assuming that they are smarter than everyone else. At the other end of the grading spectrum, students who consistently see lower marks become disillusioned with school and falsely believe that they are dumber than everyone else. There is no evidence that grades motivate or encourage learning, but there is evidence that they are demotivators.[108] On the contrary, our grading system communicates to many students that they are not and will never be successful in school.

Grading is a practice that should be eliminated from modern pedagogy.

Grades discourage further effort and collaboration. When a teacher passes back graded assignments, the inevitable comparisons begin. "What did you get?" students ask each other. But have you ever heard students voluntarily discuss what they learned on a graded assignment? Nope! Once students see a grade on a paper, they consider it "done" and are happy or defeated, depending on the mark. With a glance at the letters on their peers' papers, a student can learn to misinterpret their own value. The paper goes in the recycling bin or gets dropped on the floor in the hallway, and it's on to the next thing. A grade is final with an outward purpose: ranking for parents or GPA for college admissions. Therefore, we highly advise that you never assign grades to the SEL competencies.

It is counterproductive to use SEL assessment as part of an evaluation system for teachers and schools.

Instead of assigning grades, use formative assessments. Authentic assessments are formative, like a thermostat taking the temperature of the room and regulating the environment as needed. Who is asking a great question? Who has something worth sharing with the entire class? Who is collaborating well? Teachers should be constantly evaluating the climate of the room and adjusting the learning activities to their students.

Formative assessments have meaning. They measure learning in the moment, so teachers can adjust instruction accordingly. "Formative assessment is not a task; it is a practice. The goal is always to advance learning rather than merely check to see if students *got* what we taught them."[109] Teachers do not need to score something for it to be an important assessment. Quality feedback is the fuel of refinement.

Everything that happens in the room is a formative assessment opportunity. When you greet students at the door, you are assessing their emotional state, mood, and readiness to learn. Are they hungry or full? Are they tired or energetic? Are they calm or angry? During work time, are students engaged or distracted? Collaborative or isolated? Cooperative or argumentative? Some of the most powerful assessment tools that teachers have at their disposal are observation and listening. Conversations with students can lead to crucial discoveries about their social and emotional state, content knowledge, and SEL skills.

So, if grading does not increase learning, why do some educators spend so much time doing it? Most teachers are required to submit grades but voluntarily choose to give tedious scoring an exorbitant amount of their limited time. On the other hand, constant, formative assessment can be interspersed into the school day, yielding serious dividends for the time in-vested. The tradeoff is less time grading and more time designing quality learning opportunities. If we could summa-rize our view of assessment in a mantra, it would be as follows:

Grade less. Assess more. Plan cool stuff for kids.

Teacher and Student Tools

In Chapter 2, misconception 4 explained how research shows that Social and Emotional Learning needs to be inte-grated into the daily routines of students to be effective. SEL competencies should be taught, practiced, and assessed. Throughout this book, we have demonstrated the opportuni-ties to practice SEL competencies inside of the PBL framework. Students do not show up to class as experts in all of the SEL competencies, so how does one intentionally teach SEL to them? What does SEL teaching look like in the normal day of a PBL classroom?

Let's start with the beginning of the year. During that first week, you should design activities around the goal of empha-sizing SEL and culture building. Here are many different approaches. Pick a few to focus on and teach them immediately to establish the importance of SEL from the onset.

Team Building Activities

Most teachers use some kind of team building activities at the beginning of the year, whether it is building a spaghetti tower or escaping from the "human knot" challenge. These can be fun times for students to get to know each other and let their personalities start to shine. But sometimes teachers miss the most important opportunity of team builders: whole class debriefing. Use these activities to directly teach SEL competencies to students and have them reflect on how they applied them in the given challenge.

For example, use the popular marshmallow challenge, where students get one yard of tape, one yard of string, twenty pieces of spaghetti, and one marshmallow. The goal is to build the tallest self-supporting structure topped by the marshmallow in twenty minutes.[110] Afterward watch the short TED talk that explains how kindergarteners are more successful at the marshmallow challenge than architects and engineers because they experiment more.[111] In other words, they fail fast and often.

Next, display the CASEL chart of SEL competencies[112] with a projector and ask students to write a short reflection on what specific skills they used to complete the marshmallow challenge. Then direct a Talking Circle about the SEL skills that they used. Conclude by explaining to students that the marshmallow symbolizes the project problem that they are stuck on. Explain that, in PBL, they will get stuck frequently and will need to use these SEL skills to work through their challenges. Remind them that trial and error are a normal part of learning.

The power of teambuilding activities is that they act as shared anchor experiences that you can quickly remind students of throughout the year. Redirect struggling groups by asking what SEL skills they need to use to attack whatever challenge they are facing. Later, as students work on their projects and are struggling because they aren't communicating or collaborating, or they are wasting time, remind them of the SEL skills that they practiced in the marshmallow challenge or similar team building experience.

PULSE OF PBL

Team Building Debrief ILeva

Expanding Understanding and Application of SEL Competencies in Group Work

Steps	Rationale
1. **Activity**: Students complete one of myriad team building activities involving SEL skills such as collaboration, communication, and problem-solving.	Provides a safe, non-threatening way for students to learn and practice all of the SEL competencies.
2. **Quick write**: Display the CASEL competencies graphic and have students reflect on which skills needed to complete the task. Focus on the sub-competencies, not just the 5 main categories.	Introduces and familiarizes all of the SEL skills. At first, students may not realize the skills that they are using in the exercise.
3. **Sharing**: Use a protocol such as Turn and Talk or small group wrap around to share their thoughts.	Builds off from their personal list, showing their classmates' ideas in a safe conversation before the whole class debrief.
4. **Talking Circle**: In the first round, every student shares out how they used an SEL skill in the activity. One student writes the class list on butcher paper or a whiteboard. In the second round, students share how they might need to use this SEL skill during their project.	Creates a consistent language around what the SEL skills are and how students can use them to successfully complete their project.
5. **Anchor Activity**: Refer back to the team building activity whenever groups are struggling. *"Remember how we said during [activity], that we need to listen to everyone's opinion? I think you need to practice that right now. Why don't you stop and do a wraparound, listening to everyone's perspective before moving on?"*	Establishes the common experience as an anchor to refer back to the need to practice SEL skills in their teams. Reminds students of what successful SEL looks like.
6. **Journal**: Each student journals one SEL goal to work on based on the debrief of the activity. Check back on this goal weekly during the project.	Makes goal setting the purpose of the team building exercise and gives students a concrete experience to reflect back on.
7. **Alternative**: This same debriefing process can be used after watching a video clip of an activity or TV show that requires SEL skills. For example, Rube Goldberg machines, *Penguins of Madagascar*, or TikTok dances.	Uses an SEL rubric to evaluate characters in a show is a non-threatening way for students to see what proficiency or lacking the skills looks like.

SEL Outcomes:
- Students will learn what SEL skills look like through experience or observation of them in action.
- Students will understand SEL vocabulary and rubrics.
- Students will set and achieve SEL goals in core competencies.

Assessment Recommendations:
- During the team building activity, look for specific examples of students practicing SEL skills. Share them with students during debriefing if they don't bring them up.
- During the Talking Circle, listen for misconceptions of SEL competencies that students do not understand.
- Follow up on journals with weekly exit tickets asking students to reflect on their progress toward their SEL goal.

Another way to teach the SEL competencies of Relationship Skills is to show a fun video on YouTube demonstrating creativity and teamwork. One of our favorites is the Bottle Boys, who play music by blowing and tapping on bottles.[113] It is an entertaining way to begin or end class, but again, the magic is in the debriefing. Follow the same discussion procedure with team building activities, asking students to reflect on what SEL skills were needed to make the video and emphasizing that they need to use them too. Other videos examples are Rube Goldberg machines and flash mobs. Students of all ages love videos, and again it is an anchor experience that you can refer back to when groups are struggling.

Finally, don't just engage in team builders at the beginning of the year, consistently sprinkle them in throughout the year to remind and reinforce the need for students to practice SEL competencies.

Rubrics

Just because you may not be grading SEL skills does not mean that you shouldn't use rubrics. On the contrary, rubrics were originally intended for feedback, not grades. A common practice to teach the use of a rubric is to have students evaluate anonymous writing samples of a variety of levels: poor, average, and exemplary. This is especially powerful when students huddle around one piece of work and evaluate it as a group. For SEL skills, rubrics can be used in similar fashion. Give students a written scenario of PBL classroom interactions. Have students use a rubric to evaluate the SEL competencies used or missing from the interactions. For poor examples, students could brainstorm better approaches. For exemplars, students could explain how SEL competencies were successfully used to resolve the situation. For a fun adaptation, have students act out the scenarios while the rest of the class evaluates the skit according to a rubric of a specific SEL competency.

Rubrics can be boring to students. They tend to include a large amount of text in a small font crammed onto a single page. An enjoyable way to introduce rubrics is to watch a video clip of *The Penguins of Madagascar* (any age) or *The Big Bang Theory* (high school). Students can evaluate different characters for their collaboration skills on the rubric. Show a clip from one of the myriad reality competition shows, such as *Chopped, The Great British Baking Show, Project Runway, Sell This House, or American Idol.* Ask students whether the feedback from the judges was specific, helpful, and kind. Give students a presentation rubric and have them evaluate presenters pitching products on *Shark Tank.* Using clips of TV shows[114] is not only entertaining for students but is safe. They can give honest but appropriate criticisms, without worrying about shaming anyone in the classroom.

Rubrics aren't just for teachers! Teach students to use rubrics to assess themselves and their classmates. The most effective assessment for growing and changing behavior is self-assessment. Many people can tell a person to eat healthy and exercise regularly, but they are unlikely to do so until they analyze themself and make a personal decision to change their lifestyle.

When focusing on formative assessments instead of high-stakes summative ones, teachers should view reflection time on rubrics as academic time.[115] As previously mentioned, reflection is the Velcro moment where learning sticks. Self and peer assessments with rubrics help students get "meta" with where they are on a given SEL competency. These reflections can be written in a journal or recorded and shared with digital tools such as SeeSaw or Flipgrid. Student reflections on their SEL growth throughout a project are strong evidence that can be shared with parents.

Protocols

The primary goal of assessing SEL is to measure students as they gradually display more mature dispositions throughout the year. Some of the best tools for assessing students' SEL competencies are the many protocols that exist. Here are our favorite protocols for quick feedback or self-assessment from students:

QUICK SELF-ASSESSMENT PROTOCOLS

Fist to Five	Hold up a fist for zero or fingers from one to five to indicate their level of understanding or agreement on a question.
Thumbs Up/Down	Give a thumbs up, down, or sideways to indicate their opinion with a teacher statement or question.
Exit Tickets	Answer a short reflection question on scrap paper that is submitted as they leave the classroom.
Turn and Talks	Pair up with an elbow partner to discuss a topic or reflect.
3-2-1	Form of an exit ticket where students share 3 things learned, 2 connections to what they know, and 1 question that they still have.

For example, at the start of class, ask students to look at an SEL competency description or rubric. Explain what aspect of the competency you want them to focus on practicing today. Or you may review an SEL skill from the previous day's class that was successful or lacking as motivation to improve it today. Remind them of a movie clip or team building anchor activity where they learned about the importance of the competency. At the end of the class, give students a minute to reflect on how they individually or collaboratively performed the competency. Then ask them to silently "score" themselves with a "fist to five" or a thumbs up or down. After a quick scan of the room, ask for a few students to share some evidence for their rating. Build a climate of safety where there is no judgement of these scores, but a chance to celebrate success and problem solve how to improve in areas of struggle.

Be sure to check in with any students whose self-assessment does not match your observations. If a student surprisingly rates themself lower, make sure that they are okay. If a student rates themself higher than your observation, check in privately later or the following day. "I noticed that you gave yourself a five yesterday on teamwork, can you tell me about that?" Use a warm but direct approach to coach them. "I noticed arguing within your group and that you were not doing your fair share. Can you tell me about that?" Wrap up the conversation by having the student come up with a plan for the next group work time and follow up with them afterward to acknowledge growth or talk about further steps.

Virtually any protocol provides formative assessment data related to one of the core SEL competencies. In Chapter 6, we explained how discussion protocols are the perfect occasion to assess the Relationship Skill of communication; the Social Awareness competencies of perspective taking, empathy, and respect for others; and the Responsible Decision-Making skills of identifying, analyzing, and solving problems along with ethical responsibility. Use visible thinking routines from Harvard's Project Zero such as Leaderless Discussion, Making Meaning, the Story Routine, or Beauty and Truth to analyze content and practice Social Awareness, Relationship Skills, and Responsible Decision Making.[116] We further recommend protocols from the National School Reform Faculty and School Reform Initiative.

Choose a few protocols to repeat until students master them. Be sure to clarify for students both the content knowledge or skill and the SEL competency that they are addressing during whatever protocol you choose. Remember to do a "fun" trial run the first time before introducing content so that students figure out how it works. Don't expect everything to run smoothly the first time you employ a protocol—students are learning! You can use a printout of your class roster to document with checks or other symbols when you see SEL skills practiced. At the end of any protocol, have students reflect on both the content topic and the SEL skill exercised.

Of course, PBL has its own specific protocols that can be used to assess SEL competencies. N2K questions give a clear indication of students' background knowledge on the topic while at the same time demonstrating analytical and problem-solving skills. Feedback protocols such as the charrette, gallery walk, the Ladder of Feedback, and the Tuning Protocol are excellent opportunities to assess the Relationship Skill of communication and Responsible Decision-Making Skills. Group contracts, SEL group roles, and scrum boards help students develop Self-Management competencies and can be used as assessment data.

Peers as Experts

One of the greatest tools in your class are the students themselves. Team building encompasses the concept of learning to depend on peers for feedback, guidance, and knowledge. Students have a wealth of diverse background knowledge and untapped skills that can be harvested to lead productive student collaboration strategies such as student-led workshops. The workshops solidify content knowledge for both the student workshop facilitator and the participants.

Matinga uses a Huddle In / Huddle Out protocol with her students. Huddle In is a general call for students to gather at the front of the room and stand in a huddled semicircle around the teacher by the whiteboard or projector, much like how athletes huddle around a coach during a timeout. The purpose of Huddle In is for the students to relocate from their workspaces and mentally switch to listening and questioning mode. The teacher provides brief explicit instruction or project directives on their deliverables. Huddle In time is short. Matinga recommends a time lapse that equals the students' age (i.e., twelve-year-olds get a maximum time of twelve minutes). When the teacher calls Huddle Out, students are dismissed from the Huddle In and return to personal or group work time.

During Huddle Out Matinga has a specific spot in the room set up for student-led workshops. Student-led workshops are an optional scaffold for students who may be struggling in a specific area. There is a table with mini-whiteboards, erasable markers, and wipes. Self-selected students organically lead workshops that other students voluntarily attend.

Any student can announce a helpful workshop topic to the class, "I am doing a workshop on adding and subtracting fractions in about ten minutes" or "I am doing a workshop on how to tighten your thesis statement." Students who feel they need support sign up to attend the workshop. The teacher should encourage a student who has shown improvement or who has a particularly great way of explaining things to conduct a workshop.

An interesting trend that Matinga notices is that workshop leaders do not tend to be her top academic students, but more often they are students who simply understand a concept and want to share their knowledge with their peers. The student-led workshops are an equitable way to honor students' abilities to self-direct others. Upon completion of the workshop, the leader fills out a short feedback form for Matinga about what they noticed from each participant and whether or not they think their classmates may need more support. The students are not only helping each other through student-led workshops, but the leaders are assessing the content understanding of their peers.

Conferencing and Coaching

One of the tremendous advantages of the PBL classroom is extra time for formative assessment. Since the teacher isn't spending the entire class talking from the front of the room, they have ample time to listen, observe, and offer timely feedback. The role of the teacher shifts from content delivery to coaching. Think of the role of a coach on the athletic field or in the performing arts. Excellent coaches observe their athletes or performers and then give specific feedback to improve the performance. Coaching is relevant to individual goals and needs. With the newer emphasis on analytics in sports, athletes are given a "grade" on many specific skills, but when it comes to the game it is all about the performance. PBL teachers function in the same manner, observing students as they work in their groups and coaching them throughout the project. The presentation of the final products to the audience is like game day, and the teacher is coaching on the sidelines while students present their learning.

Group work time is the perfect chance for all kinds of formative assessment. Work time is when SEL competencies are practiced between students around real goals, presenting an authentic opportunity for students to grow in their SEL skills. During this time, teachers can conference with groups or individuals using rubrics, group contracts, or scrum boards for reflective conversations. Have a plan for what you want to accomplish each day and track each student and group in a spreadsheet or on a checklist. This could be collected as evidence to show student growth, but more importantly it is data to inform future teaching moves. For example, if you notice that many students are working independently and not participating in their groups, you may plan a team building activity to build rapport and emphasize the importance and synergy of joint effort.

There is a danger of losing student voice when you show up to observe a project team. Students tend to stop what they are doing and address the teacher with questions, or they may begin to "perform" their group role in an exaggerated fashion. When this happens, remind the group that your presence is just to listen and observe their processes. Another helpful approach is, before work time begins, to announce to the class what your role will be today. For example, one day you may be an observer noticing a specific SEL skill, such as equal participation of group members to measure collaboration. Another day, you may be an interviewer seeking to have a conversation around the student scrum board, group progress, and goals. Letting students know the teacher role for the day ahead of time helps them to be focused, prepared, and productive. Once students become comfortable with the PBL process, they will start to ignore you during observations and continue working on their project tasks.

It is not the teacher's job to be the hero, rescuing students from group struggles. Students will not learn Self-Management skills unless adults step back and allow them to work things out. This is a great time to use one of the pet lines of PBL expert and special education teacher, Kristin Uliasz:

"You're struggling with the right things right now." Or "I am comfortable with you being uncomfortable right now."

It is important to acknowledge the student's frustration without solving it for them. Instead coach students various ways to attack their difficulty as a team and iron out their differences. Use the KARE Gap ILeva from Chapter 5 to facilitate students' recognition of the source of their struggles and plan corrective measures. Of course, use your best judgment and step in if the conflict is not being negotiated in a civil manner. But instead of fixing every situation, use probing questions to help students clarify the issue and determine a path forward. Remember, coaches don't get to play in the game, they prepare players to perform to their highest ability.

Assessing the Teacher

As teachers, we are often guilty of assuming that students are happy and engaged in our class. National survey results show that this is often not the case, especially at the high school level.[117] The 2009 High School Study of Student Engagement surveyed forty-two thousand students in one hundred and three American high schools and revealed that two-thirds are bored daily and one-sixth are bored in every class.[118] A great way to model Social Awareness to our students is to elicit feedback from them. When we listen to all of our students' voices, they are empowered, and it builds a culture of respect and advocacy.

An easy way to have students assess you and your class is through a survey. Based on the Tuning Protocol, use Google Forms to have students submit their "likes" and "wonders" at the end of each project. The assessment doubles as a reflection when you ask students to consider the following:

- "What SEL competency did I improve during this project? How?"
- "What specific activities or tools helped me cultivate this SEL competency?"

- "What SEL competency do I still need to work on the most?"
- "What strategies will help me develop it?

Matinga and Mike always combine the survey with a Talking Circle because some students prefer to silently write their feedback and others like to talk it out. The conversation gives context to written responses that may be brief or incomplete. Other ways to gain feedback from students is through exit tickets or even just asking them amid everyday conversations.

**Listening is the most underrated skill
of assessment.**

By allowing students to assess you, as teacher, and following up on their comments, you are building a climate where feedback and refinement become the norm for everyone in the room, including the teacher. Embarrassment and fear of failure disappear when you put your best attempt forward knowing that it will need improvement. Instead of focusing on correct answers, students target curiosity, inquiry, and deeper learning.

Planning

What is in the lesson plan is what gets accomplished. You will not accidentally address all students' SEL needs. It is important to be intentional in how you will teach, practice, and assess SEL daily. You may already be using a number of these tools for all or some of your students, but if you want equity and full impact, then you need to intentionally plan how to

---

develop ALL of the competencies for ALL students. So how does one go about planning for SEL assessment?

Start out by creating a list of SEL learning targets. Choose learning targets based on the SEL struggles of your student population from previous years. Make a list of skills under each of the five core competencies that you expect your students to master by the end of the year. Use student-friendly language that is developmentally appropriate. Of course, this is an opportunity to teach SEL vocabulary to younger learners. As you make your list, make sure that you consider the context of your school so that you are culturally appropriate. Remember the purpose of SEL is not to "whitewash" students of color. SEL is not a tool to strong arm BIPOC and disadvantaged students to assimilate them in any way, but rather to equip them to explore, thrive in, and contribute to their own culture. If you are a white educator working with BIPOC students, invite some parents and community members to help create this list. Students' cultural identities and strengths must be respected and represented in your list.

Elementary SEL Learning Targets

Self-Awareness
I can use words to describe how I feel.
I can share my talents.
I can try things many times without giving up.
I can ask for help when I need it.
I can figure things out by myself.
I can listen and learn from feedback.

Self-Management

I can take turns.

I can follow the class norms.

I can wait my turn to speak.

I can decide how I want to learn.

I can calm myself down when I have "big feelings."

I can continue to work when I am frustrated.

I can set and complete a goal.

I can decide how to start my work.

I can clean up after myself.

I can keep track of my materials and things.

Social Awareness

I can understand my classmates' points of views.

I can share difficult ideas without arguing.

I can accept others who are different from me.

I can share how differences are strengths.

I can respect my classmates.

I can work with anyone in my class.

I can put myself in someone else's shoes.

I can consider how people in another part of the world might feel about . . .

Relationship Skills

I can present my work to others.

I can speak to a group.

I can work with others.

I can tell others how I am feeling.

I can listen to others.

I can share materials.

I can take turns.

I can help others.

I can work with adults.

I can give feedback that is specific, helpful, and kind.

I can accept feedback.

I can reflect on how I treat others.

Responsible Decision-Making

I can state a problem.

I can brainstorm solutions.

I can explore my ideas through investigations, experiments, and interviews.

I can try out my ideas.

I can decide what is the best choice.

I can do high-quality work.

I can serve others.

I can make good choices.

I can make my community better.

I can be a leader.

Secondary SEL Learning Targets

Self-Awareness

I can express my feelings in appropriate ways.

I can accurately reflect on my attitude and actions, both positive and negative.

I can apply my strengths in various situations.

I can present myself and my work confidently.

I can work through failure without quitting.

I can learn new things on my own.

I can advocate for scaffolding and support when I need it.

Self-Management

I can regulate my emotions.

I can honor our group contract.

I can deal with stress in healthy ways.

I can work through difficulties without giving up.

I can initiate work on my own.

I can follow through on my assigned tasks.

I can set and achieve goals.

I can use a scrum board to manage tasks.

I can reflect on my work for chances to improve it.

I can manage a project with my teammates.

Social Awareness

I can see more than two sides of an issue.

I can respect my classmates at all times.

I can disagree with others without arguing or offending.

I can accept differences without judging.

I can demonstrate how differences improve society.

I can empathize with viewpoints that I agree and disagree with.

Relationship Skills

I can work with everyone in my group.

I can give feedback that is specific, helpful, and kind.

I can accept feedback and refine my work.

I can give warnings when needed.

I can refocus my group on our project.

I can collaborate with adults from the community.

I can present my work and ideas confidently and clearly.

I can listen and accept ideas from others.

I can fulfill my role in the group.

I can reflect on my ability to work with others.

Responsible Decision-Making

I can identify a problem.

I can state a problem clearly and concisely.

I can brainstorm multiple solutions.

I can formulate a hypothesis.

I can test a hypothesis through experimentation, research, and investigation.

I can analyze and interpret results through an empathetic lens.

I can advocate for equity.

I can solve issues in my local community.

I can serve others.

I can lead and inspire my classmates and community.

Next map out your year so that you hit all five of the core SEL competencies, focusing on different ones for each project in your scope and sequence. Think about which competencies will mesh well with different content areas, inquiry focuses, final products, and community partners. Consider how different SEL skills will build on each other from project to project over time. This planning must be considered a draft.

Every year is different, and after school starts you should adjust how you organize your approach as you get to know your students personally.

Use a pre-planning form to plot out how you will teach, practice, and assess one SEL competency per project. This does not mean that students won't be using the other competencies but that, as a class, you will focus on one area at a time for em-phasis. Of course, in your daily interactions with individual students, you can coach them on any of the competencies as they naturally occur in the classroom. Take advantage of these spontaneous teachable moments to guide students in applying the appropriate SEL competency.

Sample SEL in PBL Pre-Planning Form

Choose one SEL core or sub competency: Teamwork or Collaboration How does this SEL skill mesh with your PBL idea? Students will need to work together to research both national and local events of CRM. Students need to collaborate to create podcasts.	What resources and scaffolding will you provide to help students meet this standard? Scrum board, rubric
List specific ways this standard will be assessed and by whom: • Exit tickets, Fist to 5 (S) • Scrum board (S) (P) (T) • Observations (T) • Google Form Final Reflection (S) (T)	List student reflection questions about this standard to use throughout the project • Rate how your group is collaborating on research. • Are we using our scrum board effectively? • Evaluate the collaboration of your team.
List specific ways that you will teach this standard: • Bottle Boys video • Chopsticks Challenge • Scrum boards on Trello	List specific ways that students will practice this standard: • Create and enforce group contract • Scrum board • Collaborative research • Creating podcast script and recording

On the planning form, determine how you will formatively assess the chosen competency on a regular basis throughout the project. How will you introduce the SEL competency in class? What team building activities, videos, or skits will you use as examples? Do you have a rubric for the SEL competency, or will you create one as a class? How will you track and report individual progress? How will students peer- and self-assess? All of these specifics must be a part of the project plan and scheduled into the calendar. Detailed plans assure that developing SEL skills remain a priority in your classroom. But do not allow fidelity to your plans to dictate over student needs. Adjust as often as necessary to match student personalities and choices. This may mean tweaks to your schedule or planned activities or even scrapping everything altogether and switching to a different competency focus entirely. Flexibility to your students' needs is key!

> *Just as our pulse regularly beats, SEL assessments are a consistent practice embedded into everything that we do in the classroom.*

The heartbeat has a constant pulse that is inconspicuous. It is always pulsating behind the scenes, but we rarely think about it. Assessing SEL in the PBL classroom does not need to be a separate, time-consuming process. Using a combination of team building activities, rubrics, protocols, and coaching means the assessment happens in real time as students are doing real work. Feedback about specific SEL targets from you and their peers alongside individual weekly reflections will lead to significant growth in confidence and skills. When teachers intentionally embed SEL skills into every lesson every day, by the end of the year students will demonstrate a high level of social and emotional intelligence.

Reflection Questions

- How will you use formative assessments to guide your students' learning process?
- How can you use scenarios and video clips to introduce SEL rubrics?
- How will you teach peer and self-assessment?
- What protocols will you make a part of your classroom culture, and how will you use them as formative assessments?
- How will you use coaching and conferencing to deep dive into individual student strengths, goals, and needs?
- How will you plan to intentionally teach, practice, and assess all of the SEL competencies throughout the calendar year?

PULSE OF PBL

Chapter 10

How Will You Revolutionize the World?

Stop preparing kids for "someday" and watch them change the world RIGHT NOW!

- Student Journey: Responsible Decision-Making
- Parent Journey: Self-Awareness
- Teacher Journey: Self-Management
- Principal Journey: Social Awareness
- Community Journey: Relationship Skills
- Pulse of PBL

Let's look at how Transformative SEL is infused into a *Shark Tank* style project at Mike's comprehensive PBL school.[119] This story is a composite of actual student experiences, parent comments, and community involvement over the years. High levels of implementation were facilitated by the district-level commitment to prioritizing PBL, providing community partnerships, and structural supports. Making the shift to Transformative SEL and PBL is hard and will not happen overnight. Results are gradual as it takes time to shift school culture and norms. Celebrate the small victories as your students develop Transformative SEL skills along the way.

Consider the perspectives of a student, parent, teacher, principal, and community partner with each viewpoint focused on one of the five CASEL competencies demonstrating how it is refined through the PBL process:

Student Journey: Responsible Decision-Making

The Revolution Project Showcase would be Sophia's first experience presenting to an audience outside of her classroom, so she was nervous. As a new student, she enjoyed the classes, even if projects were stressful at times. Her personal passions included lacrosse, her dog, and climate change. Her project teammates—James, a self-proclaimed science nerd who loved genetics, and Kim, a free-thinking artist and excellent sculptor—were second-year PBL "veterans" and assured her that the group was well prepared for the public presentation. They even dared to say out loud that their team might earn the $1,000 seed money offered for the winning idea! Sophia was personally excited about the presentation because the project challenged her and her peers to research and solve real problems in her community.

The Revolution Project began with whole school fieldwork experiences at a couple of local factories. The students knew that they were launching a new project, but they hadn't been told exactly what it was about. The first factory was a modern establishment making customized springs and conveyor parts. It had a sleek design and was brightly powered by solar panels located outside. The second factory was in a more industrial building and specialized in cutting enormous blocks of steel into smaller pieces for plastic injection molds. It was dark, dirty, and loud. Sophia was struck by the contrast of these two successful businesses.

The following day, all of the students gathered in the auditorium as a team of teachers officially launched the Revolution Project.

The Driving Question: "How will you revolutionize the world?"

The Framing Question: "How will you, as a twenty-first-century citizen, change the world so that industrialization is socially and environmentally responsible?"

In order to answer these two pivotal questions, students had to first investigate the science and history of the Second Industrial Revolution in Europe and the United States. For their final product, students would create a prototype solution for a current problem lingering from the effects of the shift to modernity. Next a guest speaker from the United Way introduced the contest aspect of the project. They would split an award of

$1,000 in seed money for the best project proposals as determined by the local chamber of commerce. Sophia was excited by the challenge and the chance to do meaningful work in her neighborhood.

After that, students watched *The Story of Stuff,* a fact-filled video looking at the underside of our production and consumption patterns.[120] This documentary was used to frame the problems of industrialization into five broad categories: extraction, production, distribution, consumption, and disposal. Students brainstormed Need to Knows, writing each question on sticky notes, which were then placed on separate posters for each industrialization category. Sophia thought about the factories they toured and wondered if all factories could become clean and efficient like the one producing springs and conveyor parts? She admired their use of solar panels for power and wondered what other ways could energy consumption be reduced? After sharing her ideas at her table, the group decided to add her question, "How could we utilize renewable resources like solar power to reduce energy use?" to the consumption poster.

After dozens of questions were generated for each category, students stood by the poster for the area that they were most interested in researching. Sophia chose the consumption poster. Alongside the other students at her poster, she brainstormed current problems about consumption. Within these poster groups, teams of three were formed. Sophia chose to work with James and Kim because she thought that their strengths and interests would coincide with her passion for climate change.

The following day, Sophia listened intently as a guest marketing expert explained the Liberatory Design Thinking process (see Chapter 8) that students would be applying in this project. She liked how the process started with empathetic questioning from the perspective of the end user. As part of an equity focus, students were expected to research multiple viewpoints, including individuals who were affected but had the least amount of power and influence. Each group had to choose a subtopic to research from their category. Other student groups investigated consumption topics such as alternative packaging, more efficient appliances, and passive solar homes. At first Sophia had no idea what to do. Kim proposed using recycled materials to create art, but the group decided that creating art out of recyclables was too literal and the approach was not broad enough.

Then James mentioned something that Sophia and Kim thought was crazy—bioluminescent plants! However, James explained that biomimicry was an expanding field that looked to nature for solutions to modern problems. For example, the bullet trains in Japan were designed after the shape of a Kingfisher's beak to prevent sonic booms, and Velcro was invented from burrs sticking to a dog's fur.[121] He shared an article with the team about biomimicry design and showed some images of biomimicry examples in industrial design. He proposed designing plants that glowed in the dark and provided a natural light to reduce energy consumption and limit artificial light pollution at night. He even had a professional connection to biomimicry to support his bizarre idea.

Once James convinced Sophia and Kim that he was serious, they contacted his geneticist contact at a local university. The scientist assured them that in fact this was a viable idea, and that scientists were researching chemicals in luminous jellyfish to see what made them glow in the dark. With her help, the students drafted a prototype of large hosta plants using the genes from a jellyfish to glow at night.

Each group sketched a poster of their initial project idea for a gallery walk. Students wrote feedback on sticky notes and posted them on each other's projects. Sophia was energized by seeing how the rest of her classmates were proposing ways to reduce climate change too. She couldn't wait to read the comments from her peers on her team's glowing hosta plant idea. Her group sorted their sticky notes into useful feedback to focus on. Some of the other students were skeptical of their concept and thought that it was too sci-fi. Many wanted to know more details about how it was possible. Her group agreed to address comments asking who would use these plants and where? Sophia suggested that an appropriate place for the glowing hostas would be the city park where she walked her dog. It had many malfunctioning, ugly, and costly sidewalk lights that could be replaced. Kim excitedly used her art skills to design bioluminescent garden beds in complex patterns and beautiful colors.

Finally, the day of the showcase arrived. Business professionals, parents, and community members toured the hallways and classrooms where each project team had a display table of their industrial problem, proposed solution, and a historical parallel innovation. There was a wide range of topics: recycling, healthier food, fitness options, reducing harmful emissions, and tracking government corruption related to regulation.

Sophia's table was located in a darkened classroom illuminated by black lights. They had a trifold poster board announcing their title in fluorescent paint, "Glow in the Park: Bioluminescent Plants." Kim's colorful garden designs were on it, along with research about jellyfish from James. Sophia had researched and created graphs calculating how much electricity and money would be saved annually by the city with the switch from streetlights to bioluminescent plants. But the highlight of their display was the props. Their geneticist partner had a colleague that allowed them to borrow a small aquarium of bioluminescent jellyfish. Sophia's team bought large, fake plants and painted them in fluorescent, neon colors. The students dressed professionally but wore neon necklaces that they passed out to visitors.

Guests were drawn into their room like moths to a fluorescent light. Sophia's group explained the science and social relevance behind their idea multiple times. Everyone loved their innovative solution, scientific knowledge, and creativity in presenting it. Sophia was proud of how her team collaborated and the effort that they put toward their problem and solution. Sophia was excited when their ecological geneticist partner brought a group of other scientists from her lab to see their project display.

The day after the showcase, students sat in a circle and used a Harkness Discussion to reflect on the project experience. Sophia was energized by the mental parallels she could draw between the design decisions made by inventers in Second

Industrial Revolution in Europe and in the United States and the design decisions her project team made using the Liberatory Design Thinking process. She shared examples of how historical designers seemed to focus on the monetary gains and political power while her team took the time to make design decisions based on feedback from the users as well as long-term sustainability goals.

During this project Sophia's team had excelled at Responsible Decision-Making in many ways. Her group designed an original solution to a persistent problem in her neighborhood. Their creative solution was based on both scientific data and empathetic listening to the community. They had connected their personal responsibility toward the planet to a wider community impact benefiting all park users. Sophia felt empowered that even though she was still in high school, she had contributed a viable idea to help the planet. She was proud, not only of their project solution, but of how her project team worked together to present in a professional and engaging fashion to an authentic audience.

One of her classes' biggest takeaways was that all students need to evaluate their families' daily habits to determine their lasting impact on the environment. Everyone has an ethical responsibility to do their part in preserving the world! At the end of class, Sophia received two incredible surprises. First the winners were announced, and her group was a finalist for the grant to continue their work! Next the ecological geneticist offered the team a paid internship in her lab the following summer because she was so impressed with their capabilities, critical eye, and drive. Sophia, James, and Kim were pumped!

Parent Journey: Self Awareness

Sophia's mother, Catalina, was apprehensive at first about switching her daughter from a traditional school to one with a PBL focus. In middle school, Sophia earned mostly Cs and Ds and constantly complained that she was bored. Catalina knew that her daughter had great potential so when Sophia showed interest in a PBL school, she immediately scheduled a visit. Their tour was hosted by two students who explained that the school used Project Based Learning as its central framework. Students learned the same content standards as they would in a tradi-tional school but gained Social and Emotional Learning skills as well. Catalina was impressed by how enthusiastic the student guides were about their learning. By the end of the day, Sophia was enrolled for the fall semester.

That summer, there was a three-day orientation for new students. Catalina saw that Sophia was both excited and nerv-ous about starting at a new school. However, when Sophia came home after the first day of orientation, she couldn't stop talking about the new classmates she had met and the fun team build-ing activities that they engaged in. For the first time in years, Sophia seemed genuinely interested in school.

Once the school year began, Catalina noticed several differ-ences in Sophia. She no longer had to beg her daughter to get out of bed to get to school on time. At the end of the day, when questioned about her classes, instead of the painful silence of the past, Sophia gushed about the projects that she was working on. Sophia enjoyed that lessons weren't spoon fed to her by teachers but that students learned through supported inquiry. School was challenging, but if she got stuck, there was always encouragement from teachers and classmates. There was the expectation that she make an attempt to "fail forward." Catalina was overjoyed to see her daughter engrossed in learning.

After a few months, Catalina saw a notable transformation in her daughter. Sophia was awakened by the responsibility of owning her learning. She was becoming more self-directed and willing to take on more responsibility at home. She was happier and even got along with her younger brothers better. Sophia started volunteering at a local farmer's market and seemed to recognize her strengths rather than wallow in detached insecurity.

One day Sophia burst through the door with an invitation for her first showcase, the Revolution Project. She was so enthusiastic that Catalina had to slow her down to understand her. Catalina had already heard all about how Sophia and her team had been developing a plan for plants that glow in the dark. It seemed absurd to her, but Sophia assured her mother that the science was legitimate. Now Catalina would get to experience it firsthand.

When Catalina arrived on the morning of the Revolution Project showcase, she was surprised by the transformation of the school. There were project displays set up in every nook and cranny of the building. Dozens of guests interacted at all of the various project tables. Catalina bumped into a couple of friends who had served as community partners to the students, even though their children did not attend there.

Catalina quickly found Sophia's room due to the black light shining out. Sophia looked so professional as she explained the science behind bioluminescent plants to a local business owner and the invited scientists. Her team was articulate and answered questions with clarity. Sophia gave a heartfelt plea for why climate change was so devastating and how it needed to be addressed by industrial actors as well as community members. Catalina was impressed with the design of the display and the quality of their presentation. She was so proud of Sophia!

Catalina's visit to the Revolution Project Showcase confirmed the decision to switch to a Project Based Learning school. Catalina witnessed, first-hand, Sophia's growth in Self-Awareness. Sophia had a new self-confidence when presenting her project to the guests. Gone was the apathy toward school and her future. No longer were they arguing about dropping out of school, instead Sophia talked about which colleges have the best environmental science programs. She had found her identity in a cross-section of her passion for science and her concern for her community. Through student voice and choice in projects, Sophia had transformed into a self-sufficient learner willing to explore her passions deeply.

Teacher Journey: Self-Management

Mr. Vargas, a former engineer, had taught freshman math for six years. He didn't teach the traditional classes of algebra and geometry. Instead students learn the same standards in an integrated path over the course of four years of high school. What Mr. Vargas appreciates about this approach is that students explore math in the context of authentic problems. They solve actual problems, not fabricated ones like "Two trains are traveling at different speeds in opposite directions . . ."

The Revolution Project is one of Mr. Vargas' favorite projects because it integrates all subjects and teachers into one big, beautiful mess. When a colleague first suggested a whole school project mixing grades and classes, he was concerned about how his content would fit in. He wasn't convinced that it would be worth the time and energy. Now the Revolution Project is a highlight of the year, and he can't imagine not undertaking it.

The teachers recognized that a huge schoolwide project was an excellent opportunity to teach, practice, and assess students' Self-Management skills. To be successful, students would need to regulate their time, tasks, and team tightly. Teachers did not want students waiting until the last minute to try and throw together a presentation without first engaging with the community.

Since project management is a pillar of quality PBL, students already knew some basic structures and protocols. The Revolution Project started with the normal PBL routines of entry event, DQ, Need to Knows, and planning next steps of inquiry toward the final product. After forming teams, students signed group contracts that identified their SEL strengths to contribute to their group and outlined expectations for equitable contributions. They used scrum boards to organize, divide up tasks, and set deadlines.

Mr. Vargas and his colleagues added some additional tools for the Revolution Project. They used the *Story of Stuff*, a short animated documentary by Annie Leonard about the life cycle of material goods, to frame categories of industrialization to sort students into more focused groups. A marketing expert taught students an empathetic design process protocol. The staff felt it was important for students to learn the tools and techniques that professionals employ to manage their work and themselves.

The mathematical focus of the project was on gathering and analyzing data to determine whether or not it supported their proposed solution. The standards were a combination of algebraic functions and statistics. It was not enough for students to design a creative solution to fix an industrialization problem. They were required to research and show mathematically both the need for and the expected results of their solution. Mr. Vargas has seen many students who "hate math" become engrossed in his content for the first time when it supported work that they were passionate about.

To facilitate collaboration, every group was assigned a home room for project work time. Each teacher was directly responsible for supporting their home room groups. Students could sign up to travel to see another teacher if they needed help from a specific content expert. Mr. Vargas's home room had many strong project ideas. He was fascinated by a group that was researching bioluminescent plants. He was not surprised by the topic choice because he knew that James was a science nerd who geeked out about stuff like this. But what impressed him the most about the group was the leadership of Sophia.

She was a new student and was the stereotypical shy, quiet girl when she arrived. At the beginning of the year in her math belief essay, she had shared her disdain for math and previous lack of success in the subject. But during this project, Mr. Vargas saw a shift. First of all, Sophia was passionate about slowing down climate change. From day one, she was vocal with tons of suggestions during the brainstorming protocol. Once her group landed on their topic, she took charge and organized their scrum board. She thought of every detail needed for her group to succeed. Sophia held her group accountable. She was not bossy, but in a friendly fashion checked in to make sure that they were always on track.

One day Mr. Vargas listened in as Sophia's group discussed how to prove the benefits that bioluminescent plants would provide. Sophia stated that they needed hard data. She volunteered to focus on that aspect of their project. She contacted the city recreation department to find the electric costs of the park where she walked her dog. She researched the type of light bulbs currently used and their consumption rates. When she walked her dog, she counted how many streetlamps were at the park. Based on this research, Sophia calculated the energy use per light post in the park and created tables, equations, and graphs to demonstrate how much energy would be saved if their bioluminescent plants replaced the streetlamps. Mr. Vargas beamed as Sophia excelled at her "worst" subject.

A few days before the planned showcase, each homeroom ran the Tuning Protocol to get feedback on their projects. Student groups were challenged with the reflection question, "What will attract visitors to your table?" Teachers encouraged students to look at trade show booths or think about the business barns at the local fair. Students realized that they needed some incentives, like visual props or giveaways of swag. Student groups spent the last few days making sure that the marketing of their tables would attract attention to their ideas.

When the day of the showcase arrived, Mr. Vargas and the rest of the teachers felt the inevitable pressure of hoping that the students would come through with quality projects that would not disappoint the community. But they weren't worried—the structures were in place for students to successfully manage themselves, and from the feedback protocols teachers knew that their students were prepared. As the guests arrived, Mr. Vargas relaxed, visited student tables, listened to their presentations, and took plenty of pictures to document student accomplishments.

Mr. Vargas loves PBL because it creates lifelong learners who make a difference in the world—not just good test takers. Students build Self-Management skills by supervising their time, tasks, and team. They become independent learners who can regulate themselves and work out problems with each other. He takes great joy in watching students find themselves and develop the skills of negotiation and collaboration with each other and the community. To Mr. Vargas, it almost feels like a bonus when students learn some mathematical critical-thinking skills in the process.

Principal Journey: Social Awareness

Ms. Brown's leadership style is to serve in the background, allowing her students and teachers to shine. She believes that after hiring and training the right kind of people, her primary job is to support their ideas. Voice and choice begin with the teachers and flow down to the students. As a former humanities teacher, Ms. Brown is passionate about her students' diversity of mind. She wants them to respectfully consider different viewpoints before locking into narrow solutions. She believes that PBL is the perfect vehicle to expose students to multiple perspectives around complex issues.

Today is one of her favorite days of the year: the Revolution Project Showcase. It is a wonderful event where students demonstrate Social Awareness when they design solutions in collaboration with community partners. Ms. Brown loves the Revolution Project because it validates how connected the school is to the real world and how passionate students are about the myriad social and environmental issues.

When teachers first pitched a school-wide project on the residue of industrialization, Ms. Brown was immediately on board. The staff spent considerable time discussing how to connect and work with community partners. They decided to make it a requirement that every group must find their own local partner to consult with during the project. In addition to the PBL framework that staff and students were already familiar with, Ms. Brown suggested using a design thinking protocol. This would help students organize their problem-solving process. She recommended the Liberatory Design Process because of its emphasis on equity and empathy with the end user.

During the weeks leading up to the showcase, there was a constant stream of calls, emails, and visits between students and the public. Students would pop into her office, excited to share who they were connecting with and what they were learning. Community contacts included social workers, business owners, scientists, chefs, professors, fitness gurus, local environmental groups, government officials, and affected neighbors. She knew her students were empathizing with many different kinds of people.

All of the various community partners were invited to the final showcase. As Ms. Brown toured the student presentations around the school, she marveled at the diversity of prototypes. Students had researched a multitude of aspects of industrialization and proposed unique solutions for sustainability. She questioned the groups and was impressed with their scientific and mathematical explanations. But what truly inspired her was students' demonstration of Social Awareness in their models. It was obvious that students had considered opinions from an array of sources and perspectives. They demonstrated empathy and compassion with both their connections and the earth as they proposed solutions for long-term results. Students understood the importance of leveraging systems to empower change. Ms. Brown saw that they had met the challenge of equitable design with the end user in mind.

It was difficult for Ms. Brown to cast her vote for just one project. Ultimately, she chose "Glow in the Park" because it was creative yet practical. The students applied the principles of biomimicry to transfer genetics from marine biology to botany. She appreciated the adaptation of natural remedies to a modern problem. Her vote was swayed by overhearing a group of visiting geneticists' admiration of the project. The scientists were so impressed that afterward they requested a meeting with her to arrange more collaboration between their lab and the school.

Community Journey: Relationship Skills

Dr. Jazmin Collins is an ecological geneticist at the local university, who specializes in how plants adapt in temperate zones. One morning, she was pleasantly surprised to receive an email from James, a local high school student who attended a STEM camp that she had volunteered at last summer. His request was intriguing. He wanted to know if there was any science to support the idea of developing bioluminescent plants. Dr. Collins knew exactly who to ask: one of her colleagues, Dr. Raj Gupta, who was studying the chemistry of how certain deep-sea creatures produce light.

Dr. Collins arranged for a video conference between Dr. Gupta, herself, and James's group. They discussed the feasibility of the students' idea of bioluminescent plants as an option to replace streetlights. Both geneticists agreed that it was scientifically possible. They assisted the students' research to discover that no one was currently working on this idea. Dr. Gupta gave the students specific places to research details on what kind of experimental study would be required to attempt this. The students were thrilled by the feedback from experts in the field. After the call, Dr. Collins and Dr. Gupta commented how impressed they were not only by the students' idea, but by their ability to engage in conversations on a professional level.

Email exchanges continued back and forth between the scientists and the students for a few weeks as the project developed. Then Dr. Collins received a formal invitation for her and Dr. Gupta to a showcase where the students would be presenting their findings to the community. She RSVP'd and invited other friends from her department. Several other scientists agreed to come along to hear about the project.

None of the scientists from the lab had ever been to the school before. Upon arrival, they were instantly struck by the energy of student presentations happening seemingly everywhere. They stopped and talked to several student groups about their projects, eventually finding their way to a dark room with glowing lights, where James's group had set up. Dr. Gupta quickly checked on his jellyfish that he had loaned the students for their presentation and was happy to see them floating peacefully.

Dr. Collins and Dr. Gupta sat back and silently observed as James, Sophia, and Kim presented their findings to their colleagues. The display was attractive, inviting, and informative. The students worked together, seamlessly explaining and answering questions about the science behind bioluminescent plants and the potential positive financial impact for the city through decreased energy consumption.

The scientists continued to tour the Revolution Project Showcase and interact with other students. Dr. Collins was introduced to the school principal, Ms. Brown. She commented how wonderful the school was and that it must be great to work at a magnet school with the city's brightest students. Dr. Collins was shocked to hear that in fact, it was not a magnet school at all, but a regular high school with a similar student population to other schools in the area. The difference, Ms. Brown assured her, is that students develop Social and Emotional Competencies through authentic projects such as the Revolution Project.

On the car ride back to the university lab, the group of scientists raved about what they had seen. They were impressed by the maturity of all the students and their Relationship Skills. Students communicatee confidently and clearly with adults. Critical thinking and creativity shone through the slew of projects presented. It was obvious that the students knew how to successfully work in diverse teams to meet deadlines with quality work. Dr. Gupta noted that he has worked with adults who can't get along as well as these students. These students were leaders who wanted to transform their world. Everyone agreed that this would not be their last collaboration with the school, but that the lab wanted to develop a long-term partnership with the authentic learning happening there.

Pulse of PBL

Schools similar to this example exist around the world. Unfortunately, this type of school is not the norm . . . yet. Transformative Social and Emotional Learning is at the heart of high-quality Project Based Learning. All students deserve training in the development of SEL skills to prepare them for life. The current K-12 philosophy emphasizes academic content to satiate the test instead of preparing individual students to be contributors in their community. When we cultivate Transformative SEL skills, we no longer have to convince students the value of the material that we teach. This book encourages educators to prioritize SEL competencies as the most vital knowledge students need for the rest of their lives. Developing these coping skills at eleven years old is preferable to unpacking these competencies with a therapist in adulthood.

Students have been taught that education is the key to success and upward mobility. We believe that this narrative does not apply to all students equally. Students who lack understanding of the most basic SEL skills are more likely to struggle in the academic context. Instead, we assert that education is the key to a satisfying and fulfilling life. Without the explicit teaching of the SEL competencies, students will grapple to fulfil the profile of the graduate that we discussed in our introduction chapter. Teachers should provide equitable learning experiences so that every student can picture themself in our envisioned graduate profile. We can spend money on character-building programs to practice SEL peripherally during morning meetings or advisory periods. However, these resources provide minimal impact if they are not integrated into daily classroom routines, experiences, and practices.

The shortest path to establishing equity in learning is to develop *ALL* students' SEL skills inside of a PBL framework.

Without a sense of Self-Awareness, it is difficult for students to understand and apply basic productive behaviors. Designing opportunities for young people to showcase their interests, strengths, and real-world potential through their academic work awakens their Self-Awareness. When students see their efforts reflected in the eyes of their community, they are empowered. Through the practice of essential strategies and protocols included in this book, students learn the value of productive behaviors in their life journey and their work. Protocols build a culture of respect and acceptance of differing viewpoints, which in turn can sharpen Transformative Social Awareness skills that can be applied to create positive contributions throughout their community and across borders. When students are explicitly taught how to forge strong Relationship Skills, they bridge paths to resolve differences among their project team members. Applying lessons on Responsible Decision-Making equips young people to benefit from the feedback process and push through challenges to improve the quality of their work.

The heart has a pulse that is constantly beating behind the scenes. SEL skills are the vital pulse of your PBL practice. Since we want students to own their learning, we give them opportunities to explore and lead their communities with powerful SEL skills. Prepare *ALL* students to create their own access to a more fair and equitable learning experience; no matter where they come from or who they are. Stop preparing kids for "someday" and watch them change the world RIGHT NOW!

Reflection Questions

- How are each of the five SEL competencies infused into the Revolution Project?
- Collaborative teacher planning time and flexible scheduling are huge benefits when shifting to PBL. What steps can you take to make the structure of your school/class a better fit for PBL?
- What are the advantages and disadvantages of cross-curricular projects?
- How could you involve parents and community partners more in your school/class?

- What specific steps could your school/class take to begin the shift to Transformative SEL infused PBL?
- What further resources or professional development support do you need?

Acknowledgements

The original idea for the *Pulse of PBL* came when Teresa Dempsey, fellow National Faculty at PBLWorks sent out a request for a crosswalk between PBL and SEL. Mike did not have one but was motivated to create it in table form. Upon completion, he saw the potential for expanding it into a book. Teresa has been a dear friend, supporting this endeavor and encouraging us from the start.

Another PBLWorks colleague, Heather Wolpert-Gawron, came up with the title. Thanks to Myla Lee, Erin Sanchez, Nate Langel, and Chris Fancher for giving us specific, helpful, and kind feedback on our ILeva concepts.

We owe special thanks to the many teachers who shared their stories with us: Erin Gannon for the detailed and amazing Trickster Tales Project that anchors Chapter 3. Vickie Weiss, Jacky Lyimo, Wendy Turner, Ryan Sprott, John Derian, Melissa Riggs, Tracy Saylor, Karen Cormony, Jim Bentley, Heather Creelman, Rebecca Lovelace, Matt McCullough, Matt Webster, Nate Langel, and Lisa Yuk Kuen Yau. Thank you for sharing the amazing work of your students.

I, Matinga, would like to thank Mike for inviting me into this book project and sharing his endless PBL knowledge to enrich this experience. Nancy Ragatz, my awesome mother-in-law, provided a conservative perspective to balance the narrative around politically contested education topics. My husband Dan Ragatz engaged in countless conversations to workshop me pedagogical practices that were difficult to explain. My sons

Trey Ragatz, Nile Ragatz, and Rio Ragatz provided a student point of view on many of the strategies mentioned in the book. Finally I would like to acknowledge my Auntie Iya Djali (Amalia Ebuka Besebo) and my indomitable cousin Nardi (Bernarda Modu Ebuka) for their guidance in explaining Ndowe traditions and specifically the ILeva concept. Their reminder of the contributions of our people and their patient feedback made this project more purposeful. I am forever grateful for their inspiration and selflessness.

I, Mike, would like to thank Andrew Holly, my coteacher for years at Kent Innovation High. He was the ultimate partner who cocreated every project that is referenced in this book. Nate Langel and Trevor Muir were my other partners in crime, joining in brainstorming sessions and offering feedback on project ideas. Kym Pawelka, principal of Kent Innovation High, was the best leader because she gave teachers voice and choice and never hesitated to support all our crazy ideas.

I would like to shout out to all the students of Kent Innovation High, a bunch of crazy kids who aren't afraid to be their own unique selves and change the world! You are the ones who made me the teacher that I am today. It is and always has been about students.

Lastly, I would like to thank my wife, Jodi, a living thesaurus and editor who made countless sections of this book sound intelligent and cohesive. I could not have accomplished this book without your loving support throughout the entire process.

End Notes

The following are all of the citations throughout the entire book.

---

[1] Petrone, P. (2019). The Skills Companies Need Most in 2019 – And How to Learn Them. Retrieved July 13, 2020, from https://learning.linkedin.com/blog/top-skills/the-skills-companies-need-most-in-2019--and-how-to-learn-them

[2]SEL: What Are the Core Competence Areas and Where are they Promoted? (2020). Retrieved October 17, 2020, from https://casel.org/sel-framework/

[3] Bleiberg, J. (2021). Does the common core have a common effect? An exploration of effects on academically vulnerable students. *AERA Open, 7*, 233285842110107. doi:10.1177/23328584211010727

[4] Mcleod, S. (2016, March 16). The biggest indictment of our schools is not their failure to raise test scores. Retrieved July 13, 2020, from http://dangerouslyirrelevant.org/2016/03/the-biggest-indictment-of-our-schools-is-not-their-failure-to-raise-test-scores.html

[5] Jones, S.M. & Kahn, J. (2017). The Evidence Base for How We Learn Supporting Students' Social, Emotional, and Academic Development. National Commission on Social, Emotional, and Academic Development. Washington, DC: The Aspen Institute Gabrieli, C., Ansel, D., & Krachman, S. B. (2015). Ready to be counted: The research case for education policy action on non-cognitive skills Boston: Transforming Education.

[6] Saavedra, A., Rapaport, A., Morgan, K., Hu, A., Hoepfner, D., Garland, M., . . . Ying, L. (2021, February 22). *Knowledge in Action Efficacy Study Over Two Years* (Publication). Retrieved

https://cesr.usc.edu/sites/de-
fault/files/Knowledge%20in%20Action%20Efficacy%20Study
_18feb2021_final.pdf

Krajcik, J., Schneider, B., Miller, E., Chen, I., Bradford, L., Bartz, K., .
. . Codere, S. (2021, January 11). *Assessing the Effect of Project-Based Learning on Science Learning in Elementary
Schools* (Tech.). Retrieved https://mlpbl.open3d.sci-
ence/sites/default/files/MLPBL-technical-report.pdf

[7] Goleman, D., (1995) Emotional Intelligence, New York, NY, Eng-
land: Bantam Books, Inc. *Disclaimer:* Goleman has been highly
critical of PBL and advocated for things like drill and practice for
"low-income students."

[8] History. (2020). Retrieved September 02, 2020, from https://ca-
sel.org/history/

[9] Simmons, D. (2019, February 19). Is Social-Emotional Learning
Really Going to Work for Students of Color? Retrieved July 13, 2020,
from https://www.edweek.org/tm/articles/2017/06/07/we-need-to-
redefine-social-emotional-learning-for.html

[10] Robert J. Jagers, Deborah Rivas-Drake & Brittney Williams (2019)
Transformative Social and Emotional Learning (SEL): Toward SEL
in Service of Educational Equity and Excellence, Educational Psychologist, 54:3, 162-184, DOI: 10.1080/00461520.2019.1623032

[11] Atwell, M., & Bridgeland, J. (2019) Ready to lead: A 2019 update of
principal's perspectives on how social and emotional learning can
prepare children and transform schools. https://casel.org/wp-con-
tent/uploads/2019/10/Ready-to-Lead_FINAL.pdf

[12] SEL: What Are the Core Competence Areas and Where are they
Promoted? (2020). Retrieved October 17, 2020, from https://ca-
sel.org/sel-framework/

[13] SEL: What Are the Core Competence Areas and Where are they
Promoted? (2020). Retrieved October 17, 2020, from https://ca-
sel.org/sel-framework/

[14] SEL: What Are the Core Competence Areas and Where are they Promoted? (2020). Retrieved October 17, 2020, from https://ca-sel.org/sel-framework/

[15] SEL: What Are the Core Competence Areas and Where are they Promoted? (2020). Retrieved October 17, 2020, from https://ca-sel.org/sel-framework/

[16] SEL: What Are the Core Competence Areas and Where are they Promoted? (2020). Retrieved October 17, 2020, from https://ca-sel.org/sel-framework/

[17] THE 17 GOALS | sustainable development. (n.d.). Retrieved August 09, 2021, from https://sdgs.un.org/goals

[18] Lev, S., Clark, A., & Starkey, E. (2020). Implementing project based learning in early childhood: Overcoming misconceptions and reaching success. New York, New York: Routledge, Taylor & Francis Group.

[19] Jackson, C., Porter, S., Easton, J., Blanchard, A., & Kiguel, S. (2021, January 05). Linking Social-Emotional Learning to Long-Term Success. Retrieved January 18, 2021, from https://www.educationnext.org/linking-social-emotional-learning-long-term-success-student-survey-responses-effects-high-school/
Lawson, G. M., McKenzie, M. E., Becker, K. D., Selby, L., & Hoover, S. A. (2019). The Core Components of Evidence-Based Social Emotional Learning Programs. Prevention science : the official journal of the Society for Prevention Research, 20(4), 457–467. https://doi.org/10.1007/s11121-018-0953-y

[20] Berger, T. (2020, September 23). How to Maslow Before Bloom, All Day Long. Retrieved January 18, 2021, from https://www.edutopia.org/article/how-maslow-bloom-all-day-long

[21] Duchesneau, N. (2020, August 6). Social, Emotional, and Academic Development Through an Equity Lens. Retrieved

February 13, 2021, from https://edtrust.org/wp-content/uploads/2014/09/Social-Emotional-and-Academic-Development-Through-an-Equity-Lens-August-6-2020.pdf

[22] Durlak, J. A., Weissberg, R. P., Dymnicki, A. B., Taylor, R. D. & Schellinger, K. B. (2011). The impact of enhancing students' social and emotional learning: A meta-analysis of school-based universal interventions. Child Development, 82(1): 405–432.

[23] Meraji, S., Riculan, C., Michael, N., Perry, A., Devarajan, K., Yi, L., & Hammar, N. (2020, December 11). Video: Is 'poc' outdated? Maybe. but it also has a measurable superpower. Retrieved July 11, 2021, from https://www.npr.org/2020/12/11/944291001/video-is-poc-outdated-maybe-but-it-also-has-a-measurable-superpower The word BIPOC was popularized the summer of 2020 in the United States. BIPOC replaced the term People of Color (POC) which placed non-White Americans into one category. BIPOC specifically emphasizes the lived experience of Black and Indigenous people. We understand that names that generalize non-White people have changed over time and will continue to change.

[24] Srinivasan, M. (2019) SEL Every Day: Integrating social and emotional learning with instruction in secondary classrooms. New York: W. W. Norton & Company. Duchesneau, N. (2020, August 6). Social, Emotional, and Academic Development Through an Equity Lens. Retrieved February 13, 2021, from https://edtrust.org/wp-content/uploads/2014/09/Social-Emotional-and-Academic-Development-Through-an-Equity-Lens-August-6-2020.pdf

[25] Simmons, D. (2019, February 19). Is Social-Emotional Learning Really Going to Work for Students of Color? Retrieved July 13, 2020, from https://www.edweek.org/tm/articles/2017/06/07/we-need-to-redefine-social-emotional-learning-for.html

Chatmon, L., & Osta, K. (2020, April 27). 5 Steps for Liberating Public Education From Its Deep Racial Bias. Retrieved July 13, 2020, from https://www.edweek.org/ew/articles/2018/08/22/5-steps-for-liberating-public-education-from.html

[26] Griffith, Janelle. "Black Beauty Products Kept under Lock and Key at Some Walmart Stores, Raising Complaints." *NBCNews.com*, NBCUniversal News Group, 10 Feb. 2019, www.nbcnews.com/news/us-news/walmart-s-practice-locking-black-beauty-products-some-stores-raises-n967206.

[27] KENDI, I. X. (2019). HOW TO BE AN ANTIRACIST. New York: One World.

[28] Simmons, D. (2019, April). Why We Can't Afford Whitewashed Social Emotional Learning. Retrieved January 19, 2021, from http://www.ascd.org/publications/newsletters/education_update/apr19/vol61/num04/Why_We_Can't_Afford_Whitewashed_Social-Emotional_Learning.aspx

[29] LOVE, B. (2020). WE WANT TO DO MORE THAN SURVIVE: Abolitionist teaching and the pursuit of educational freedom. S.l.: BEACON.

[30] Mehta, J. and Fine, S. (2019) In search of deeper learning: The quest to remake the American high school. Cambridge, MA: Harvard University Press.

[31] Postman, N. & Weingartner, C. (1969) Teaching as a Subversive Activity New York: Dell.

[32] Allen, A., Scott, L.A., & Lewis, C.W. (2013). Racial microaggressions and African American and Hispanic students in urban schools: A call for culturally affirming education. Interdisciplinary Journal of Teaching and Learning, 3(2), 117-129;

Yeager, D.S, Purdie-Vaughns, V., Hooper, S.Y., & Cohen, G.L. (2017). Loss of institutional trust among racial and ethnic minority adolescents: A consequence of procedural injustice and a cause of life-span outcomes, Child Development, 88 (2), 658-676.

[33] Duchesneau, N. (2020, August 6). Social, Emotional, and Academic Development Through an Equity Lens. Retrieved February 13, 2021, from https://edtrust.org/wp-content/uploads/2014/09/Social-Emotional-and-Academic-Development-Through-an-Equity-Lens-August-6-2020.pdf

[34] Robert J. Jagers, Deborah Rivas-Drake & Brittney Williams (2019) Transformative Social and Emotional Learning (SEL): Toward SEL in Service of Educational Equity and Excellence, Educational Psychologist, 54:3, 162-184, DOI: 10.1080/00461520.2019.1623032

[35] Fisher, D., Frey, N., & Smith, D. (2019). All learning is social and emotional: Helping students develop essential skills for the classroom and beyond. Alexandria, VA: ASCD.

[36] Hammond, Z. (2015) Culturally responsive teaching and the brain: Promoting authentic engagement and rigor among culturally and linguistically diverse students. Thousand Oaks, CA: Corwin, a SAGE Company.

[37] https://www.today.com/popculture/science-guy-tackles-issues-older-fans-wbna8132457

[38] Gannon, E. (2019, October 09). A Literature Study Made Awesome with Art and Science. Retrieved July 13, 2020, from https://www.pblworks.org/blog/literature-study-made-awesome-art-and-science

39 ABC. (n.d.). ABC 20/20 What Would You Do? Confronting Racism in America. *20/20 What Would You Do?* Season 1 Episode 1.
40 Note that this activity was an introduction to talking points about whether or not students had implicit bias. The Implicit Bias Test is not scientifically proven and should not be taken as evidence of prejudice or bias. Lopez, G. (2017, March 07). For years, this popular test measured anyone's racial bias. but it might not work after all. Retrieved November 21, 2021, from https://www.vox.com/identities/2017/3/7/14637626/implicit-association-test-racism

[41] English language Arts standards " SPEAKING & listening " grade 3 " 4. (n.d.). Retrieved July 15, 2021, from http://www.corestandards.org/ELA-Literacy/SL/3/4/

[42] Epstein, A. S. (2003). How planning and reflection develop young children's thinking skills. *Young Children, 58(5)*, 28-36.

[43] Joseph, M., & David, A. (n.d.). *Tuning Protocol* [PDF]. School Reform Initiative.

[44] Busse, A. (2017, October 30). Take an Interactive Tour of Grand Rapids Civil History. Retrieved July 13, 2020, from https://www.experiencegr.com/blog/post/take-an-interactive-tour-of-grand-rapids-civil-history/

45 Chris was proud to have his story included in our book and agreed with the use of his dead name and female pronouns at the beginning.

[46] Ruler. (2020). Retrieved February 13, 2021, from https://www.ycei.org/ruler

[47] Turner, W. (2020, March 05). Rubber bracelets to support emotional regulation? Absolutely! Retrieved February 13, 2021, from https://www.fosteringresilientlearners.org/blog/2019/4/8/rubber-bracelets-to-support-emotional-regulation-absolutely

[48] *Using SF-CESS Discourse Cards* [PDF]. (2016). San Francisco: San Francisco Coalition of Essential Small Schools.

[49] The Myers & Briggs Foundation - MBTI® Basics. (2021). Retrieved February 13, 2021, from https://www.myersbriggs.org/my-mbti-personality-type/mbti-basics/

[50] ***Myers-Briggs Personality Test:** We are aware that the Myers-Briggs Personality test is inconsistent and may provide inaccurate results. **This activity is not designed to give student labels or create an inflexible characterization of their personalities**. We are simply using this test mechanics and its results to provide

a starting point into a generally difficult conversation. Young children and teens often have difficulty verbalizing emotional triggers and justifying their reactions, which often results in conversations full of "I don't know" and shoulder shrugs. The Myers-Briggs Type Indicator provides easily understandable base re-sults that most school age students can relate to. Students should be allowed to take the test again if they feel that their results do not fully describe them or be allowed to create their own descriptions of their perceived personalities. Either way, the end game is to teach young people that regardless of their personality or disposition, they can learn to quickly analyze unpleasant events or scenarios and determine productive ways to resolve issues or push through.

Please NEVER use the results to classify or pigeonhole students. Individual re-sults can change over time due to maturity, growth, or trauma. Our personalities and characteristics are never fixed. Students are placed in folx* groups to create more engaging, nonjudgmental, and dynamic discussions about personal behav-iors and personal choices.

The Myers & Briggs Foundation - MBTI® Basics. (2021). Retrieved February 13, 2021, from https://www.myersbriggs.org/my-mbti-personality-type/mbti-basics/

[51] White, S. V. (2019, October 09). Creating a learning environment where all kids feel valued. Retrieved September 06, 2021, from https://www.edutopia.org/article/creating-learning-en-vironment-where-all-kids-feel-valued
See also this video explanation: https://youtu.be/yNm3xM4B00s

[52] Jagers, R. J., Rivas-Drake, D., & Borowski, T. (2018). Equity and social-emotional learning: A cultural analysis. CASEL Assessment Work Group Brief series. Retrieved from https://measuringsel.ca-sel.org/wp-content/uploads/2018/11/Frameworks-Equity.pdf

[53] Fisher, D., & Frey, N. (2013). *Better learning through structured teaching: A framework for the gradual release of responsibility.* ASCD.

[54] Perkins, D. (2009) Making learning whole: How seven principles of teaching can transform education. San Francisco, CA: Jossey-Bass: A Wiley Imprint.

55 Attributed to John C. Maxwell https://www.good-reads.com/quotes/1309491-fail-early-fail-often-but-always-fail-forward#:~:text=Quote%20by%20John%20C.,%2C%20but%20al-ways%20fail%20forward.%E2%80%9D

[56] Anderson, S. (Director), Anderson, S., Bernstein, J., Spitz, M., Hall, D., Greno, N., Redson, A., & Mateo, J. (Writers), & McKim, D. (Producer). (2007). Meet the Robinsons [Video file]. United States: Buena Vista Pictures.

[57] Hammond, Z. (2015) Culturally responsive teaching and the brain: Promoting authentic engagement and rigor among culturally and linguistically diverse students. Thousand Oaks, CA: Corwin, a SAGE Company.

[58] Talking circles overview from the first nations pedagogy online project. (n.d.). Retrieved June 06, 2021, from http://firstna-tionspedagogy.ca/circletalks.html

Many cultures hold the circle as a sacred formation used in rituals and customs. To many, it represents wholeness, connected-ness, and balance. On the American continent, ethnic groups from the Canadian First Nations to Native Americans in the United States to the South American indigenous nations like the Muiscas of the Cundiboyancence plains of Colombia use the circle as an educa-tional and democratic tool to encourage listening, sharing, and learning in communal inclusivity. The tradition of the Talking Cir-cle is a powerful ancestral custom where the speaker speaks without interruption, to everyone present, not to one person. Everyone in the circle can opt to express themselves or can choose to only listen. Many teachers use the Talking Circle protocol in their classroom. To avoid inadvertent cultural appropriation of Native people's contri-butions, it is important that teachers take the time to honor the origins of this custom by ensuring that all participants understand the background of the Talking Circle and practice it respectfully.

[59] Lev, S., Clark, A., & Starkey, E. (2020). Implementing project based learning in early childhood: Overcoming misconceptions and

reaching success. New York, New York: Routledge, Taylor & Francis Group.

[60] Gallup, I. (2020, December 16). Measure what matters most for student success. Retrieved February 12, 2021, from https://www.gallup.com/education/233537/gallup-student-poll.aspx

[61] Pink, D. (2015, June 24). RSA Animate: Dan Pink - Drive: The Surprising Truth About What Motivates Us. Retrieved from https://youtu.be/y1SDV8nxypE

[62] Pink, D. (2018) Drive: The surprising truth about what motivates us New York: Riverhead books.

[63] What is the qft? (2020, June 26). Retrieved February 12, 2021, from https://rightquestion.org/what-is-the-qft/

[64] The QFT on One Slide. (2020). Retrieved July 14, 2020, from https://rightquestion.org/resources/qft-card-template/

[65] Pascoe, M., Hetrick S., & Parker, A. (2020) The impact of stress on students in secondary school and higher education, International Journal of Adolescence and Youth, 25:1, 104-112, DOI: 10.1080/02673843.2019.1596823

[66] Derian, J. (2019). How to Create More Meaningful Team Contracts. Retrieved July 14, 2020, from https://www.pblworks.org/blog/how-create-more-meaningful-team-contracts

67 Metzger, A. N., & Hamilton, L. T. (2021). The stigma of ADHD: teacher ratings of labeled students. *Sociological Perspectives*, 64(2), 258-279.

Ibrahim, N., Amit, N., Shahar, S., Wee, L. H., Ismail, R., Khairuddin, R., ... & Safien, A. M. (2019). Do depression literacy, mental illness beliefs and stigma influence mental health help-seeking attitude? A cross-sectional study of secondary school and university students from B40 households in Malaysia. *BMC public health, 19*(4), 1-8.

68 Zemeckis, R. (1994). Forrest Gump. Paramount Pictures.

[69] Card, O. (1977) Ender's Game New York: A Tor Company.

[70] Hill, B. (2021). It's good to talk: Speaking up for oracy in the management classroom. The International Journal of Management Education, 19(2), 100462.

[71] Oracy Skills Framework. (n.d.). Retrieved from https://www.educ.cam.ac.uk/research/programmes/oracytoolkit/oracyskillsframework/

[72] Voice 21. (n.d.). Retrieved March 18, 2021, from https://www.school21.org.uk/voice21

[73] "The Amazing Harkness Philosophy". *Phillips Exeter Academy*. Retrieved 2021-10-02

[74] Sprott, R. (2019, July 17). 3 Tips for Exploring Controversial Issues in PBL. Retrieved July 14, 2020, from https://www.pblworks.org/blog/3-tips-exploring-controversial-issues-pbl

[75] Glankler, E., & Pool, E. (2019, November 15). BONUS: SXSW EDU "Teaching in the era of fake news" - ANTI-SOCIAL STUDIES. Retrieved February 20, 2021, from https://antisocialstudies.org/2019/03/05/bonus-episode-sxsw-edu-teaching-in-the-era-of-fake-news/

[76] Exploding atom. (n.d.). Retrieved February 20, 2021, from https://dbp.theatredance.utexas.edu/node/26

[77] Anderson, L. (2017, April 15). Guest Post From Lorin W. Anderson, Co-Author Of The Revised Bloom's Taxonomy. Retrieved August 25, 2020, from https://larryferlazzo.edublogs.org/2017/04/15/guest-post-from-lorin-w-anderson-co-author-of-the-revised-blooms-taxonomy/

78 Krathwohl, D. R. (2002). A revision of Bloom's taxonomy: An overview. *Theory into practice, 41*(4), 212-218.

[79] Berger, R. (2016, December 13). EL Education's Ron Berger on Field Trips, Fieldwork, and Maximizing Learning. Retrieved August 26, 2020, from https://eleducation.org/news/el-educations-ron-berger-on-field-trips-fieldwork-and-maximizing-learning-in-the-field

[80] PBLWorks. (2020, October 13). *Ocean Plastics Project* [Video file]. Retrieved September 07, 2021, from https://youtu.be/66zelGJ8pd0

[81] Bariso, J. (2018, September 19). There are actually 3 types of empathy. Here's how THEY DIFFER—AND how you can develop them all. Retrieved February 28, 2021, from https://www.inc.com/justin-bariso/there-are-actually-3-types-of-empathy-heres-how-they-differ-and-how-you-can-develop-them-all.html

[82] Tulenko, J. (2016, August 10). What one assistant Principal learned from shadowing a student for a day. Retrieved February 15, 2021, from https://www.pbs.org/newshour/show/one-assistant-principal-learned-shadowing-student-day

[83] *I Used to think...Now I think* [PDF]. (2019). Cambridge: Project Zero Harvard Graduate School of Education.

[84] Raymond A. Mar, Keith Oatley, Jacob Hirsh, Jennifer dela Paz, Jordan B. Peterson, Bookworms versus nerds: Exposure to fiction versus non-fiction, divergent associations with social ability, and the simulation of fictional social worlds, Journal of Research in Personality, Volume 40, Issue 5, 2006, Pages 694-712, ISSN 0092-6566, https://doi.org/10.1016/j.jrp.2005.08.002.

Kidd, D. C., & Castano, E. (2013). Reading Literary Fiction Improves Theory of Mind. Science, 342(6156), 377-380. doi:10.1126/science.1239918

[85] Hammond, Z. (2015) Culturally responsive teaching and the brain: Promoting authentic engagement and rigor among culturally and linguistically diverse students. Thousand Oaks, CA: Corwin, a SAGE Company.

[86] Pattani, A. (2019, July 10). Seeing classmates struggling, these 5th graders wrote a book of poems to inspire those with depression. Retrieved July 14, 2020, from https://www.inquirer.com/health/depression-mental-health-poems-students-children-kirkbride-elementary-school-20190709.html

[87] Kraft, M. A., Blazar, D., & Hogan, D. (2018). The effect of teacher coaching on instruction and achievement: A meta-analysis of the causal evidence. Review of Educational Research, 88(4), 547–588. doi:10.3102/0034654318759268

[88] Baldwin, J. (1979, July 29). If Black English isn't a Language, Then Tell Me What is? Retrieved January 19, 2021, from https://archive.nytimes.com/www.nytimes.com/books/98/03/29/specials/baldwin-english.html

[89] Hammond, Z. (2015) Culturally responsive teaching and the brain: Promoting authentic engagement and rigor among culturally and linguistically diverse students. Thousand Oaks, CA: Corwin, a SAGE Company.

[90] Blogush, P. (2019, March 15). Blogush. Retrieved July 14, 2020, from https://blogush.edublogs.org/

[91] Hattie, J., & Timperley, H. (2007). The power of feedback. Review of Educational Research, 77(1), 81–112.

[92] Berger, R. (2012) Austin's Butterfly from https://youtu.be/hqh1MRWZjms

[93] Brown, B. (2018) Dare to lead: Brave work, tough conversations, whole hearts New York: Random House.

[94] Murphy, B. (2005). Need to get your students talking? Try speed Dating! *Teaching Professor, 19*(7), 1-4.

[95] Alcalde Delgado, R. (n.d.). *Gallery Walk Activity Protocol* [PDF]. Education Consortium, LLC.

[96] National School Reform Faculty. (n.d.). Four "A's" Text Protocol. Retrieved July 18, 2021, from https://www.nsrfharmony.org/wp-content/uploads/2017/10/4_a_text_0.pdf

[97] Robinette Kowal, M. (2012, November 28). How and why I use online alpha-readers while writing novels. Retrieved July 14, 2020, from http://maryrobinettekowal.com/journal/how-and-why-i-use-online-alpha-readers-while-writing-novels/

[98] Charrette protocol. (2017, March 30). Retrieved July 18, 2021, from https://www.schoolreforminitiative.org/download/charrette-protocol/

[99] Bonda, Penny (2007). Sustainable Commercial Interiors. John Wiley & Sons. p. 29. ISBN 9780471749172.

[100] Ladder of feedback. (2018). Retrieved July 18, 2021, from https://pz.harvard.edu/resources/ladder-of-feedback

[101] Adapted from TerBorg, S. (2018, October 23). Ladder of feedback. Retrieved September 05, 2021, from https://sonyaterborg.com/2018/10/21/ladder-of-feedback

[102] Koenka, A. C., Linnenbrink-Garcia, L., Moshontz, H., Atkinson, K. M., Sanchez, C. E., & Cooper, H. (2019). A meta-analysis on the impact of grades and comments on academic motivation and achievement: A case for written feedback. Educational Psychology. Advance online publication. https://doi.org/10.1080/01443410.2019.1659939

[103] Wexton, J. [@RepWexton]. (November 20, 2019). Hey @GoshenPostES—we just passed the Shark Fin Sales Elimination Act! With this bill, we will ban the commercial sale of shark fins and products containing shark fins. Thank you for bringing this important issue to my attention! [Tweet]. Retrieved from

https://twitter.com/search?q=shark%20fins%20%40repwex-ton&src=typed_query

On November 20, 2019, The US House of Representatives passed HR.737, The Shark Fin Sales Elimination Act of 2019, which would make it illegal for any person to possess, buy, or sell any product containing shark fins. https://awionline.org/content/shark-fin-sales-elimination-act

[104] Plummer, M. (2019, October 27). A Short Guide to Building Your Team's Critical Thinking Skills. Retrieved July 14, 2020, from https://hbr.org/2019/10/a-short-guide-to-building-your-teams-critical-thinking-skills

[105] Ritchhart, R. and Church, M. (2020) The power of making thinking visible: Practices to engage and empower all learners. Hoboken, NJ: Jossey-Bass: A Wiley Brand.

[106] Anaissie, T., Cary, V., Clifford, D., Malarkey, T. & Wise, S. (2021). *Liberatory Design.* http://www.liberatorydesign.com.

National Equity Project. (2021). Liberatory Design For Equity Process. https://www.nationalequityproject.org/frameworks/liberatory-design

[107] Berger, R. (2016, December 13). EL Education's Ron Berger on Field Trips, Fieldwork, and Maximizing Learning. Retrieved August 26, 2020, from https://eleducation.org/news/el-educations-ron-berger-on-field-trips-fieldwork-and-maximizing-learning-in-the-field

[108] Pink, D. (2018) Drive: The surprising truth about what motivates us New York: Riverhead books.

[109] Ritchhart, R. and Church, M. (2020) The power of making thinking visible: Practices
		to engage and empower all learners. Hoboken, NJ: Jossey-Bass: A Wiley Brand.

[110] Wujec, T. (n.d.). Marshmallow Challenge. Retrieved July 14, 2020, from https://www.tomwujec.com/marshmallowchallenge

[111] Wujec, T. (2010, April 22). Build a Tower, Build a Team. Retrieved from https://youtu.be/H0_yKBitO8M

[112] Found at https://casel.org/sel-framework/

[113] Boys, B. (2014, May 26). Bottle Boys - Bille Jean (Michael Jackson cover on Beer Bottles). Retrieved from https://youtu.be/NkbZlautuUc

[114] Honor Fair Use and only show short video clips from TV or movies. You would need to pay a licensing fee if you're showing a whole episode

[115] Hammond, Z. (2015) Culturally responsive teaching and the brain: Promoting
        authentic engagement and rigor among culturally and linguistically diverse
        students. Thousand Oaks, CA: Corwin, a SAGE Company.

[116] Ritchhart, R. and Church, M. (2020) The power of making thinking visible: Practices to engage and empower all learners. Hoboken, NJ: Jossey-Bass: A Wiley Brand.

[117] Brenneman, R. (2019, February 20). Gallup Student Poll Finds Engagement in School Dropping by Grade Level. Retrieved July 13, 2020, from https://www.edweek.org/ew/articles/2016/03/23/gallup-student-poll-finds-engagement-in-school.html
Sparks, S. (2020, June 23). Part of Global Trend, 1 in 3 U.S. High Schoolers Felt Disconnected From School Before Pandemic. Retrieved July 13, 2020, from http://blogs.edweek.org/edweek/inside-school-research/2020/06/us_students_UNESCO_school_engagement.html

[118] Yazzie-Mintz, E. (2010) *Charting the path from engagement to achievement: A report on the 2009 high school survey of student engagement.* Bloomington, IN: Center for Evaluation & Education Policy.

[119] All students and adults are fictious but the narrative is based on actual feedback from students, parents, and the community.

[120] Leonard, A. (2007). The Story of Stuff. Retrieved July 14, 2020, from https://www.storyofstuff.org/movies/story-of-stuff/

[121] Goddard, G. (n.d.). Biomimetic design: 10 examples of NATURE inspiring technology. Retrieved June 06, 2021, from https://www.sciencefocus.com/future-technology/biomimetic-design-10-examples-of-nature-inspiring-technology/

Mike Kaechele

Mike is a teacher who leads Project Based Learning and Social and Emotional Learning workshops around the country helping educators make the shift to student-centered inquiry. He earned national exposure as an avid blogger and has been featured in Edutopia, PBLWorks, Edweek, New Tech Network, WeGrowTeachers, and TeachThought. He is National Faculty Emeritus with PBLWorks (Buck Institute of Education).

During his 20 year career, he has integrated projects across all four core content areas and electives in both middle and high school settings. While living abroad, Mike gained international experience teaching in China. Mike was a founding teacher at Kent Innovation High School, a nationally recognized PBL school of the New Tech Network. His passion is inspiring edu-cators to design SEL infused PBL curriculum for all content areas and age levels. Mike is convinced that we don't need to prepare students for "someday," but that they should take on meaningful work right now!

Matinga E. Ragatz, Ph.D

Matinga Ragatz is a multiple-award winning educator, author, keynote speaker, and consultant. As an innovative teacher, she redefined learning and developed a trusted voice striving to revolutionize the way children learn and the way teachers teach. Among many accolades, she served as Michigan Teacher of the Year and in 2017 was inducted in the National Teacher Hall of Fame. She holds a PhD in Education with a spe-cialty in Learning, Instruction, and Innovation and is National Faculty at PBLWorks (Buck Institute of Education).

Matinga's international background and her own challenging learning experiences inspire a unique perspective on the cultivation of students' talents and abilities. In 2017, she opened a PBL food science school in Tanzania focusing on children of extreme poverty and their learning needs. In 2020, she founded a scholarship and advocacy program for school children to support parents financially affected by COVID-19 in Malabo, Equatorial Guinea.

Matinga inspires school leaders to create real-world engagement within their schools utilizing the innovative strategies that she has developed and successfully implemented over 20 years. She believes that accessible and effective education is the keystone of economic development and imperative in the geopolitical discourse. To this end, she has carried this message to educators in Asia, Africa, Europe and the Americas. She is currently an NPR Michigan Radio education commentator where she speaks about education issues throughout the state of Michigan.

Pulse of PBL Workshops

Cultivating Equity Through Social Emotional Learning

Teaching Social and Emotional Learning skills is the latest fad but **what does it actually look like in the classroom?** This session features the tools, strategies and practical approaches for traditional and PBL teachers to teach the five core SEL competencies to ALL of their students integrated into daily learning experiences.

Pulse of PBL

Transformative Project Based Learning cultivates academic content and Social and Emotional Learning skills simultaneously. In this workshop educators will design their own SEL integrated project through experiencing the PBL process themselves. Teachers from all levels and content areas will partake in a PBL environment full of SEL protocols instantly transferable to any classroom.

*To learn more about our other workshops and consulting services, go to **PulseofPBL.com***

Made in the USA
Middletown, DE
08 May 2024

54040870R00199